THE DÁIL
IN THE
21ST CENTURY

THE DÁIL
IN THE
21ST CENTURY

ANTHONY O'HALLORAN

MERCIER PRESS
IRISH PUBLISHER – IRISH STORY

MERCIER PRESS

Cork

www.mercierpress.ie

Trade enquiries to CMD BookSource,
55a Spruce Avenue, Stillorgan Industrial Park,
Blackrock, County Dublin

ISBN: 978 1 85635 636 7

10 9 8 7 6 5 4 3 2 1

A CIP record for this title is available from the British Library

Printed and bound in the EU.

Contents

Acknowledgements   9

Glossary of Terms   14

Preface   17

1   Dáil Éireann in a Changing Ireland   23

2   Dáil Éireann in an Era of Multiple Revolutions   50

3   Parliamentary Decline and Post-Parliamentary Governance   67

4   Contemporary Liberal Democracy: A Flawed Model?   94

5   Democratic Politics   103

6   An Ideal Typical Parliament   115

7   Separation of Powers and Resources   132

8   Fiddling about with Dáil Éireann's Standing Orders   154

9   European Union and Civil Society   168

10   Social Partnership and Expert Sovereignty   200

11   Dáil Éireann as an Advocate for the Common Good?   208

12   Contemporary Dáil Éireann   239

Appendix 1   247

Appendix 2   250

Appendix 3   261

Bibliography   262

Index   283

DEDICATED WITH LOVE AND AFFECTION TO MY PARENTS
PATRICK AND MARY O'HALLORAN
WHO TAUGHT ME THE DIFFERENCE BETWEEN A HOUSE AND A HOME

A Cheann Comhairle, I regret to say this but I consider that your position is no longer tenable. I think you will either have to resign or be removed from office.

E. Gilmore, Dáil Éireann, 6 October 2009

In all the discussion and speculation about who might replace the departing John O'Donoghue, there was one unquestioned assumption: the post would be in the gift of the Taoiseach. That this should be taken for granted is depressing evidence of the weakness of the Dáil.

Editorial, *The Irish Times*, 17 October 2009

The drab proceedings went on for an hour and a half and then the current TDs made their way over to the Dáil's largely vacuous parliamentary proceedings. Not that the issue discussed was not of significance: the nationalisation of Anglo-Irish Bank. But the proceedings made nonsense of any pretence of any parliamentary democracy, except in its formalities.

V. Browne, *The Irish Times*, 21 January 2009

A well-adjusted US Senator needs to combine a sincere interest in public policy with a joyful acceptance of the need to demean oneself while begging for votes and donations.

G. Collins, *New York Times*, 21 January 2009

Acknowledgements

Many individuals have helped me complete this book. My PhD supervisor Dr Seamus Ó Tuama deserves special mention. As a supervisor, Seamus brought the practice of attention to detail to new heights! Apart from his academic support, Seamus was supportive in a more holistic way. When confidence levels were low, he injected me with a sense of renewed energy. Suffice to say, Seamus fully understands that life is rarely a linear straightforward path. Thank you, Seamus!

My parents, Patrick and Mary O'Halloran, have proved extraordinarily patient and supportive. Since I entered the Waterford Institute of Technology as a legal studies student in 1991, they have come to realise that there is more to learning than exam preparation. Neither they nor I realised at the time that my studies would take me to University College Galway, University College Dublin, Southern Illinois University Carbondale and University College Cork. Their support has included the emotional and spiritual, not to mention the financial. However, most of all, our house in Ardfinnan, County Tipperary, is a home, which operates on an 'open door' policy. Close to the Knockmealdowns and the River Suir, we live in a place of beauty. This book could not have been completed without the positive energy which Ardfinnan generates for me.

My father, Patrick O'Halloran, left school in fifth class of primary school to work on the family farm. My mother, Mary O'Mahoney, left school during the first year of her secondary education to work in Ardfinnan Woollen Mills. College life was to be an experience confined to their children. I have seen at first hand the marginalisation and fear a lack of formal education can generate. Whilst their lack of formal education has been more than compensated for by natural intelligence, astuteness and remarkable coping skills, they deserved a fairer treatment from Irish society. I dedicate this book to Patrick and Mary O'Halloran for rising so admirably to the economic challenges of life.

The former Ceann Comhairle of Dáil Éireann, Seamus Pattison, must be singled out for particular mention and praise. Two lectures which Seamus delivered in University College Cork acted as a significant catalyst for my research. Tom O'Connor, vice-president of the Institute of Public Administration, has proved extraordinarily helpful. Tom and I worked very closely over a period of some five years as co-authors of *Politics in a Changing Ireland 1960–2007: A Tribute to Seamus Pattison*. I thank Tom for his guidance and support whilst researching and writing this book.

I had the privilege of working with Piet Strydom of the Department of Sociology, University College Cork on a Higher Education Authority funded research project. One of Piet's many areas of expertise is public sphere theory. As a newcomer to this field, Piet pointed me in many fruitful directions. Our weekly seminars in the early stages of the project proved particularly beneficial.

The library staff of University College Cork are deserving of special praise. Courteous and warm, I have always found them a pleasure to work with. Ann McCann, senior executive assistant with University College Cork's Department of Government, is also deserving of my gratitude. I thank Ann for her guidance and warmth during my time at University College Cork. Southern Illinois University Carbondale has been a very positive space in my life. My period as a Fulbright Fellow in Carbondale was one of the most enriching periods in my life. I thank Carbondale's Political Science Department for being such wonderful hosts. It was at Carbondale that I met my good friend from Argentina, Professor Cristina Diaz. Cristina has been an infinite source of intellectual and emotional support.

A number of other people are deserving of gratitude. These include Mark Ryland, Rose Scheneeweiss, Dr Clodagh Harris, Seanie Lonergan, MCC, Tom Tobin and Claire Tobin, Gráinne O'Flynn and Bridget Carroll. The staff of the Houses of the Oireachtas are worthy of special commendation. Time and time again, on frequent visits to Leinster House, I encountered staff who are models of courtesy and helpfulness. In particular, I thank Kieran Coughlan, Derek Dignam, Art O'Leary, Paul Conway and Elaine Gunn for providing me with important clarifications and data.

My thanks as well to Eoin Purcell for his initial enthusiasm for the project and my publishers, Mercier Press, for having confidence in my original proposal. One of the great privileges of academic life is sharing one's thoughts with wider audiences beyond the 'Ivory Tower'. Mary Feehan, Patrick Crowley and Wendy Logue at Mercier Press have helped me reach this objective and challenge dominant narratives on Dáil Éireann's actual and future role in Irish politics.

I also wish to thank the Institute of Public Administration for allowing me to draw on papers that I contributed to their well-established journal *Administration*. For the record, these papers are: 'Changing the Rules: Fiddling Around with Dáil Éireann's Standing Orders?' *Administration*, Vol. 57, No. 2, pp. 25–42; 'Transformation in Contemporary Ireland's Society, Economy and Polity: An Era of Post-Parliamentary Governance?', *Administration*, Vol. 53, No. 1, pp. 54–79; and 'The Privatisation of Citizenship? Exploring Frameworks for Membership of the Irish Polity', *Administration*, Vol. 52, No. 1, pp. 19–34. I especially thank the journal's editor, Tony McNamara, who has provided me with a valuable platform to share my evolving thoughts on a range of themes from citizenship to post-parliamentary governance.

I also have more long-term debts to acknowledge to people who have shaped my life in a positive way. They include my good friend Dr Douglas Butler, the late Michael Ferris, TD (Tipperary South), and of course the late Harold Walker, MP, who served as Deputy Speaker of the British House of Commons for almost a decade. Douglas and I have been hunting together for twenty years. Apart from our mutual love of country life, we both cherish stimulating political conversation. On more than one occasion, Douglas has compelled me to reconsider an entrenched position. On one highly memorable occasion Harold, his wife Mary (a Tipperary woman!) and I stood at the dispatch box on the floor of the House of Commons together. For just one moment, I was Prime Minister taking questions! Michael gave me my first tour of Dáil Éireann. It was a day that I still deeply cherish. I regret that neither Michael nor Harold lived to see me complete this book. I miss both of them enormously. May they rest in peace.

Professor Mayra Besosa's home in Vista, California, has provided me with ideal surroundings in which to make corrections and revisions. Without Mayra's expert proofreading eye many of my projects would have not been completed. I thank Mayra for her love and patience during often testing circumstances. Howard and Susan Besosa's home in Monterey, California, also provided me with a pleasant research and writing environment, too pleasant at times as temptations such as sun-drenched porches and cold beer constantly beckoned. I apologise to Howard and Susan for being over-absorbed with academic matters during visits.

Finally, I wish to acknowledge an invaluable source of data for students of Irish politics. I refer of course, to Nealon's Guides to Dáil elections, the first of which was published after the 1973 general election. Whilst the two most recent editions (2002 and 2007) out of a series of eleven were published under the aegis of *The Irish Times*, Ted Nealon deserves special acknowledgement for initiating and sustaining the series over a period of almost three decades. Of course, Nealon's Guide has become the 'bible' for junkies of Irish politics, including me! General election statistics in this book derive largely from these indispensable guides.

GLOSSARY OF TERMS

Ceann Comhairle: Ceann Comhairle is the Chairperson of Dáil Éireann.

Dáil Éireann: Dáil Éireann is the Lower House of the Oireachtas. Dáil Éireann and 'the Dáil' are interchangeably used in academic, media and general political discourse.

Deloitte and Touche Report: The Deloitte and Touche Report published in March 2002 was an 'independent staff resource analysis of the Houses of the Oireachtas conducted by Deloitte and Touche Management Consultants and overseen by a Steering Group of Members of the Dáil and Seanad. Deloitte and Touche, as professional independent analysts, were specifically asked to review staff resources'.[1]

DIRT: DIRT stands for deposit interest retention tax. A Sub-Committee of Dáil Éireann's Public Accounts Committee investigated allegations that Irish depositors evaded this tax using bogus accounts. It was alleged that the banking sector facilitated this tax evasion. The Sub-Committee published two reports on the allegations. Its findings acted as a catalyst for significant Dáil reform.

Discursive: Discursive in this book is employed as an umbrella term for all kinds of verbal communications including conversations, talk, discussions, dialogues, arguments and debates. The term discursive is intrinsically social as it involves a relationship between two or more people.

---

1 Deloitte & Touche, 2002: *Foreword.*

Empirical: Empirical in this book is taken to mean observing and describing actually existing reality.

Kildare Street: Kildare Street, Dublin 2, is the street where both Houses of the Oireachtas are located.

Leas-Cheann Comhairle: Leas-Cheann Comhairle is the Deputy Chairperson of Dáil Éireann.

Leinster House: Leinster House is the building on Kildare Street where both Houses of the Oireachtas sit.

Merrion Street: Merrion Street is in Dublin 2 where Government Buildings, which house the Department of An Taoiseach and the Cabinet Room, are located.

Normative: Prescribing how things ought to be.

Oireachtas: The Oireachtas consists of both Houses of Parliament and a non-executive president.

Polity: A political community which in contemporary terms is usually equated with the geographically bounded sovereign state. Classically, the term can be traced to the city states of ancient Greece, most notably Athens.

Seanad Éireann: Seanad Éireann is the Upper House of the Oireachtas.

Taoiseach: The Prime Minister of the Republic of Ireland.

TD: TD (*Teachta Dála*) is a member of Dáil Éireann.

Treaty of Nice: A treaty agreed in 2000, which made very little progress in the process of EU reform, but which did manage to include an agreement about how many votes member states should have in the Council of Ministers and how many members of the European Parliament should be allowed for each member state after the enlargement of 2004.[2]

---

2 Warleigh, 2004: 129.

Nice 1: Nice 1 refers to the Treaty of Nice rejected by Ireland in a 2001 constitutional referendum. For a new treaty to become law, it must be ratified by all member states. Ireland's rejection of the treaty therefore caused a crisis.

Nice 2: Nice 2 was the Treaty of Nice which was put to the Irish electorate for a second time during 2002. On this occasion, voters approved the treaty, thereby avoiding its collapse.

PREFACE

Asked by an American tourist when I was an undergraduate student in University College Galway what subjects I was studying, I proudly replied 'Law and Politics'.

The tourist in question exclaimed: 'Why would you be studying to join two of the most corrupt and dishonest professions?'

Pride turned to a mumbling and defensive reply the content of which I cannot recall. In the intervening seventeen years I have frequently been exposed to such statements. And as one with a particular interest in Irish parliamentary politics, I have witnessed what at face value might be described as an open contempt for politics and politicians from my fellow citizens. Of course, the whole picture is more complicated. Alongside this general hostility, I have observed at constituency level relationships of mutual respect between governors and governed. Equally, Irish citizens are not indifferent to the political process – politics and sport are key parts of many conversations in Irish pubs.

I have never shared my fellow citizens' general hostility towards politics. On the contrary, I believe politics is a profoundly important endeavour. We in Ireland know more than many what happens when politics becomes dysfunctional, when differences are resolved through guns rather than words. My approach to politics is unambiguously clear. Democracy affords us the opportunity to resolve our differences and chart our futures peacefully, and parliaments such as Dáil Éireann ought to be crucial players in the democratic process.

That is not to say that I am naive about the exercise of power in parliamentary democracies. On the contrary, I am acutely aware that society affords very different life chances depending on social class, gender or race. I am equally aware that political outcomes frequently reflect the preferences of the strong and powerful to the obvious detriment of the poor and socially excluded. Neither can it be forgotten that parliamentarians in most countries, including Ireland, are usually upper middle-class males. Of course, parliamentary democracy is not a panacea but, at a minimum, it deserves to be given a robust and fair hearing. Given that Dáil Éireann 'celebrated' its ninetieth anniversary on 21 January 2009, the hearing is at least timely.

Speaking broadly, I have two core objectives. Firstly, how can the contemporary Dáil Éireann be most appropriately classified? Is it an irrelevant institution in a state of perpetual decline? Is it an institution populated by self-serving politicians whose view of public service is drawing from generous expense accounts? Or is Dáil Éireann a modern parliament which is coping with and even embracing change? Perhaps contrary to media narratives, can the Dáil be described as central to the democratic life of contemporary Ireland? In the language of political science, this first exercise is empirical: describing how things are or, to put it another way, observing actually existing political reality. Again, in the language of political science this exercise involves choosing an appropriate theoretical framework and marshalling the available evidence. Secondly, I seek to chart an innovative democratic role for Dáil Éireann under the conditions of early 21st-century politics. In the language of political science, this exercise is normative: prescribing how things ought to be. It is a question of thinking outside real world constraints, embracing ideals but ultimately ensuring that proposals are feasible. Themes such as democratic accountability, selfish consumerism and the common good are important facets of this normative exercise.

MacCarthaigh asserts that:

> After all, the accountability of the Government to the people, via Parliament, is the most fundamental element of a democratic polity.[1]

However, in my view the discipline of legislative studies tends to neglect the most crucial dimension of democratic politics: the *Demos* or people. There is an over-emphasis on internal parliamentary procedures, practices and processes. The discipline is like a play without an audience. Scholars study the actors, dialogue and equipment on stage but leave out the audience. Legislative studies suffer from disciplinary insularity.

I therefore adopt a very different approach which clearly recognises that internal procedures are important and relevant. Thus, Standing Orders may inhibit or enhance a parliament's capacity to function democratically. Similarly, whether a parliament is well resourced or under-resourced will influence its ability to discharge its accountability functions. But an approach which relies solely on the internal workings of parliaments limits our horizons. I break with conventional approaches by bringing the public centre stage. I do so by employing deliberative democratic and public sphere theories (see chapter one). It is the first time that a research project on Dáil Éireann has adopted such an approach. It may even be the first time that any parliament has been studied in this fashion. Therefore, my book constitutes a significant departure from previous approaches.

---

1 MacCarthaigh, 2005: 1.

It is the culmination, though not the end, of a journey, the seeds of which were planted twenty-seven years ago, in the early years of secondary school. A passing plea by an eccentric history teacher named Dan Green in St Joseph's College, Cahir, County Tipperary, encouraged me to start listening to parliamentary reports on BBC Radio 4. The impact of this fleeting comment was more profound than Dan Green could possibly have imagined. Since then I have possessed a passionate interest in parliamentary politics.

My book marks what I hope will be the beginning of another journey, the seeds of which were planted a mere six years ago. I refer to the contribution deliberative democratic theory might make to some concept of the common good. Mentored by Dr Seamus Ó Tuama of University College Cork's Department of Government, I have found my exposure to deliberative democratic theory extraordinarily enriching. As such, my book constitutes an intellectual marriage, a meeting at the crossroads as it were, of two different, but not entirely separate, journeys.

In June 1972 two young American political scientists, Frank M. Bryan and Jane Mansfield, met for the first time to discuss research ideas on direct democracy. Their meeting took place in a cow pasture beside a New England river. Frank M. Bryan wanted to write the definitive book on New England town democracy. He started to complain to Jane Mansfield about over-teaching, lack of resources and other obstacles, which would prevent him from achieving this objective:

> The glint in her eyes danced between reproach and amusement. 'Then it will become your life's work, Frank,' she said. And so it has.[2]

---

2 Bryan, 2004: x.

In 2004 Frank M. Bryan achieved his ambition when he published *Real Democracy: The New England Town Meeting and How it Works.* Unlike Bryan, I cannot claim to have dedicated my academic life to one core objective. My journey has been erratic and at times very uncertain. However, I clearly envisage that deliberative democratic theory will occupy the central place in my future scholarship. I doubt that I will ever write the definitive book on the topic. That is, unless, I get a pep talk from Jane Mansfield on a balmy summer's day on the banks of the River Suir in County Tipperary. However, assuming that I am not the beneficiary of such a talk, I intend to write at least one definitive paper.

Anthony O'Halloran
Ardfinnan, County Tipperary, and Vista, California

I

Dáil Éireann in a Changing Ireland

The Government shall be responsible to Dáil Éireann.[1]

Few academics of any discipline could have predicted the dramatic political, economic, social, cultural and religious changes of the middle and late 1990s on the island of Ireland.[2]

The present farce of Deputies addressing empty seats has had the additional impact of greatly reducing the quality of Dáil speeches as good oratory or great research has no impact on empty seats and in turn the reportage thereof has greatly diminished. Parliamentary reputations, unlike in the past, are no longer made in the Dáil chamber and this has impoverished the parliamentary tradition.[3]

On Tuesday 14 October, 2008, the Minister for Finance Brian Lenihan delivered the annual budget statement to Dáil Éireann. An atmosphere of anticipation hung over the chamber as the Minister rose from his seat. However, on this occasion anticipation was accompanied by deep anxiety. The national budgetary situation had deteriorated drastically since 2007. Exchequer income was

---

1 Article 28.4.1, 1937 Constitution.
2 Keogh, 2005: 400.
3 Mitchell, 1999.

falling whilst expenditure was rising. The language of budgetary cuts, deficits and increased borrowing re-entered politics. Global markets were in turmoil and confidence in the banking sector was collapsing. Government backbenchers were particularly nervous, as they expected the customary backlash from voters as cuts in public expenditure became a reality.

Their anxiety, on this occasion, was warranted. One budgetary measure in particular generated deep public hostility, namely the decision to remove the right of all citizens over seventy years of age to free medical care. A universal right of free access to healthcare, enjoyed by the elderly since 2001, was replaced with a means-tested system. Within one week the Government was forced into an embarrassing and humiliating climbdown. The authority of the Government was severely damaged and references to an early general election appeared in the media.

How and why was the Government forced into this budgetary *volte-face*? Three inter-related factors can be identified: firstly, elderly citizens and their representatives mobilised effectively and very vocally to resist the measure. The sheer scale and intensity of this mobilisation surprised politicians and observers. Secondly, Dáil Éireann also became an important site of parliamentary agitation for Opposition parties. The principal Opposition party, Fine Gael, put a motion before the House calling on the Government to reverse the decision. Two Government supporters voted with the Opposition. Ultimately though, whilst the Government survived the parliamentary vote, it was clear that it had lost the parliamentary, and broader public, debate. As the debate took place within Leinster House, 15,000 elderly protesters assembled in Kildare Street. Government speakers who addressed the gathering received a very hostile response; in effect, they were shouted down. The third factor to be considered is that the citizenry at large engaged in a broader public debate. This episode was not just another example of a lobby group pressuring the Government on a specific policy issue: the issue of medical care for the elderly touched a chord with the public. The measure was perceived as draconian and unfair, focusing as it did on a vulnerable group in Irish society. Commenting on the entire episode, *The Irish Times,* in an editorial asserted that:

> There is something good about what has emerged in recent days. There is a new engagement with the political system, a sense that politics and what happens in Dáil Éireann does matter and has an effect on people's real lives.[4]

This particular assertion by *The Irish Times* that the Dáil does matter stands in sharp contrast to the dominant discourse on Dáil Éireann where it is assumed that Dáil Éireann *does not matter.* Commentators mourn the declining relevance of the Dáil. The Dáil, for example, is berated for sitting insufficient days. Some of the media coverage tends to be trivial:

> For three weeks now, while others have made the daily trudge to work on cold mornings, our TDs have turned over in their cosy beds for another long lie in, like the blissful couple in that old Lotto Ad.[5]

And yet more of the coverage seems designed to sensationalise issues, as was surely the case with a front-page story in the *Irish Daily Mail* on TDs' and senators' expenses which led with the headline 'Snouts in the Trough'.[6]

---

4 Editorial, *The Irish Times,* 2008b.
5 Anderson, 2007.
6 Lyons, 2008.

Members are also criticised for devoting too much time to constituency affairs. The tag of constituency messenger still resonates. According to Fianna Fáil Minister Noel Dempsey there is a 'craven focus on the parish pump' in the Irish political system. And Dempsey adds:

> If we want our national politicians to be constantly looking into potholes and giving the impression that they are fixing individual planning permissions and getting planning permissions, then we should accept the fact that the Oireachtas will become more irrelevant.[7]

An editorial in *The Irish Times* referring to the 'pernicious curse of clientelism' states that the clientelist system:

> ... rewards those who write the most letters, attend the most funerals, sponsor the most football shirts, those from whom service in the Dáil is largely a permanent campaign for re-election. It punishes those who see their role primarily as legislator and who don't keep ahead of party colleagues snapping at their heels, as many a former TD will attest.[8]

Former Taoiseach Garret FitzGerald also expresses concerns about the clientelist pressures which politicians face. FitzGerald argues that there is a constant tension in a politician's life between serving the particular interests of his/her constituency and the common good of the electorate as a whole. He emphasises that politics is frequently about balancing these two conflicting forces.[9]

In the aftermath of Ireland's rejection of the Lisbon Treaty in June 2008 another *Irish Times'* editorial referred to a 'disconnect between

---

7   Quoted in O'Halloran, 2001.
8   Editorial, *The Irish Times*, 2007.
9   FitzGerald, 2006.

voters and their Oireachtas members'.[10] The editorial rehearsed the all too familiar (but not necessarily invalid) assessment of Dáil Éireann, focusing on the summer recess, TDs' pay, sitting days and the damage done to the political system by revelations of political corruption.

Similarly, much of the discourse suggests that power remains concentrated in the executive branch. Reform is understood as overhauling the Dáil's internal procedures or changing the electoral system. In a climate where political corruption is continuously exposed, members tend to be treated as an undifferentiated monolith. One might easily form the same impression of Dáil Éireann as Ashdown holds of the House of Commons, namely that Britain's Lower House of Parliament is 'puerile, pathetic and utterly useless'.[11] And the following quote from an opinion piece in the *Los Angeles Times* would probably go down well in the world of Irish political satire:

> No wonder satirist Mark Russell closes many of his shows by telling his audiences what members of Congress tell their colleagues every Wednesday: 'Have a nice weekend'.[12]

In the Irish polity of the early 21st century, Dáil Éireann is commonly described as entirely irrelevant. An editorial in the *Irish Independent* stresses this point:

> Dáil Deputies, or some of them, dragged themselves back to work yesterday after their long Christmas holidays. But only in a manner of speaking. They dragged themselves back into Leinster House, but not to do the work for which they are paid, the work allocated to them by the Constitution ... Leinster House has almost become

---

10   Editorial, *The Irish Times*, 2008a.
11   Ashdown, quoted in Ward, 2004: 45.
12   Mann and Ornstein, 2006.

irrelevant to the public business carried on by the civil service and state agencies.[13]

A new member of the 30th Dáil adds his voice to the chorus:

The Oireachtas is an archaic body, governed by rules and regulations that were already outmoded in the 20th century, never mind the 21st. The Dáil has become little more than a talking shop, with very little real work being done in the chamber.[14]

However, the public discourse is rarely subject to in-depth analysis. When it is suggested that the Dáil is irrelevant, redundant and meaningless, what does this actually mean? Does talk of parliamentary decline mean that in some previous era Dáil Éireann exercised significant political power? When it is stated that Deputies are constituency messengers, is the representative role of parliamentarians being ignored? Is the contemporary Dáil Éireann an archaic body? Or has it for example embraced information technology as a means of modernising and professionalising parliamentary business? When the Dáil is berated for being a talking shop, are commentators ignoring the very essence of parliamentary democracy, which is that political differences are best resolved through the medium of talk? In short, much of the public discussion appears to be shallow and devoid of analytical rigour.

The key point to be stressed at this early stage is that it is time to look at Dáil Éireann through a different analytical lens. It is time to question the dominant discourse. Contemporary Ireland has experienced deep change since the mid-1990s. Economically, socially and politically there

---

13 Editorial, *Irish Independent*, 2007.
14 Sherlock, 2008.

is a 'new game in town'. But the 'script' on Dáil Éireann remains in a pre-transformation time warp, lagging behind recent societal, economic and political transformations. I argue that the literature on Dáil Éireann is located within tightly circumscribed theoretical frameworks that ignore transformations which have significant implications for its future role. Inevitably, the analytical power and normative potential of these frameworks is considerably impoverished.

I present two frameworks, namely the post-parliamentary governance model[15] and the public sphere.[16] The post-parliamentary governance model holds that the powers of parliaments are being systematically eroded. It argues that profound changes in modern societies, polities and economies have led to the evolution of a so-called post-parliamentary governance era, whereby collectively binding and authoritative decisions are made in arenas other than parliament, arenas which are being crowded out by an array of actors at the national, supranational and global levels.

I explore the position of the contemporary Dáil through the theoretical lens of the post-parliamentary governance model. In other words, I employ the post-parliamentary governance model as a means of understanding the political reality of contemporary Dáil Éireann. The model falls into the 'what is' (descriptive) category rather than the 'ought to be' (normative) category. It should be observed that to argue, as Andersen and Burns do, that citizens are living in a *post*-parliamentary era, is both radical and provocative, given that European polities are commonly described as parliamentary democracies. Parliaments are, after all, the very embodiment of

---

15 Andersen and Burns, 1996.
16 Habermas, 1984, 1987, 1989, 1996; Fraser, 1992, 2007; Young, 1997a, 1997b, 2001, 2002; Strydom, 2002a.

democratic life for many citizens. Crucially, it must be strongly stated that the post-parliamentary governance model moves well beyond theories and polemics which suggest that parliaments are in decline. In this regard, the post-parliamentary governance model is sharply distinguished from the decline of parliament thesis which is discussed in chapter three.

Normatively, I employ public sphere theory to chart an enhanced democratic role for Dáil Éireann in the early 21st century:

> The public sphere denotes a space, real or virtual, in which individuals, who otherwise live private lives and have their own private concerns, come together to discuss issues of common concern with the purpose of thrashing out their different views and arriving at a common position.[17]

The public sphere can, therefore, be understood as a communicative and discursive space. It is a space in which a vast range of actors, individual and collective, state (including parliaments) and civil society, debate and discuss a wide range of issues before an observing, judging and evaluating audience. Young explains the functions of the public sphere as follows:

> The public sphere is the primary connector between people and power. We should judge the health of the public sphere by how well it functions as a space of opposition and accountability on the one hand, and policy influence on the other hand. In the public sphere political actors raise issues, publish information, opinion and aesthetic expression, criticise actions and policies, and propose new policies and practices.[18]

---

17 Crossley, 2005: 227–228.
18 Young, 2002: 173.

Parliaments are important participants in the public sphere. Reference was made at the beginning of this chapter to the controversial budgetary statement which was announced in Dáil Éireann during October 2008. As the controversy surrounding this budget demonstrates, events in Parliament clearly have the potential to ignite major debates in the public sphere. Equally, as was clearly illustrated in the aftermath of this budget, civil society can shape and influence matters under consideration in Parliament via the public sphere. Writing on the relationship between parliaments and civil society in the public sphere, Welton puts it well:

> The parliamentary system cannot simply proceed instrumentally or strategically. They are forced into dialogue with civil society, with morally infused communication as civil society's power source.[19]

Habermas offers us a sophisticated understanding of the public sphere's input potential. He places a strong emphasis on the respective roles of parliamentary institutions and civil society.[20] Civil society via the public sphere acts as a 'sounding board/sensor' for themes and problems. Whilst the public sphere detects, categorises and dramatises problems, it does not make decisions. Rather, opinions are formed in the public sphere, which are translated into communicative power in the parliamentary system and administrative power in the bureaucracy. On the Habermasian reading, therefore, the public sphere generates opinions which are potentially translated into decisions by the parliamentary and administrative systems. Civil society via the sensitive public sphere possesses the capacity to trigger initiatives and responses in parliamentary systems.[21]

---

19 Welton, 2001: 23.
20 Habermas, 1996.
21 *Ibid.*: 299–359.

Like Habermas, Hendricks affords a crucial role to civil society in the public sphere.[22] Theorists who focus on what she terms macro deliberative spaces are interested in:

> How informal, open, and unstructured deliberation in civil society can shape public opinion and in turn, political institutions.[23]

From my perspective, the public sphere provides Dáil Éireann with a tangible real world space in which it can promote the common good.

A number of issues and concerns have shaped my approach to this book. Firstly, I am deeply concerned with the implications that a peripheral Dáil has for democratic life. I argue that, as the core source of democratic legitimation, the Dáil ought to be a key actor. Secondly, members of the Dáil constantly complain that they have no real say in the political decision-making process.[24] Typical of this perspective are comments made by the All-Party Oireachtas Committee on the Constitution:

> There is a widespread and powerful sense that the two Houses are not fulfilling their functions as effectively as they should, and that their standing and relevance are in decline.[25]

Thirdly, as will become evident, the so-called decline of parliament thesis has occupied a key space in legislative studies literature for over a century. Parliaments, it is argued, have become actors subservient to

---

22 Hendricks, 2006.
23 *Ibid.*, 2006: 491.
24 Mitchell, 1991; Bruton and Mitchell, 2000; Brennock, 2000; Rabbitte, 2003; Quinn, 2005.
25 All-Party Oireachtas Committee on the Constitution, 2002: 9.

the executive branch of government. Fourthly, the primary origin of the approach I adopt can be traced to the proposition that the current era is one of deep and profound transformation in the political, economic and social spheres, a period of 'multiple revolutions', as Giddens suggests.[26]

The transformations associated with the current period have enormous implications for all existing institutional structures. In short, existing institutions as currently constituted, including parliaments, have diminishing capacity to cope with these transformations. Dahl argues that, unless existing institutions adapt to the new circumstances, democratic erosion will occur. Whilst Dahl remains quite optimistic about the capacity of democratic institutions to adapt, he does not under-estimate the challenges posed by the sheer scale of contemporary changes.[27]

I seek a new normative and real-world frame of reference for Dáil Éireann, namely the public sphere. But why the public sphere? After all, why *should* Dáil Éireann be a proactive member of the contemporary public sphere? I cite three reasons: firstly, the public sphere is primarily a discursive arena; in essence, it is an arena in which multiplicities of actors vie with each other for the public's attention. In contemporary polities, the public sphere is primarily a mediated arena, since actors tend not to address publics directly on a face-to-face basis but rather through national and global communication networks. The communications revolution has ensured that actors are much less restrained by time and space.

In contemporary politics, this mediated public sphere is of crucial importance. It may be as important as many of the more formal political spaces. The skills required to participate in this sphere are partly, but not

---

26 Giddens and Hutton, 2001: 213.
27 Dahl, 2000: 187–188.

exclusively, discursive. Debate, discourse, discussion and rhetoric have historically been essential tools of the parliamentarian. When we think of Parliament, debate and argument immediately come to mind. Discursive skills may even be more important for modern parliamentarians. As such, these parliamentary skills are readily transferable to the public sphere. To be succinct, there is a match between the discursive orientation of Parliament and the public sphere.

Secondly, I am interested in theoretical frameworks which place the common or public good at their ethical centre. A heavy emphasis on consumerism in contemporary Ireland erodes notions of the common good in favour of market success, neo-classical economics and selfish individualism. As a result, the polity is becoming increasingly atomised. Suffocating notions of citizenship, consumerism elevates self-regarding acts to the detriment of other-regarding acts. A consumerist discourse seems to have taken root. According to Gibbons:

> Yet so deeply entrenched has consumption become in our understanding of who we are that we barely notice, let alone complain, when our politicians, trade unions, business and media refer to us collectively as consumers. This contagion is everywhere.[28]

A counter-discourse is, therefore, required to challenge this contagion. Drawing on civic republican values, I will offer such a counter-discourse and I contend that concepts of the common good ought to be advocated by parliaments in the contemporary public sphere. Relying on their strong democratic mandates, parliaments, including Dáil Éireann, bring particularly strong credentials to any discussions in the public sphere.

---

28 Gibbons, 2008.

Thirdly, I am interested in frameworks which move beyond the normative assumptions of liberal democracy. Arguing that there is an increasing gap between the normative expectations of citizens and contemporary political conditions, I challenge certain core assumptions of liberal democracy. In particular, I challenge liberal democracy's normative supposition that the institutions of parliamentary government largely determine public policy outcomes. Employing the post-parliamentary governance model to illuminate contemporary political conditions, I advocate that both citizens and leaders ought to adjust their normative orientations. This adjustment will necessitate a radical transformation in the normative underpinnings of liberal democracy. I propose an alternative democratic role for parliaments, the contemporary public sphere.

CHANGE AND TRANSFORMATION IN CONTEMPORARY IRELAND

As if to emphasise the striking force of contemporary change, by September 2008 Ireland's so-called Celtic Tiger economy seemed like a historical memory as the Government struggled to cope with a global economic crisis. As the Bush Administration in the United States bailed out banks, governments around the world, including Ireland, appeared helpless and very fragile as the crisis deepened. Ireland had clearly entered the 'post-Celtic Tiger era'.[29] Rising unemployment, a rapidly deteriorating budgetary situation, a collapse in economic growth, political paralysis on the part of the Government, cuts in educational spending, house repossessions and a banking crisis were the themes which dominated the media coverage of 2008 and 2009. There was a sense that the forces of economic

---

29 Spring, 2008.

globalisation were beyond the control of governments. Equally, there was a sense that business and banking elites were receiving preferential treatment compared to ordinary citizens. The language of golden circles re-entered the lexicon. Ideologically unregulated free market capitalism *a la* Thatcher and Reagan was exposed to a rigorous analysis. Nevertheless, a fatal blow to Thatcherite/Reaganite economics does not necessarily herald a new dawn for left wing politics. By mid-2009, citizens, it seemed, were living in a very different and less optimistic Ireland than that of just twelve months earlier and they knew it would be at least five years before the country would recover, assuming the economy did not experience a literal systemic collapse.

Yet it would be foolish to dismiss how much Ireland had changed before late 2008. Post-Celtic Tiger Ireland has not diluted some of the most profound changes which have occurred in Ireland, particularly since the 1950s. I will focus specifically on those changes which are relevant to the post-parliamentary governance model and as I said earlier the post-parliamentary governance model holds that parliaments are being displaced and bypassed by an array of actors at the national, supranational and global levels. In the Irish context, these actors include European Union (EU) institutions, social partnership, interest groups and experts.

One of the most significant political events in the Republic of Ireland's recent history was accession to the then European Economic Community (EEC) on 1 January 1973. Membership of this supranational entity radically transformed the exercise of politics in Ireland. Given the sheer pace of the integration project since the Single European Act came into force in 1987, the transformation has been ongoing, dynamic and radical. More and more policy areas come within the competence of the Union. The Maastricht Treaty was the most radical amendment to the founding treaties. Legally establishing Economic and Monetary Union, it was the most significant advance for integrationists since the founding treaties were signed in the 1950s. Members of the euro zone, including Ireland, agreed to a set of macroeconomic parameters, a timetable for the single currency and transferred responsibility for interest rate management to an independent European Central Bank. Thus, the policy-making process is being 'Europeanised'. In the words of McGowan and Murphy, 'EU institutions evolve and member states adjust to EU membership'.[30]

At a purely formal level, sovereignty, as classically understood in the 1937 Irish Constitution, has been undermined. Couched in the language of classical sovereignty, Articles 5, 6 and 15 of the Constitution have a dated air about them:

> Article 5: Ireland is a sovereign, independent, democratic State.

> Article 6.2: These powers of government are exercisable only by or on the authority of the organs of State established by this Constitution.

> Article 15.2.1: The sole and exclusive power of making laws for the State is hereby vested in the Oireachtas: no other legislative authority has power to make laws for the State.

The political reality is simple: in the polity of the early 21st century, classical concepts of sovereignty are largely defunct. The organs of constitutional government do not exercise exclusive competence as envisaged in the Constitution. It is not necessary to look beyond the European Court of Justice's seminal rulings on supremacy to realise the changing architecture of sovereignty for all member

---

30 McGowan and Murphy, 2003: 185.

states, including Ireland. In a radical departure from Westphalian principles, which emphasise the pre-eminence of the independent state, the European Court of Justice declared during 1964 that, in the integration project, Community law takes precedence over national law in particular circumstances.[31] As such, Union law prevails over the Irish Constitution. As Stein notes:

> The Court of Justice has fashioned a constitutional framework for a federal type structure in Europe.[32]

Ireland is, therefore, not a classically sovereign, self-contained political system. Rather, it shares sovereignty with its fellow members of the European Union. Writing on aspects of Ireland's membership of the European Union, Laffan emphasises the collective nature of the EU:

> In the Union power is exercised by the member states acting collectively within the institutional and constitutional framework established by treaties and evolving custom and practice.[33]

The collective nature of European Union governance means that the project does not simply involve a transfer of sovereignty from the national to the supranational. Such an interpretation would amount to a gross over-simplification of European Union politics. The situation is in fact far more complex. Laffan captures this complexity:

> Yet the Union is not simply a creature of its member states: its institutions have a capacity for autonomous action, its legal order is

---

31 Costa *v* Enel, Case 6/64.
32 Stein, 1981: 1.
33 Laffan, 2001: 1.

federal in character and membership of the Union shapes national preferences and constrains independence.[34]

Membership of the European Union seems to have been particularly beneficial for the Irish economy. Released from its dependence on the British market, Irish exporters grasped the opportunities of the common European market. An economy once based on protectionist principles was exposed to the threats and opportunities of the Common Market. Union membership paved the way for the State's arrival on the competitive stage of footloose global capital. Until recently Ireland has been a net beneficiary of European funds, with agriculture in particular heavily subsidised via the Common Agricultural Policy. It is hardly surprising that membership of the Union has been sold by the political elite in economic terms. Membership of Economic and Monetary Union establishes macroeconomic parameters. The power to set interest rates lies with the independent European Central Bank. Thus, Ireland and other euro-zone countries have lost a vital instrument of economic policy.

Within the political science literature, much has been written on the European Union's democratic deficit.[35] I have identified five dimensions, including, crucially, the marginalisation and displacement of national parliaments in the Union's decision-making process.[36] I ask in chapter nine how Dáil Éireann has reacted to Union membership since entry into the EEC in 1973. Specifically, I will examine what

---

34 Laffan, 1996: 14.

35 Chryssochoou *et al*, 1998; Chryssochoou, 2000; Dogan, 1997; Eriksen and Fossum, 2000; Decker, 2002; Featherstone, 1994; Laffan, 1999; Lord, 1998; Lord and Beetham, 2001; Lord and Magnette, 2004; Raunio, 2005; Raworth 1994; Rumford, 2003; Scharpf, 1996; Weiler, 1995; Weiler *et al*, 1995.

36 O'Halloran, 2003.

measures the Dáil has put in place to scrutinise European Union legislation.

Since 1987, Ireland has adopted the so-called social partnership approach to public policy, although it should be noted that in the post-Celtic Tiger economy of autumn 2009 it is not at all clear whether social partnership will survive as a central bulwark of Irish public policy-making. The social partnership agreements have consisted of two core parts, namely macroeconomic policy and centralised wage bargains. In its original format the social partners consisted of state, labour and business representatives. However, departing from this classical tripartite model, a community and voluntary pillar was included, which resulted in the successful negotiation of the Programme for Prosperity and Fairness (PPF) during 2000. This pillar represents a broad spectrum of civil society, particularly groups which represent the disadvantaged and socially excluded.

The social partnership agreements, ostensibly at least, take the form of tortuous make or break negotiations. Once agreement is reached, the broad parameters of public policy are set for successive years. Many commentators argue that the social partnership model has been one of the key ingredients of recent economic success associated with the Celtic Tiger era.[37] Others have suggested that, whilst interest groups have gained privileged access to the public-policy-making process, it has come at the price of eroding parliamentary politics.[38] Commenting on this aspect of social partnership, Roche and Cradden suggest:

> It is also seen to be undemocratic in elevating the influence of interest groups in economic policy-making over that of the elected Parliament.

---

37 MacSharry and White, 2000: 144.
38 Ó Cinneide, 1998; FitzGerald, 2000; Collins, 2004.

This has been an important strand of commentary on the Irish experience; but as social partnership seemed to prove its economic worth as the 1990s proceeded, this view was pressed less forcefully.[39]

And, speaking in a post-Celtic Tiger context, a member of Seanad Éireann expressed his frustration:

> One would pinch oneself on what passes for democratic debate and scrutiny in this country because the Government goes to the social partners in the first instance and not the Houses of Parliament.[40]

Dáil Éireann's role in the social partnership process will be examined in chapter ten. Breaking down the partnership into four different phases, I will examine the Dáil's input at each stage. Given the central role which social partnership has played in contemporary Irish politics, Dáil Éireann's exclusion from the partnership process could be held to create a democratic deficit. Democratic principles clearly demand that the Dáil should be afforded either an input or accountability role in the partnership process.

INTEREST GROUPS AND EXPERTS

The anecdotal evidence strongly suggests that the contemporary Dáil has become a hive of interest-group activity. At present, it is very common to observe adverts by Parliamentary Committees seeking observations from groups. When deliberating upon specific policy issues it has become a regular practice that a process of public consultation is undertaken. Similarly, groups make oral presentations

---

39 Roche and Cradden, 2003: 74.
40 White, quoted in Collins, 2008.

to Committee members. A vibrant Committee system has facilitated the mobilisation of interest groups. The anecdotal evidence suggests that Committees have become an important target for groups.

There is support in existing literature for this. For example O'Halpin and Connolly suggest that interest groups lobby intensively in and around Leinster House.[41] However, it has to be observed that their findings are void of any empirical evidence. In the British case, Norton has argued that, since the early 1970s, interest groups are very active in Westminster Palace.[42] In Denmark, Parliamentary Committees have become increasingly important sites of interest-group activity since the mid-1970s.[43] In the Irish case, there has been an explosion in the number of interest groups in recent decades. I will explore whether the contemporary Dáil Committee system has facilitated the mobilisation of interest groups in Kildare Street. In particular, I will ask whether interest groups are bypassing Dáil Éireann in its Committee guise.

In addition to interest groups, experts have become significant actors in the public policy-making process. Consultants' reports have become an important part of the political vernacular. Before progressing with major policy initiatives, Government Departments frequently seek an 'independent' overview of the policy options.

The post-parliamentary governance model emphasises the central role experts play in contemporary governance. Employing the concept of 'expert sovereignty', Andersen and Burns argue that the complexities of contemporary governance afford experts a crucial political role.[44]

---

41 O'Halpin and Connolly, 1999.
42 Norton, 1994.
43 Damgaard, 1994.
44 Andersen and Burns, 1996.

I will address the topic of 'expert sovereignty', providing empirical evidence on the role of experts and consultants in contemporary Irish politics. More specifically, I will ask whether Dáil Éireann is marginalised by expert sovereignty.

Historically, Dáil Éireann as an institution pre-dates the present 1937 Constitution. The first meeting took place in January 1919. From 1800 to 1918 Irish Members of Parliament sat in the British House of Commons. However, the 1918 general election transformed the Irish political landscape. A separatist party, Sinn Féin, gained a massive electoral victory, securing 73 of Ireland's 105 Westminster seats. Sinn Féin interpreted this result as a mandate to break all constitutional links with the British crown. Refusing to send its MPs to Westminster, Sinn Féin decided to establish an independent Irish Parliament. It was in these revolutionary circumstances that Dáil Éireann assembled for its first historic meeting in the Mansion House, Dublin, on 21 January 1919.

Conventional wisdom has it that Ireland imported the Westminster model of government. This, however, is only partially correct. The Irish system of government has always been far less parliament-centred than its Westminster equivalent. The 2003 debates on the Iraq war in the House of Commons demonstrated how even a Prime Minister with an overwhelming majority can incur the wrath of Parliament. Dáil Éireann, on the other hand, has always tended to be culturally and systemically subservient to the Cabinet. Many of the Dáil's deficiencies can be traced to this subservience.

Members of Dáil Éireann are elected in forty-three multi-member constituencies for a maximum term of five years. A key objective of Ireland's electoral system of Proportional Representation by means of the Single Transferable Vote (PRSTV) is electoral proportionality. It is designed to ensure that, if a political party gets 10% of the national vote, it gets *approximately* 10% of the seats in Dáil Éireann. Gallagher observes that, historically, the system has tended to achieve quite a high degree of proportionality. But trends are changing:

> Ireland, having been well towards the more proportional scale for most of the post-war period, is now exhibiting disproportionality levels of the same order as the less proportional PR-using countries such as Spain and Greece.[45]

The 2002 general election results provide a useful example. Fianna Fáil won 49% of Dáil seats on a vote of 41%. As such, it enjoyed a significant positive bonus winning twelve more Dáil seats than it was proportionately entitled to. The Progressive Democrats also enjoyed a positive bonus gaining two more seats. On the other hand, Fine Gael and Sinn Féin were victims of a negative bonus, both winning six fewer seats than they were proportionately entitled to.[46]

Nevertheless, compared to the United Kingdom's first-past-the-post system, Ireland's system does not generate severe disproportionality. The 1997 British general election provides a good example of severe disproportionality. Whilst the Liberal Democrats secured 16.8% of the vote this translated into only 7.0% of parliamentary seats; Labour, on the other hand, secured a massive 63.6% of parliamentary seats on a national vote of 43.3%.[47]

Ireland's electoral system is simple to understand from the voters' perspective:

---

45 Gallagher, 2003: 110.
46 Coakley, 2003: 33; Gallagher, 2003: 111–112.
47 Gallagher, Laver and Mair, 2001: 306.

All that is needed in order to use the system to the full is the understanding of the notion of ranking a set of candidates according to one's preferences.[48]

The elector simply votes for candidates in order of his/her preferences. Thus, if there are ten candidates on the ballot, a maximum of ten preferences can be exercised. There is of course no obligation on the elector to exercise all of his/her preferences. The electorate, it seems, is content with the system as proposals to abolish it during 1959 and 1968 were rejected.

Constitutionally, the Dáil enjoys three core functions. Firstly, the Dáil appoints and dismisses the Government. Secondly, it holds the Government to account. Thirdly, it enacts legislation in partnership with Seanad Éireann, subject to the right of the President to refer the bills to the Supreme Court to test their constitutionality.

The method of appointing the Government is set out in Articles 13.1.1 and 13.1.2 of the Constitution:

The President shall, on the nomination of Dáil Éireann, appoint the Taoiseach, that is, the head of the Government or Prime Minister.

The President shall, on the nomination of the Taoiseach with the previous approval of Dáil Éireann, appoint the other members of the Government.

After each general election the Dáil convenes to discharge two immediate tasks, the election of the Ceann Comhairle (Chairperson) followed by the election of the Taoiseach (Prime Minister). The Taoiseach, having been formally appointed by the President, presents his/her Government (fifteen senior Ministers) to the Dáil. The

48 Sinnott, 2005: 110.

President formally appoints the Ministers subsequent to this vote of parliamentary approval.

The Government holds office only as long as it maintains the confidence of the Dáil. Ultimately the Dáil may dismiss the Cabinet through the medium of a no confidence motion. The key article in the Constitution is Article 28.10:

> The Taoiseach shall resign from office upon his ceasing to retain the support of a majority in Dáil Éireann unless on his advice the President dissolves Dáil Éireann and on the reassembly of Dáil Éireann after the dissolution the Taoiseach secures the support of a majority in Dáil Éireann.

It should be noted that, when the Taoiseach resigns, all of his/her Ministers automatically resign too.

Holding the Government to account is an important parliamentary function in all liberal democracies. In this regard, Article 28.4.1 of the Irish Constitution is unambiguously crisp in stating that 'the Government shall be responsible to Dáil Éireann.' In discharging this function, members have three main instruments at their disposal. Parliamentary questions (oral and written) are perhaps the most important instrument available to members. Oral question time in particular provides members with the opportunity to scrutinise a Minister using supplementary questions. Party leaders enjoy a special privilege at the start of Dáil business. They can put oral questions without formal advance notice to the Taoiseach. The Order of Business determines the Dáil's daily business. However, Opposition Deputies frequently use the Order of Business to raise issues which may prove embarrassing for the Government.

A further instrument available to Deputies is Private Members' Business. Just three hours per week are allocated for Private Members'

Business. The relevant political party will frame a motion designed to highlight a particular issue.

The final instrument is the Parliamentary Committee. During Committee hearings members have the opportunity to pursue Ministers in some detail on relevant matters. Since 1993, there are specialist Parliamentary Committees to shadow departments. Membership reflects the relevant party's strength in the chamber. In effect, this means Government-appointed members will always enjoy a voting majority. The Government also nominates a majority of Committee chairs.

In all liberal democracies, parliaments enjoy important legislative functions. The legislative procedures within Dáil Éireann are based on the Westminster model. Essentially, a bill passes through five stages. The greatest scrutiny takes place at Committee level. Here the relevant specialist Committee may question the mover (invariably a Minister) of the bill in some detail. Most legislation enacted by the Oireachtas originates with the Government. Very few private members' bills make it onto the statute books. As MacCarthaigh observes, only fifteen became law in the sixty-five year period from 1937 to 2002.[49]

Until the late 1980s, the seats in the Dáil were usually divided among three political parties and a few independent Deputies. The two larger centre right parties, Fianna Fáil and Fine Gael, in combination took on average over 80% of the national vote. The share of the national vote usually obtained by the smaller social democratic Labour Party hovered around 10%. Government formation consisted of two basic choices: a single party Fianna Fáil Government which occurred for two unbroken periods between 1932 and 1948 and between 1957 and 1973, or a coalition of Fine Gael and Labour which occurred between 1973 and 1977 and again in 1981 and between 1982 and 1987. Fianna Fáil was

---

49 MacCarthaigh, 2005: 11.

thus perceived as the natural party of government, with Fine Gael and Labour destined to spend long periods on the opposition benches.

However, since the late 1980s the average vote of Fianna Fáil and Fine Gael combined has declined by almost 15%. Fine Gael has fared the worst accounting as it does for 9% of the combined loss.[50]

The Dáil arithmetic changed significantly in 1987 when a newly formed party, the Progressive Democrats, stood in that year's general election. Standing on a right-wing Thatcherite platform, they gained 11.85% of the national vote, which translated into fourteen parliamentary seats. The arrival of the Progressive Democrats on the political scene has had a significant impact on Government formation. Since 1989, Fianna Fáil has never led a single-party Government, having instead to rely on coalitions with the Green Party, the Progressive Democrats or Labour. The days of single-party Fianna Fáil Government in Ireland appear to be over. In the 1992 general election Labour enjoyed what, with the benefit of hindsight, was a false dawn. Its share of the national vote soared to 19.31%, giving it an unprecedented thirty-three parliamentary seats. However, its share of the vote fell back to 10.4% in 1997.

A significant transformation in Irish parliamentary politics took place during the 2002 general election. Firstly, the Fine Gael party returned to the 29th Dáil having won just thirty-one seats, a drop of twenty-three from the 28th Dáil. Secondly, the election yielded an increased number of independent members. Thirteen independent members were returned. Thirdly, Sinn Féin, the Greens and the Progressive Democrats returned to the 29th Dáil with increased representation. Four new seats brought Sinn Féin's membership to five in the 29th Dáil. The Green Party increased its representation from two to six. Contrary to pre-

---

50   Mair and Weeks, 2005: 152.

election media speculation of the virtual elimination of the Progressive Democrats, the party doubled its representation securing eight seats. Fourthly, the Fianna Fáil and Labour share of the national vote only changed marginally.

The net effect of these changes is that the 29th Dáil was probably the most fragmented since 1948. However, the fragmentation was confined to the opposition benches. The Fianna Fáil–Progressive Democrat coalition was returned to office with a secure majority.

The 2007 general election witnessed a significant reduction in the number of independents elected. Just five independents were returned to the 30th Dáil. Fine Gael returned to the 30th Dáil with fifty-one seats, a net gain of twenty on their disastrous 2002 result. Fianna Fáil lost three seats, returning with seventy-eight Deputies whilst Labour secured twenty seats, just one less than their 2002 performance. The Progressive Democrats lost six seats returning just two members which ultimately led to a decision to dissolve the party in November 2008. Sinn Féin returned with four members, down one on 2002, whilst the Greens remained unchanged at six seats.

The 30th Dáil is therefore a much less fragmented institution. When the 30th Dáil met on 14 June 2007, a three-party coalition of Fianna Fáil, the Green Party and the Progressive Democrats formed the new Government. Fianna Fáil negotiators also made deals with four independents to ensure that the smaller coalition partners would enjoy less leverage over Fianna Fáil. The Greens thus entered Government for the first time whilst Bertie Ahern, defying the odds, became Taoiseach for a third time. Brian Cowen replaced Bertie Ahern as Taoiseach on 7 May 2008. Mr Ahern resigned from office on the back of allegations that he received improper financial donations from businessmen during the 1990s, a matter that has been investigated by a Tribunal of Inquiry.

2

Dáil Éireann in an Era
of Multiple Revolutions

So that one cannot abuse power, power must check power by the arrangement of things.[1]

People sometimes complain that since the war MPs have had to waste too much of their time as welfare officers. I profoundly disagree. Every MP should act as a Miss Lonelyhearts. The busier a politician is with national or international affairs, the more important is his constituency casework.[2]

People expect to find politics in the arenas prescribed for it, and performed by the duly authorised agents: Parliament, political parties, trade unions and so on. If the clocks of politics stop here, the political as a whole has stopped ticking ...[3]

My primary purpose in this chapter is to place Dáil Éireann in the context of changes and transformations associated with the current era. I explore what the literature (primarily Irish) has to say on Dáil Éireann. What emerges is a picture of three models dominating the

---

1 Montesquieu [1748], 1994: 155.
2 Healey, 1989: 139–140.
3 Beck, 1994: 17.

literature since the 1960s. Subsequently, frameworks in the social sciences which place the themes of change and transformation at their explanatory centre are examined. The implications of these frameworks for parliamentary institutions are highlighted.

A cursory examination of the political science literature on Dáil Éireann yields one clear conclusion: Dáil Éireann operates within narrow analytical and normative frameworks. Firstly, adopting Montesquieu's executive–legislative relations framework, the literature suggests that the Dáil rubberstamps the wishes of a dominant Executive.[4] Typical of this approach is Chubb, who concludes that:

> The corollary of a powerful Government with a monopoly of initiative and great power to manage is a puny Parliament peopled by members who have a modest view of their functions and a poor capacity to carry them out.[5]

Chubb addressed this issue as early as 1963 in a seminal paper entitled 'Going about Persecuting Civil Servants'. O'Halpin explains Chubb's key argument, namely that most TDs are:

> …engaged primarily in interventions with national and local bureaucracy on behalf of their constituents, all but oblivious to their constitutional roles as legislators and scrutineers of the actions of the Executive, and constrained from useful contribution to the parliamentary discussion of public affairs by strict party discipline.[6]

A former Labour Party TD who obviously found life as a Government backbencher particularly restrictive supports this view:

---

4 Arkins, 1990; Ward, 1996.
5 Chubb, 1992: 189.
6 O'Halpin, 1998: 127.

The ideal one is a Lady or a Gentleman who has virtually no ideas or proposals and in the event of such backbenchers being contaminated by an idea, they will have the good sense to keep their mouth shut.[7]

O'Halpin observes that Chubb's framework 'has predominated in academic discussion of the Oireachtas ever since'.[8] Indeed, O'Halpin argues that culturally Dáil Éireann 'took the absolute dominance of the Executive for granted'.[9] A tightly-whipped party system ensures that both Opposition and Government TDs follow the party line. It is hardly surprising that only two Governments have fallen to a no confidence motion since the foundation of the State in 1922.[10] No wonder MacCarthaigh observes that:

… for most of the State's existence, its Parliament has been seen as effectively powerless to challenge the dominant Government that it elects.[11]

And Murphy argues that contemporary Dáil reform processes have:

… in some ways produced even stronger Government in Ireland. A feature of strong Government is that it is not typically responsive to Parliament.[12]

Dáil reform, therefore, needs to be closely monitored as to its effect on executive–legislative relations. Murphy's contribution is highly

---

7   Upton, 1996.
8   O'Halpin, 1996: 127.
9   *Ibid.*: 134.
10 Gallagher, 2005: 216.
11 MacCarthaigh, 2005: 1.
12 Murphy, 2006: 450.

useful because it compels us to consider that Dáil reform is not necessarily a parliamentary panacea. On the contrary, she reminds us that reform efforts may enhance the capacity of executives to 'manage' parliaments.

Secondly, adopting a clientelist/brokerage model, literature contends that TDs spend a significant proportion of their time nursing constituencies:

> The political broker who intervenes on behalf of constituents to help them obtain Government benefits and the constituent who rewards the politician with his vote has become an acceptable and even fashionable model of political life.[13]

The constituency role of Dáil members has been extensively examined under this particular model.[14] Rather than behaving as parliamentarians, members devote their time to 'persecuting civil servants'.[15] O'Halpin reiterates the conventional critique:

> It has frequently been argued that the traditional preoccupation with constituency affairs renders many parliamentarians oblivious to wider national issues.[16]

In other words, TDs behave as constituency servants rather than legislators.[17] Members are expected to deliver the goods for their

---

13 Komito, 1984: 173.
14 Bax, 1976; Carty, 1980, 1981; Collins, 1985; Collins and O'Shea, 2003; Collins, 2004; Collins and Butler, 2004; Gibbon and Higgins, 1974; Higgins, 1982; Kelly, 1987; Komito, 1984, 1989, 1992, 1997; O'Halpin, 2002; Sacks, 1976; Whyte, 1966.
15 Chubb, 1963.
16 O'Halpin, 2002: 118.
17 Geoghegan-Quinn, 1998.

constituency and individual constituents. This is not to suggest that Deputies actually control the distribution of resources as a patron would. Rather, they may influence:

> ... minor administrative decisions where some additional information may produce a fairer or more efficient outcome.[18]

Former Minister Barry Desmond makes a distinction between clientelism and representative duties, arguing that there is:

> ... a democratic obligation on all Deputies to make themselves available to community groups and individual constituents and to take their views on board, if possible.[19]

Even in an ostensibly less constituency-oriented polity such as the United Kingdom, support can be found for Desmond's view. Former Chancellor of the Exchequer Denis Healey paints a colourful picture:

> People sometimes complain that since the war MPs have had to waste too much of their time as welfare officers. I profoundly disagree. Every MP should act as a Miss Lonelyhearts. The busier a politician is with national or international affairs, the more important is his constituency casework.[20]

Nevertheless, clientelism in its constituency representation guise has its critics. In the following passage from his autobiography, former Minister Noel Browne recalls the antics of one of his fellow

---

18 Collins, 2004: 606.
19 Desmond, 2000: 52.
20 Healey, 1989: 139–140.

Government Ministers during the 1948–51 Inter-Party Government:

> Having carefully 'clocked' into the Cabinet meetings on those days in which the County Council sat in Wicklow, Everett would gather his largely unread sack full of briefs, utter his apologies, and slip away. He had little time for Cabinet meetings compared to the supreme importance of Wicklow County Council.[21]

In the example just cited, it appears that local constituency work had a significant impact on ministerial behaviour. The Minister in question obviously felt his primary loyalties lay at constituency level. Continuing the theme of ministerial behaviour, former Taoiseach Garret FitzGerald notes that Ministers are expected to give preferential treatment to their constituencies:

> … there is ample evidence that Ministers do in fact, set out to distort resource allocation and decentralisation of units of the civil service, thus retrospectively 'justifying' the popular demand that ministries be distributed on a geographical basis.[22]

As discussed before, an *Irish Times* editorial strongly condemned what it referred to as the 'pernicious curse of clientelism'.[23] And in an article entitled 'A Culture TD Fixers Thrive On', Fintan O'Toole argues that TDs are 'wedded' to the existing clientelist system.[24] In addition, Garret FitzGerald, in an opinion article entitled 'Clientelism Still Blights Political Life of the Nation', raises the tension between

---

21 Browne, 1986: 194–195.
22 FitzGerald, 2003: 67.
23 Editorial, *The Irish Times*, 2007.
24 O'Toole, 2007.

addressing constituency and individual grievances and promotion of the polity's general welfare:

> A basic problem for politicians is that the private interests of individual citizens will often, perhaps even usually, be in conflict with the general good of the electorate as a whole.[25]

Thirdly, adopting an electoral systems model, the literature discusses whether the electoral system (Proportional Representation Single Transferable Vote – PRSTV) is one of the core causes of brokerage within the Irish polity.[26] Intuitively, it appears plausible to contend that multi-member competitive constituencies force TDs to focus excessively on constituency work to the apparent detriment of their parliamentary duties. Calls for radical reform of the system are common. During the 1997–2002 Dáil the then Minister for the Environment, Noel Dempsey, led calls for reform advocating the adoption of the additional member system, which is used in both New Zealand and Germany. Under this system, half of Dáil Éireann's membership would be elected from single seat constituencies and half from a party list system. According to the Minister, this system would enhance parliamentary scrutiny of the Executive, reduce clientelism and lead to a more representative Dáil.[27]

However, proposals for change cannot be approached casually as the PRSTV system is constitutionally enshrined. Any changes, therefore, require the approval of the people in the form of a constitutional amendment and as noted in chapter one, on two previous occasions,

---

25 FitzGerald, 2006.

26 Carty, 1980; Farrell, 1985; Fitzgerald, 2003; Gallagher, 1996; Gallagher and Komito, 1999; Laver, 1998; Sinnott, 1999.

27 Quoted in All-Party Oireachtas Committee on the Constitution, 2002: 20.

1959 and 1968, the people rejected proposals to abolish PRSTV. In the light of these experiences, politicians are obviously cautious. The *Seventh Progress Report of the All-Party Oireachtas Committee on the Constitution*, published in 2002, examined alternatives. But the Committee recommended that the current system be retained. In any event, it is unwise to ascribe all the ills of Irish parliamentary politics to the electoral system. There is no guarantee that a different electoral system would reduce the brokerage pressures on Irish politicians. As Gallagher and Komito argue:

> Members of Parliament in countries with a range of different electoral systems undertake a lot of constituency work.[28]

In the British case, for example, there has been a significant increase in constituency work since the 1960s.[29]

MULTIPLE REVOLUTIONS

The current era is the era of 'posts'. Post-industrial, post-national, post-materialist, post-modern, post-Fordist, post-corporatist, post-communist, post-Catholic-Ireland, post-9/11 and post-parliamentary. And as of 2009, post-Celtic Tiger. Social scientists and citizens struggle to understand changes and transformations in this world of 'posts' as it is the era of 'multiple revolutions'.[30] Change, transformation and mutation occupy a pivotal theoretical position within the contemporary social science literature. Here I explore three positions

---

28 Gallagher and Komito, 1999: 220.
29 Norris, 1997: 30.
30 Giddens and Hutton, 2001: 213.

which place change and transformation at their theoretical centre. These are globalisation, the risk society and multi-level governance.

The concept of globalisation has been subject to wide-ranging and in-depth analysis. It is of interest to political scientists, challenging as it does state-centric analytical frameworks. In particular, the Westphalian assumption that sovereignty is rooted in the nation state appears to have decreasing relevance at present. For international relations scholars, globalisation undermines the state-centric assumptions of the realist paradigm, which interprets the world order as a collection of power-driven separate states who vie with each other for superiority. A supranational entity such as the European Union defies realist expectations. Normative democratic theorists are offered the tantalising prospect of democratic governance above the level of the nation state. Globalisation demands that political sociologists re-examine the normative underpinnings of citizenship. Public policy experts explore the extent to which globalisation shapes statal policy preferences. Globalisation has become a ubiquitous concept in the social sciences as it appears to challenge all existing orthodoxy.

The very nature of the concept of globalisation places change and transformation at its theoretical centre. However, this theoretical position differs from previous approaches (modernisation theory), which adopted a linear approach to change and transformation. Globalisation, on the other hand, seems to adopt a dynamic and non-linear approach. It is a highly complex concept, which incorporates change in many different spheres.[31] Giddens identifies four key dimensions, namely the communications revolution, the knowledge economy, the post-1989 world order and transformations in everyday life. Giddens contends that combining these four sets of changes

---

31 *Ibid.*: 33.

means that 'the level of global transformation they signal is nothing short of spectacular'.[32]

Footloose capital, international law and emergent global governance structures are concrete political examples of these changes. Footloose global capital is genuinely *supranational* in its organisation. Transcending national boundaries, it enjoys the capacity to act independently of the nation state. As such, it must be clearly distinguished from *international* trade between sovereign nation states. However, that is not to say that states are mere creatures of global capitalism. Rather:

> States retain a good deal of scope for policy choice, resulting in enduring diversity both in social policy provisions and in overall features of economic performance.[33]

There is also evidence that a global legal order is emerging. Whilst these legal structures are primarily international in their orientation, global tendencies are not entirely absent. Most notably, many international legal instruments, such as the Universal Declaration of Human Rights, claim universal application. Of course, the European Union is the world's only truly supranational legal entity. The Union's institutions enjoy an independent law-making capacity above the level of the nation state. Crucially, the European Court of Justice enforces these laws. Global governance structures have also been formed. These include the World Trade Organization, the International Monetary Fund, the World Bank and the various organs of the United Nations. Unlike the European Union, these organisations do not enjoy an

---

32 *Ibid.*: 2.
33 Hardiman, 2002: 1.

autonomous law or policy-making capacity. Nevertheless, these organisations do:

> To some extent enforce a host of transworld norms, rules and procedures in wide-ranging areas including technical standards and (purportedly) universal human rights.[34]

There is also a social and cultural dimension to globalisation. Transnational social movements, emerging global identities and the information technology revolution fall under this category. Crucially, changes in the social/cultural category create a global communicative space. Thus, citizens, particularly when they combine collectively, are central actors in the social and cultural dimensions of change. This point is important because it demonstrates that citizens collectively have the capacity to shape the future direction of globalisation. Whilst technological and economic determinism may indeed be features of the globalisation process, it would be unwise to exclude the power of human action.

The communications revolution may provide particularly fertile soil for the emergence of an embryonic global citizenship. National citizenship relies on an 'us and other' relationship to sustain it. Global communication, whether in electronic or face-to-face form, should theoretically break down such relationships. Similarly, global civil society provides spaces for supranational social and cultural intercourse. As of 2000, approximately '16,500 global/transnational civil society associations' existed.[35] In overall terms, state-centric understandings of citizenship are eroded.

---

34 Scholte, 2000: 53.
35 *Ibid.*: 58.

Is such a cosmopolitan-centred account justified? A more realistic analysis would proceed as follows. Citizenship is conventionally defined as membership of a political community. Membership of this community brings with it a package of rights and obligations. Crucially, members share a sense of common identity, whether ethnic or civic in kind. Put another way, members share a sense of belonging. For at least two centuries, the sovereign nation state has constituted community. Citizenship is the glue which holds the nation state together. Citizenship and identity are hence rooted in the nation state. As such, citizenship is understood in state-centric, not supranational, terms.

There is, however, an increasing recognition that multiple identities are not only feasible but are already a feature of our everyday lives at statal level. There does not have to be an either/or dualism between state-centric and cosmopolitan notions of identity. Rather, different identities can co-exist. The forces of globalisation will not displace territorially based citizenship. However, state-centric citizenship will most probably continue to be undermined. The extent of this process is, of course, an unknown at this moment. In time, citizenship may be divorced from singular, state-centric notions of identity.

The second position I examine is Beck's risk society.[36] Like the concept of globalisation, his risk society offers a provocative perspective on the nature of current transformations. Beck defines risk as:

> ... a systematic way of dealing with hazards and insecurities induced and introduced by modernisation itself.[37]

---

36 Beck, 1992, 1994, 2001.
37 *Ibid.*: 21.

In the risk society Beck argues that:

> ... the problems and conflicts relating to distribution in a society of scarcity overlap with the problems and conflicts that arise from the production, definition and distribution of techno-scientifically produced risks.[38]

The language of dangers and hazards enters the discourse, much of which revolves around how risks are and ought to be distributed.[39] Risk becomes the driving dynamic of change. According to Beck, risk society is an example of 'epochal and systemic transformation'.[40] Risks in the latter half of the 20th century result from the scientific and technological actions of humans rather than the forces of nature. Human beings acquire the capacity to destroy the human race itself, so the destructive dimensions of technology and science are highlighted. Significantly, the processes, changes and outcomes of risk society do not respect national borders:

> Risk society, fully thought through, means world risk society. For its axial principle, its challenges are dangers produced by civilisation, which cannot be socially delimited in either space or time.[41]

Beck's sub-politics framework offers a challenge to the liberal democratic ideological supremacy.[42] Politics takes place in arenas other than liberal democratic institutions. According to Beck, current transformations necessitate a broad and fluid understanding of what

---

38 *Ibid.*: 19.
39 Strydom, 2002a.
40 Beck, 1994: 7.
41 Beck, 2001: 20.
42 *Ibid.*: 91–108.

constitutes politics. Politics is not confined to parliamentary elections, the election of executives and the granting of privileged access to neo-corporatist and policy-network actors. Thus, citizens, experts and social movements become potentially powerful political actors. Sub-politicisation, therefore, involves a decrease in the power of central government. New actors enter the changing political arena.

Changes and transformations ensure that liberal democratic institutions no longer enjoy a privileged space in the sphere of 21st-century politics. Beck observes that:

> People expect to find politics in the arenas prescribed for it, and performed by the duly authorised agents: Parliament, political parties, trade unions and so on. If the clocks of politics stop here, the political as a whole has stopped ticking ...[43]

In Beck's sub-politics framework the clock of politics does not stop at the door of formal organs of government and other privileged actors. These actors remain important. However, the clock of politics ticks in new spaces, which are occupied by hitherto non-political actors. Politics is thus re-invented.

The final position I examine in this section is the theory of multi-level governance, which seeks to capture the complex and dynamic nature of contemporary changes and transformations. Originally conceived in an EU-specific context, it has increasingly been applied across all sub-fields of political science. Operating at both spatial and organisational levels, multi-level governance occupies a key position in contemporary political science literature. Bache and Flinders offer the following understanding of the concept:

---

43   Beck, 1994: 17.

Multi-level referred to the increased interdependence of Governments operating at different territorial levels, whilst 'governance' signalled the growing interdependence between Government and non-governmental actors at various territorial levels.[44]

The theory is a marriage of two terms, namely governance and multi-level. Governance has become an all-pervasive concept in the social science and public discourse generally. Governance is the notion that a multiplicity of actors, governmental and non-governmental, influence and shape political processes and outcomes. The concept of governance moves beyond a purely institutional understanding of politics. The institutions of state do not exercise a political monopoly. Decision-making is dispersed across a wide range of actors rather than concentrated in the state's classical organs of government.

The term 'multi-level' refers to the notion that the exercise of contemporary politics is becoming less state-centric. Whilst the state level remains crucial, it nevertheless does not enjoy a monopoly on the exercise of politics. The territorially bounded nation state is but one, albeit a crucial, spatial entity. Politics operates at local, regional, state, international, supranational and global levels and is not interpreted as spatially bounded within the nation state. A wide range of actors interact at these different levels. Governmental and non-governmental actors may operate at different levels either simultaneously or concurrently.

It should be highlighted that the concept 'multi-level governance' differs substantially from its much older predecessor, 'government'. The concept of government favours formal institutions of state such as parliaments and executives. Multi-level governance, whilst recognising the importance of these formal organs, incorporates a much broader

---

44   Bache and Flinders, 2004: 3.

range of actors. Thus, multi-level governance emphasises that contemporary politics is characterised by 'multi-actorness'.[45]

A government-centred approach would contend that political decisions are the outcome of formal political processes. But, under the multi-level governance model, both formal and informal processes are accorded key roles. Similarly, the concept of government tends to be synonymous with the state. Multi-level governance, on the other hand, transcends state-centric approaches. It is spatially unbounded and fluid, and operates at different spatial levels, from the subnational to the global, but both concepts divide sharply on the issue of sovereignty. A government perspective is state-centric, conflating sovereignty with the territorially bounded nation state. Sovereignty is firmly rooted in the nation state. Multi-level governance implies that this classical Westphalian approach to sovereignty is obsolete. Sovereignty is shared at different levels.

All three perspectives, globalisation, the risk society and multi-level governance, share a number of characteristics. Firstly, at a territorial level the nation state no longer enjoys a highly privileged political space. This is not to say that the end of the state as a political entity is imminent. Rather, the state is one of several key players in contemporary politics. It has not been displaced. It has not been transcended. However, its role has been both transformed and relativised. Secondly, an increasing and diverse range of actors are involved in the political process. These actors may operate at several different territorial levels concurrently. Thirdly, modern politics is highly complex and dynamic. In reality, it is in a state of ongoing flux. As such, it consists of both formal and informal processes. If anything, informal processes may be becoming more important.

---

45 Rosamond, 2000: 111.

Political analysis is, therefore, particularly challenging. Theories must take cognisance of complexities.

What are the implications of these approaches for the role of contemporary parliaments? Firstly, parliaments are statal institutions. In a less state-centric world, parliaments will most likely be required to operate at different territorial levels. Secondly, parliaments will need to embrace informal processes. Parliaments need to concede that many major decisions are made outside the formal institutions of parliamentary government. This is not to say that such political decisions ought to be beyond parliamentary scrutiny. On the contrary, scrutiny of authoritative decisions ought to be an important function of parliaments. Thirdly, given the dynamic nature of contemporary politics, parliaments will have to adapt to ever-changing political circumstances. Prescriptive approaches need to be sensitive to this dynamism.

The existing literature on Dáil Éireann tends to be dated, narrow in its theoretical scope and shallow in its empirical depth. Failing to take account of transformations associated with early 21st-century politics, the literature accordingly offers an impoverished understanding of Dáil Éireann. Not allowing for the reality that the current era is indeed one of 'multiple revolutions' and 'epochal transformations' the literature is situated in a pre-transformation time warp. Whether spatially, temporally or in terms of sheer volume, these transformations pose a significant challenge for all parliaments including Dáil Éireann. The scholarship has *not* addressed the role of Dáil Éireann either explicitly or implicitly in the context of the radical transformations which are shaping contemporary politics. Consequently, this book marks an important departure.

3

PARLIAMENTARY DECLINE AND POST-PARLIAMENTARY GOVERNANCE

So well is our real Government concealed that if you tell a cabman to drive to Downing Street he most likely will never have heard of it, and will not in the least know where to take you.[1]

It is indeed more appropriate to talk about decline of governments and resurgence of parliaments in Scandinavia. Weaker governments are the other side of the coin.[2]

Distrust of the Legislature is a feature of post-War political practice. It is a distrust based, in some cases, on a deteriorating parliamentary personnel, in others on a belief that the Legislature of the 19th century is unsuited to deal with the problems of the 20th. Its more obvious expression is in the diminution of the powers of the Legislature.[3]

Focusing on the decline of parliament thesis and the post-parliamentary governance model, in this chapter I analyse, compare and sharply distinguish both approaches to parliamentary analysis. The post-parliamentary governance model might appear to be a

---

1 Bagehot [1867], 1966: 266 n.1.
2 Damgaard, 1994: 100.
3 Mansergh, 1934: 212.

variant of its much older predecessor, the decline of parliament thesis, however, both approaches are creatures of different times. Informed by different assumptions, they possess contrasting explanatory and normative orientations. Perhaps, unwittingly, much of the public discourse in Ireland remains informed by the decline of parliament thesis. I argue that the decline of parliament thesis, because of its 19th-century political origins and associated narrow parameters, lacks the capacity to come to terms with the complexities of modern politics. Whilst aspects of the decline of parliament thesis remain highly useful, I employ a different set of assumptions and understandings about the role of parliaments under conditions of modern politics.

The so-called decline of parliament thesis has occupied a central place in political discourse for over a century.[4] Proponents of the thesis hold that parliaments are declining and becoming weaker, especially relative to executives. Executive control of and dominance over parliament means that 'parliamentarians are merely lobby fodder'.[5] Essentially, once the governing party enjoys a parliamentary majority, the executive can 'dictate' policy and other outcomes. Rather than enjoying autonomous legislative and accountability functions, parliament becomes an instrument of an increasingly powerful executive. As Elgie and Stapleton explain:

> In contrast to times past, so the argument goes, parliaments are little more than talking shops. The real decisions are now made elsewhere.[6]

---

4 Bryce, 1921; Crick, 1965; Elgie and Stapleton, 2006; Flinders, 2007; Foot, 1959; Hill and Whichelow, 1964; Hollis, 1971; Loewenberg, 1971, 1972; Lowenberg and Patterson, 1979; Wheare, 1968.

5 Elgie and Stapleton, 2006: 466.

6 *Ibid.*

James Bryce's two-volume text, *Modern Democracies,* published in 1921, has become synonymous with the decline of parliament thesis. But as the following quote demonstrates, Bryce's interpretation of decline ought not to be understood solely in institutional terms. Rather, there is a strong elitist/aristocratic tone to his work:

> They tell him, in terms much the same everywhere, that there is less brilliant speaking than in the days of their own youth, that the tone of manners has declined, that the best citizens are less disposed to enter the Chamber, that its proceedings are less fully reported and excite less interest, that a seat in it confers less social status, and that, for one reason or another, the respect felt for it has waned.[7]

In reading Bryce's nine-page chapter entitled 'The Decline of Legislatures', one is struck by his obsession with the apparently declining status and prestige of parliaments. Throughout the chapter, he frequently refers to the declining admiration, respect, prestige and deference afforded to parliaments. It is easy to speculate that what concerned Viscount Bryce was not the decline of parliament *per se,* but the declining influence of his aristocratic class within the institutions of democratic government.

Bryce cites a number of examples where, he believes, legislatures have experienced decline. In the United States, state legislatures have declined due to increasing control by the party machine as well as by direct democracy through initiatives and referenda. In France, high turnover of cabinets and political brokerage are damaging parliament. In Britain, party discipline and obstructionist parliamentary tactics are factors that contribute to the House of Commons' declining esteem.[8]

---

7 Bryce, 1921: 335.
8 *Ibid.*: 336–337.

According to Bryce, it is not accurate to talk of decline in Australia and Canada 'for the level was never high'.[9]

Bryce's overall position on parliamentary decline is less than clear. He contends that paying MPs *'has been supposed* to lower the status and fetter the freedom of a representative' [my emphasis].[10] Reviewing political changes, such as the increasing influence of trade unions and left-wing parties, he concludes that these:

> ... account for the disappointment felt by whoever compares the positions held by legislatures now with the *hopes once entertained* [my emphasis].[11]

The question arising from this quote can be posed as follows: Is Bryce 'measuring' parliamentary decline against vague historical standards of a normative nature? Bryce's conclusion is that, although the influence of parliaments is declining, they remain a crucial cog in the machinery of government.

Bryce's account on parliamentary decline, at least until the 1970s, 'had become a dictum' for scholars of legislatures.[12] Or as another source puts it, Bryce clearly:

> ... established the decline of Parliament thesis as the dominant interpretation of executive-legislative relations, not just in the UK but more generally as well.[13]

---

9   *Ibid.*: 338.
10 *Ibid.*: 339.
11 *Ibid.*: 341.
12 Loewenberg, 1972: 5.
13 Elgie and Stapleton, 2006: 467.

Therefore, what is important to understand is the fact that Bryce's work had a highly significant impact on legislative studies' scholarship.

In his classic text *The English Constitution*, Walter Bagehot provides an account of British parliamentary politics in the pre-1867 era and makes his well-known distinction between the 'dignified' and 'efficient' parts of the English Constitution. In modern terms, the dignified parts are those institutions which generate socio/psychological emotional attachments to the polity. Flags, symbols and music are obvious examples. These institutions are designed to 'excite and preserve the reverence of the population'.[14] The efficient parts of the Constitution are those institutions which actually govern by making decisions.

Perhaps, the most well-known line in Bagehot's work is:

> The efficient secret of the English Constitution may be described as the close union, the nearly complete fusion of the executive and legislative powers.[15]

The result of this fusion is a relatively new institution termed the Cabinet, which is 'a Committee of the legislative body selected to be the executive body'.[16] Bagehot contends that his contemporaries failed (deliberately or in error) to observe that the true workings of British politics were based on a Cabinet elected by and accountable to the House of Commons. Rather, his contemporaries peddled the myth that the executive and legislative branches were separate. And, crucially, the centrality of the Cabinet was hidden from the public at large. In a fascinating footnote, Bagehot states:

---

14 Bagehot [1867], 1966: 61.
15 *Ibid.*: 65.
16 *Ibid.*: 66.

So well is our real Government concealed that if you tell a cabman to drive to Downing Street he most likely will never have heard of it, and will not in the least know where to take you.[17]

Bagehot depicted parliamentary life as one where the House of Commons exercised significant influence and power. The executive branch was indeed a committee of the House of Commons rather than an institution which dominated it:

We are ruled by the House of Commons; we are indeed, so used to being ruled, that it does not seem to be at all strange.[18]

The House of Commons was no mere talking shop. Debates really mattered because:

The deciding catastrophes of Cabinet Governments are critical divisions preceded by fine discussions.[19]

It should be noted that Bagehot, as a member of the English ruling class, was clearly an opponent of the emerging trends towards universal suffrage. In the introduction to the second edition of *The English Constitution*, Bagehot did not disguise his thoughts on the evils of increased democracy:

It must be remembered that a political combination of the lower classes, as such and for their own objects, is an evil of the first magnitude; that a permanent combination of them would make them (now that so many of them have the suffrage) supreme in the country; and that their

---

17 *Ibid.*: 266 n.1.
18 *Ibid.*: 155.
19 *Ibid.*: 72.

supremacy, in the state they now are, means the supremacy of ignorance over instruction and of numbers over knowledge. So long as they are taught not to act together, there is a chance of this being averted.[20]

Bagehot may very well have been describing an era (real or illusionary) of classical parliamentary government, often referred to as the 'golden age' of parliaments. However, on Bagehot's understanding, it was a 'golden age' which should exclude the working class.

Writing the foreword to the 1966 edition of *The English Constitution*, Richard Crossman convincingly maintains that Bagehot's description of parliamentary life was accurate for the period 1832–67. Crossman repeatedly emphasises, however, that post-1867, with the advent of Disraeli's Reform Act which extended suffrage, 'Britain had left the epoch of classical parliamentary Government'.[21] Crossman holds that the House of Commons during this period of pre-universal suffrage, pre-state civil service, pre-welfare state and pre-strongly organised political parties, was indeed 'the place where the most vital decisions were still taken'.[22] Citing empirical research, Crossman reminds us that party divisions were rare and that, during the period 1850–65, the Government was defeated no fewer than ten times per session and did not have to resign.[23]

To maintain that the Commons retained sovereignty in the 1960s is deemed a legend by Crossman. Rather, the Commons had become 'a forum of debate between well disciplined armies'.[24] There is a transition from independent to party MP and parliamentary

---

20 *Ibid.*: 277.
21 Crossman, 1966: 38.
22 *Ibid.*: 136.
23 *Ibid.*: 135.
24 *Ibid.*: 39.

control of the Executive is a fiction. Real parliamentary control is exercised not by the official opposition, but by dissenting government MPs.[25] Power has shifted from the floor of the chamber to the party committee rooms and cabinet government has been replaced with prime ministerial government.

Actually, Bagehot clearly acknowledges that five years after the publication of his first edition parliamentary circumstances had changed radically. Contending that: 'in so short a period there have rarely been more changes', Bagehot himself clearly recognised that he was describing an era that had already passed.[26] Thus, what will always be disputed about this classic is whether it is an accurate historical description.

In his 1965 publication, *The Reform of Parliament*, Bernard Crick adopts a similar position to Crossman. He provides a delightfully crisp and provocative definition of British politics as one where the:

> ... Prime Minister dominates a Cabinet which in turn dominates a Party majority in the House of Commons; this Party under the same leaders has to fight periodic general elections: if the Party wins the elections, then the Prime Minister and his Cabinet control the entire machinery of legislation and administration.[27]

Painting an almost despotic picture of British politics, Crick contends that the only effective constitutional limit:

> ... rests on the ultimate check of the general election, not on the day to day results in Parliament.[28]

---

25 *Ibid.*: 44.
26 *Ibid.*: 267.
27 Crick, 1965: 16.
28 *Ibid.*: 19.

Wheare continues the theme of parliamentary decline in his 1968 publication, *Legislatures*, holding that:

> If a general survey is made of the position and working of legislatures in the present century, it is apparent that, with a few important and striking exceptions, legislatures have declined in certain important respects and particularly in powers in relation to the Government.[29]

Wheare contends, however, that there has been a relative rather than an absolute decline in the power of parliaments. Executives have not taken power from parliaments. Rather, the power and policy scope of executives have increased relative to those of parliaments. To put it simply, in an era of the expansive and interventionist state, the executive branch does more. The detrimental impact which delegated legislation has on parliament is also acknowledged. And where governments and organised interests combine, parliament can easily become 'a rubber stamp'.[30] The setting up of Ombudsman-type offices threatens parliament's role as a committee of grievances. Whilst radio and television can be interpreted as threats to parliament, they also allow parliamentarians to reach a wider audience. In overall terms, though, Wheare concludes that it is difficult to reach definitive conclusions on the decline of parliament thesis:

> The fact is that the decline of legislatures may be an interesting question to discuss in general terms, but it is difficult if not impossible to decide.[31]

---

29 Wheare, 1968: 148.
30 *Ibid.*: 154.
31 *Ibid.*: 156.

Looking to the future, Wheare injects a realistic note into debates surrounding the decline of parliaments:

> It is not the function of a legislature to be the sole forum of debate or the sole committee of grievances in its country's political system; these functions must and should be shared with other bodies. It is not the function of the legislature to govern.[32]

Wheare recognised that in the post-Second World War era, when the political sphere was expanding and becoming more complex, parliaments could not expect to exercise a discursive or decision-making monopoly. Parliaments would clearly have an important place in democratic politics, but it would be a shared, rather than a monopolistic, role. Perhaps the following was Wheare's wisest advice:

> To do less and perhaps, thereby, do it better, may often prove to be the best safeguard against the decline of legislatures.[33]

These parting words from Wheare are even more relevant for parliaments of the early 21st century.

The decline of parliament thesis can also be detected within the scholarship on Dáil Éireann. Mansergh's 1934 publication, *The Irish Free State: Its Government and Politics,* is a case in point. Writing of the reality of Executive dominance, he is clearly concerned about the fantasy of Dáil control of the Executive Council of 1922–36. According to Mansergh, by the early 1930s 'there is no question but that the hegemony of the Executive is complete'.[34] He contends:

---

32 *Ibid.*: 156.
33 *Ibid.*: 157.
34 Mansergh, 1934: 212.

Distrust of the Legislature is a feature of post-War political practice. It is a distrust based, in some cases, on a deteriorating parliamentary personnel, in others on a belief that the Legislature of the 19th century is unsuited to deal with the problems of the 20th. Its more obvious expression is in the diminution of the powers of the Legislature.[35]

Mansergh asserts that whilst the intention of the framers of the 1922 Constitution was to afford the Dáil a central role in the State's political machinery, the Executive quickly became the dominant organ of Government.[36] Later sources, including Ayearst, Chubb and MacCarthaigh, provide retrospective endorsement of Mansergh's analysis. Ayearst explains:

> It was the intention of the framers of the original Free State Constitution that the Dáil should be the real seat of power, the body that would freely debate and determine policies and the master rather than the servant of Ministers.[37]

According to MacCarthaigh, departing from the parliamentary-centred provisions of the 1922 Constitution, the Executive branch 'sought to consolidate and centralise its power at the expense of parliamentary oversight'.[38] By 1937, when the State adopted its new Constitution, Fianna Fáil 'effectively governed in a "rubber stamp" Parliament'.[39] Thus, in Ireland's case there was clearly a decline of parliament. But it was a decline only in the sense that it departed from the *de jure* role which the 1922 Constitution envisaged for Dáil

---

35 *Ibid.*: 85.
36 *Ibid.*: 103–104.
37 Ayearst, 1970: 135.
38 MacCarthaigh, 2005: 65.
39 *Ibid.*: 67.

Éireann. *De facto* Executive dominance took root in the formative years of the State. As McCracken comments:

> The Cabinet system brought with it what the framers of the Free State Constitution would have regarded as its attendant evils. The Dáil did not become a deliberative assembly.[40]

The decline of parliament thesis has been challenged in recent decades. Suggesting that a 'golden age' of parliaments never existed, the counter-thesis holds that:

> Parliament has not been totally marginalised and, depending on the circumstances, it maintains the capacity to embarrass the Government and Prime Minister.[41]

Acknowledging that following the Second World War the decline of parliament thesis had become accepted, Menzey, nevertheless, casts a sceptical eye on the literature. Also doubting whether a 'golden age' of parliaments ever existed, he notes that the thesis has suffered from an absence of empirical data.[42] For American political scientists, 'the theme of historical decline was joined with the assumption of political marginality'.[43] Menzey contends that in the 1990s, however, parliaments were enjoying a resurgence, including:

* The consolidation of parliamentary government in Portugal, Spain and Greece.

---

40 McCracken, 1958: 166.
41 Elgie and Stapleton, 2006: 468.
42 Menzey, 1995: 196.
43 *Ibid.*

* In Scandinavia, weak minority governments led to an enhanced role for parliaments.
* The break up of the USSR from 1988 onwards has created a wave of new parliaments.
* In the United States, there are increasing references to a resurgent Congress.
* In the UK, party government and Executive domination cannot be taken for granted.[44]

Menzey observes that parliaments are both independent and dependent variables. Therefore, whilst parliaments can shape their own collective preferences (independent variables), many changes are not self-induced (dependent variables). In overall terms, therefore, parliaments are:

> … nested in a set of political institutions, which in turn is nested in a larger socio-economic-political context.[45]

Scholars of parliamentary institutions, therefore, need to be acutely sensitive to the contexts in which parliaments are rooted. Flinders offers an interesting counter-perspective to the decline of parliament thesis, arguing that in Britain the House of Commons has advanced because:

> Recent reforms have strengthened its position vis-à-vis the Executive but in a way that has not threatened the Executive's dominant position within the broader constitutional configuration.[46]

This is an interesting position because it is not simply the case that

---

44 *Ibid.*: 196–197.
45 *Ibid.*: 199.
46 Flinders, 2007: 174.

one institution's gain is another's loss. Rather, according to Flinders, executives can maintain a dominant position, whilst parliaments strengthen their position via reform processes. Of course, this clearly implies that there is a reform threshold; in other words, executives will only facilitate reform processes which do not threaten their overall dominant position within the political architecture. Flinders argues that parliamentary reform processes can be divided into three categories, namely cosmetic, moderate and fundamental.

Under cosmetic reform exercises, the distribution of power remains largely unchanged. Moderate reform processes involve a shift in the balance of power to some degree but the executive retains control over core components and power centres. When fundamental reform occurs there is a stark departure from previous constitutional arrangements.[47] Developing a concept termed 'incremental bounded reform', Flinders emphasises that reform processes can have a spill-over or domino-like effect. As such, it may be difficult to discern major turning points in the reform process, and it may be an incremental process over time. Flinders contends that under incremental bounded reform processes, parliamentary scrutiny of the executive can be improved without necessarily threatening the centrality of executive government.

Patterson and Copeland refer to 'The Age of Parliaments', contending that:

> We are living in a world of remarkable re-establishment, reinvention, and transformation of Parliaments around the globe.[48]

---

47 *Ibid.*: 177.
48 Patterson and Copeland, 1994: 8.

Cotta, addressing the subject of the pre-1992 Italian Parliament, questions the salience of the executive dominance model. In fact, Cotta contends that executive dominance has been conclusively proven.[49] Norton and Wood conclude that modern Britain possesses 'a more active, more specialised, and less marginal House of Commons'.[50] Similarly, Damgaard highlights the strong position of Scandinavian parliaments.[51] Explicitly rejecting the decline of parliament thesis, he contends that 'weak minority Governments produce rather strong Parliaments'.[52] In the Scandinavian case, Damgaard concludes that:

> It is indeed more appropriate to talk about decline of governments and resurgence of parliaments in Scandinavia. Weaker governments are the other side of the coin.[53]

The United States Congress has always stood out as the great exception to the executive dominance model.[54] The notion of a supreme, sovereign and fiercely independent parliament is certainly a 'rather antiquated concept'.[55] Antiquated or not, however, the United States Congress most closely approximates independence. Congress is not a mere tool of the Executive. Neither does Congress fit with the European debate around the decline of parliament thesis. In fact if the Opposition controls Congress it can considerably reduce the

---

49 Cotta, 1994: 62.
50 Norton and Wood, 1993: 3.
51 Damgaard, 1994.
52 *Ibid.*: 102.
53 *Ibid.*: 100.
54 Huitt, 1966: 9; Norton and Wood, 1993: 2; Davidson and Oleszek, 2000: 6.
55 Hennis, 1971: 66.

influence of a sitting President. In short, Congress is not a quiescent legislature. The sitting US President can never rely on party support to the same extent as his/her prime ministerial counterpart in a parliamentary democracy where both the executive and legislature are *de facto* fused. In the USA, there is no parliamentary equivalent of the whipping system. The White House can apply significant pressure, but members of both Houses can and do adopt an independent line. It is for these reasons that Damgaard classifies the United States Congress in the following terms:

> Classical parliamentarianism is today most closely approximated to the United States, where there are no disciplined parties and where the legislature has retained a considerable degree of independence and control over the legislative process.[56]

However, the crucial point to note is that it was not always so. In fact in its embryonic phase Congress was a weak legislature. Patterson and Copeland make the following point:

> Today, the US Congress is acknowledged to be one of the world's most powerful legislative bodies. But in the early 19th century, Congress was a somewhat feeble, incipient organisation.[57]

In Dáil Éireann's case, Elgie and Stapleton have challenged the decline of parliament thesis. The authors measure, by way of an advanced computer programme, whether the parliamentary interventions of the Taoiseach decreased or increased during the period 1923–2002. Reduced interventions (speeches, statements and taking questions) by

---

56 Damgaard, 1994: 101.
57 Patterson and Copeland, 1994: 3.

a state's chief executive are equated with parliamentary decline. Less participation in parliamentary proceedings implies that chief executives are less frequently scrutinised and that they attach less importance to parliament. The reverse obviously applies where there is increased participation in parliamentary proceedings by prime ministers. Elgie and Stapleton's research reveals that parliamentary interventions by the Taoiseach, during the 1990s in particular, have been 'relatively high'.[58] According to the authors:

> Measured by the parliamentary activity of the head of Government, the results suggest that there has not been a decline of Parliament in the Irish case since 1923. On the contrary, they indicate that in the 1990s Parliament was more central to the political process than at any time since the formation of the State.[59]

This conclusion will come as a surprise to many scholars of Dáil Éireann because, as previously explained, there is a substantial literature on Executive dominance within the Irish political science literature. Nevertheless, it is important to emphasise that this conclusion is based on just one quantitative measure, namely parliamentary intervention by the chief executive. Even allowing for the fact that Elgie and Stapleton supplement this quantitative analysis with a brief qualitative examination of the changing nature of the Order of Business, caution is required before accepting broad generalisations based on one variable.[60]

---

58 Elgie and Stapleton, 2006: 477.
59 *Ibid.*: 480.
60 *Ibid.*: 481–482.

POST-PARLIAMENTARY GOVERNANCE

Andersen and Burns have offered the following characterisation of the post-parliamentary governance model, namely that in modern polities:

> The direct influence of the people through formal representative democracy has a marginal place.[61]

Other actors are displacing parliaments. In effect, citizens are living in a post-parliamentary era. Non-parliamentary actors are becoming more important. In modern polities parliament as an institution is becoming increasingly irrelevant because:

> The opportunities for popular representatives and their institutions to play their 'proper roles' are very limited, if not becoming largely unfeasible.[62]

In the era of post-parliamentary governance, interest groups, policy networks and experts become key actors. Bypassing parliament, both interest groups and experts shape political processes and outcomes. Parliament becomes a political spectator and bystander. Non-parliamentary arrangements, such as policy networks and neo-corporatism, are therefore in the ascendant. The emergence of post-parliamentary governance results from the increased differentiation and complexity of contemporary society. Contemporary politics is characterised by a huge volume and very diverse range of policy spheres. These spheres frequently demand highly specialised and expert analysis. Parliaments do not possess the necessary capacity or expertise and

---

61 Andersen and Burns, 1996: 227.
62 *Ibid.*: 228.

simply cannot cope with the demands of modern politics and society. On the other hand, an array of interest groups, policy networks and experts can bring their expertise and specialist knowledge to bear on particular policy spheres. These actors colonise the vacuum which parliaments cannot fill. In an era when politics and society demanded less specialisation and expertise, parliaments had less difficulty coping. A lesser volume and narrower range of policy spheres did not pose the same challenges.[63]

The condition of post-parliamentary governance:

> … erodes and destabilises established institutions of Government that may have been previously effective.[64]

Thus, there is a sense that contemporary politics is simply overwhelming parliaments. It is clear that the model has much in common with perspectives examined earlier on globalisation, multi-level governance and the risk society. All perspectives emphasise how complex and dynamic modern politics is. Likewise, the assertion that contemporary politics is characterised by 'multi-actorness' is a common theme. As Beck emphasises, much of contemporary politics occurs outside 'the officially classified political sphere'.[65] Political parties and the official constitutional organs of state, including parliaments, do not enjoy a monopoly on political activity. Beck goes on to ask:

> Who says that politics is possible only in the forms and terms of Governmental, Parliamentary and party politics?[66]

---

63 *Ibid.*: 227–251.
64 *Ibid.*: 236.
65 Beck, 2001: 91.
66 *Ibid.*: 91.

As already noted, he clearly contends that politics is possible outside the aforementioned forms. But it is a different matter to argue that politics is becoming increasingly impossible within conventional political spaces such as parliaments, executives and political parties. Politics is clearly possible outside formal institutional spaces, but is it plausible, as Andersen and Burns believe, that citizens are living in a post-parliamentary era? Beck opines that it may indeed be necessary to abandon conventional politics. However, interestingly, he leaves open the possibility to 'expand, rethink and recompose' conventional political spaces.[67]

An initial criticism is that the post-parliamentary governance model makes two questionable assumptions, namely that post-parliamentary governance has replaced parliamentary government and that interest groups displace parliaments.

Like the decline of parliament thesis it is assumed that in an earlier phase of parliamentary government parliaments were deemed important political actors exercising power in the polity. However, there is little evidence to support the assumption that a 'golden age' ever existed, but even if it did, it did so in a pre-democratic age, not under conditions of late or post-modernity. The model's second assumption is that interest groups displace parliaments. Whilst it would be foolish to dispute the assertion that interest groups are important actors in modern polities, it is a different matter to argue that they are displacing parliaments. In fact, some sources suggest that, in the Irish context, interest groups may be working through, rather than bypassing, Dáil Éireann.[68] Far from undermining parliaments, interest groups may provide representative institutions with an opportunity to enhance their standing, particularly in the eyes of powerful executives.

---

67 *Ibid.*: 93.
68 O'Halpin and Connolly, 1999; Murphy, 1999.

Rather than bypassing parliaments, interest groups may increasingly work through parliament to highlight policy concerns. A strong and vibrant committee system which regularly considers submissions from interest groups may facilitate such interaction.

The model suffers from three further deficiencies. Firstly, it operates at high levels of generalisation and offers little in the way of empirical rigour. This is likely to have implications for the model's utility. Secondly, it fails to appreciate that parliaments, like all institutions, are capable of adapting to new circumstances. Parliaments may indeed be changing with the times. Thirdly, whilst the model offers an alternative understanding of contemporary governance, it fails to offer an alternative role for contemporary parliaments.

The absence of empirical rigour is a significant weakness. For example, can we assume that there are no cross-national differences among parliaments? Most certainly not. I contend that there are significant cross-national variations in the institutional architecture of parliaments. Whilst certain generalisations can be made about contemporary governance that is not to say that all parliaments behave the same. Parliaments cannot be treated as an undifferentiated monolith. Country-specific institutional settings are likely to be of significant importance. Unfortunately, Andersen and Burn appear to treat all parliaments as undifferentiated. Whilst it remains to be seen whether this is a fatal weakness in the model, it clearly invites both country-specific and comparativist scholars to be cautious.

Like all institutions, parliaments are capable of adapting to new circumstances. It is surprising that Andersen and Burns do not discuss this reality. Parliaments need not sink in a sea of change and transformation. It is worth noting a number of significant changes in their procedures. Activity is moving away from the chamber into committee rooms. Parliaments have responded to a heavier and more complex workload by reforming and significantly upgrading the committee systems.[69] Norton observes a move away from the chamber in the British House of Commons:

> There has, in short, been a shift in emphasis from the chamber (the domain of Parliament man) to Committee (the domain of policy advocate).[70]

The impact of European integration has also been significant. For example, there has been a mushrooming of European Affairs committees. Whilst the committees vary in their remit and powers, their growing importance cannot be ignored. The Danish Parliament, for instance, subjects Union proposals to rigorous scrutiny via its European Union Committee. In fact, it adopts *ex ante* control measures.[71] The growing significance of European Affairs committees demonstrates the dynamic nature of parliamentary responses to the challenges posed by supranational governance. Damgaard similarly concludes that the Nordic countries have adapted to new challenges by 'making use of new control instruments'.[72]

Finally, whilst the model offers an alternative understanding of contemporary governance, it fails to offer an alternative role for contemporary parliaments. In other words, it fails in any comprehensive way to sketch an alternative role for parliament in a post-parliamentary era. This is partly due to the fact that nowhere in Andersen and Burns does one find a systematic exposition of parliamentary functions. This methodological deficiency erodes the model's normative salience.

---

69   Longley and Davidson, 1998: 2.
70   Norton, 1997: 29.
71   Larsen-Jensen, 2002.
72   Damgaard, 2000: 167.

Despite these apparent deficiencies, the post-parliamentary governance model has significant strengths. It places a strong emphasis on current transformations. As noted earlier, across the social sciences there is considerable support for the proposition that this current period in world history is one of profound change and mutation. Andersen and Burns seek to make sense of these transformations, which is not an easy task. Their approach is to trace the transformations to several different sources. Thus the role of experts, interest groups and processes such as globalisation are examined. Parliaments are not immune from these wider societal and other transformations. As Dror contends:

> In the face of escalating needs, governance is increasingly obsolete, with a growing incapacity to govern caused by the relatively static nature of the main features of governance in contrast with rapid transformations in the issues with which it must cope.[73]

This focus on change and transformation is particularly useful in the Irish case. However, the literature on Dáil Éireann has not addressed contemporary transformations, let alone the implications. In the context of the most recent transformations, the impression is formed that the literature is trapped in a time warp, but it can no longer credibly ignore transformations which have major implications for the future role of Dáil Éireann. These transformations include: EU membership, globalisation, social partnership, a vibrant civil society and the role of experts. The literature has largely neglected the impact these changes are having upon the Dáil. Andersen and Burns offer an entirely fresh and new perspective. Even if deficient in some respects, it encourages scholars to break free from the chains of traditional

---

73 Dror, 2001: 2.

models which are incapable of capturing the dynamics of current transformations.

The post-parliamentary governance model raises a challenge to the literature on Dáil Éireann and perhaps to legislative studies generally. The home of legislative studies is clearly in the field of political science, but researchers may benefit from looking beyond political science to enrich their analytical and normative frameworks. In particular, legislative studies may benefit from importing sociological and other approaches such as those offered by Andersen and Burns, particularly at the level of normative analysis. In this regard, the complexity of contemporary polities and societies suggests that the liberal democratic framework alone can no longer exclusively inform normative responses.

It is important not to confuse the empirical and normative underpinnings of the post-parliamentary governance model and the decline of parliament thesis. Both perspectives share two characteristics. They tend to assume, either explicitly or implicitly, that a previous era existed where parliaments were key political actors. In this respect, they suffer from the 'golden age of parliaments' syndrome. Additionally, both perspectives are concerned with the erosion of parliamentary power and influence, suggesting that parliaments can no longer fulfil their 'proper' roles.

However, the post-parliamentary governance model can be sharply distinguished from the decline of parliament thesis. In reality, the post-parliamentary governance model interprets parliament through a radically different analytical lens. It is a product of the early 21st century, belonging to the era of 'posts', 'epochal transformations' and 'multiple revolutions'. It is shaped by the observation that the current era is one where the pace and depth of change are truly staggering. As such, the post-parliamentary governance model is rooted in late or post-modernity. The decline of parliament thesis owes its origins to a different era. Politically, as both Bagehot and Bryce illustrate, the thesis is shaped by 19th-century assumptions. Born in an era of government as distinct from governance, it focuses primarily on executive–legislative relations. On the other hand, the post-parliamentary governance model shares the contemporary assumptions associated with globalisation, multi-level governance and the risk society. It should also be noted that the decline of parliament thesis looks primarily at the British model whereas the post-parliamentary governance model is more contemporary European in its orientation.

For theorists who hold that parliaments should be key democratic actors, both perspectives invite different normative responses. Logically, the post-parliamentary governance model compels scholars to think outside the 'liberal democratic box'. Distinctions between parliamentary modernisation, parliamentary reform and even incrementally bounded reform, whilst highly useful, are insufficient. Rather, the key demands are innovation and creativity. Relationally, scholars are compelled to think in multilateral (multi-actorness) rather than bilateral (legislative–executive) terms. The following table provides a comparison of both perspectives.

Comparing the Decline of Parliament Thesis with the Post-Parliamentary Governance Model

	Decline of Parliament Thesis	Post-Parliamentary Governance Model
Origins	19th century	Late or post-modernity
Shared assumptions	Parliamentary golden age	Parliamentary golden age

Shared concerns	Parliamentary marginalisation	Parliamentary marginalisation
Political organisation	Government	Governance
Parliamentary relationships	Bilateral	Multilateral
Prescriptive remedies	Reform/modernisation	Innovation/creativity
Normative responses	Reform/modernisation	Innovation/creativity
Democratic orientation	Liberal democracy	Post-Parliamentary democracy
Key concepts	Separation of powers/ dominant executive	Change, complexity, multi-actorness

Since the early 20th century, there has been extensive literature on the decline of parliament thesis. I have demonstrated that the thesis in its own right is highly contentious, not least because the very existence of a period of parliamentary ascendancy is disputed. If such an era ever existed it did so in a pre-democratic age, specifically in mid-19th-century Britain, a period that might well be described as one of parliamentary government but clearly not one of parliamentary democracy. To be succinct, the question of what *great heights* parliaments are supposed to have *declined from* remains very open indeed. In overall terms, public commentators in particular would do well to cast a highly sceptical eye upon the existence of a parliamentary 'golden age'. Such scepticism is particularly warranted in Dáil

Éireann's case. In reality, Executive dominance has been a feature of Irish parliamentary life since 1919, a feature that became entrenched when the 1937 Constitution became the polity's fundamental law.

The most positive scholarly legacy of the decline of parliament thesis concerns that ubiquitous theme in legislative studies: executive dominance. But whilst models of executive dominance remain highly useful, they are limited in their analytical reach. In a political era of complexity and 'multi-actorness', the central challenge facing students of parliamentary institutions is to situate analytical frameworks in these and other broader contexts of late modernity. It is for this reason that the post-parliamentary governance model, particularly its underlying assumptions and conceptual orientation, provides scholars with a better 'take' on the realities confronting modern parliaments.

The model offers a fresh theoretical perspective on the position of contemporary parliaments. The model's strength lies in its holistic theoretical orientation. Positioning parliament within the context of broader societal and political transformations, it challenges parliamentary studies to transcend an exclusively institution-focused theoretical orientation. Provocative in its conclusion that citizens are living in a post-parliamentary era, it explicitly rejects the normative underpinnings of liberal democracy. In this and other regards, the model can be sharply distinguished from the decline of parliament thesis. However, it should be observed that the model suffers from empirical deficiencies.

4

CONTEMPORARY LIBERAL DEMOCRACY: A FLAWED MODEL?

The ballot box is king.[1]

To decide once every few years which member of the ruling class is to repress and crush the people through Parliament – this is the real essence of bourgeois parliamentarism, not only in parliamentary-constitutional monarchies but also in most democratic republics.[2]

Professional politicians govern, in the sense of making policy and taking decisions; the general public is merely engaged in the task of selecting which group of politicians should be entrusted with Government power.[3]

Here I explore whether certain of liberal democracy's core assumptions about the politics of public policy-making are outdated in the political conditions of the early 21st century. I contend that there is an increasing chasm between the normative expectations of citizens, who are informed by liberal democratic assumptions, and the political conditions of the 21st century. The liberal democratic framework places parliaments and executives at its decisional centre. However,

---

1 Landy, 2001.
2 Lenin [1917], 1970: 46.
3 Heywood, 1992: 282.

contemporary politics is much more complex than the liberal democratic framework would suggest. From a public policy-making perspective, there is no one decisional centre; rather, there are multiple and fluid decisional centres. I argue that citizens and political elites should adjust their normative orientations.

Western parliamentary government is embedded in the liberal democratic framework. This framework is a union of 19th-century liberalism and early 20th-century representative democracy. Liberalism's contribution to this is a set of constitutionally entrenched civil rights which open up a space in the polity for debate, discussion and argument. Classically, these rights consist of freedom of expression, assembly and association. However, liberalism also brought Western free market capitalism to the union. In reality, liberal democracy and free market capitalism are synonymous. Democracy's key contribution is universal adult suffrage. Adult citizens elect parliamentary representatives in a free, fair and competitive electoral process. It should be remembered, however, that the union between liberalism and democracy is not tension free. In particular, there is a tension between the majoritarian features of democracy and liberalism's emphasis on protection of individual rights. Nevertheless, despite inherent tensions, liberal democracy is deeply rooted within Western polities.

What assumptions does the liberal democratic framework make about the politics of public policy-making? And do these assumptions make any sense in the early 21st century. According to the liberal democratic framework, the institutions of parliamentary government determine public policy outcomes. As Held states, elected politicians 'alone can make political decisions (that is, decisions affecting the whole community)'.[4] Or to put it another way:

---

4 Held, 1993: 21.

> Professional politicians govern, in the sense of making policy and taking decisions; the general public is merely engaged in the task of selecting which group of politicians should be entrusted with Government power.[5]

Writing on the equilibrium model of liberal democracy, MacPherson makes a similar point: the citizens' function 'is to choose the men who will do the deciding'.[6] The parliamentary and executive branches of government make collective and binding policy decisions. These actors, it is assumed, have the capacity to determine and control public policy outcomes. Crucially, both organs of government are held responsible to the citizenry for these outcomes. Furthermore:

> Democratic theory has tended to assume a 'symmetrical' and 'congruent' relationship between political decision-makers and the recipients of political decisions.[7]

In other words, the polity is definable.

In effect, parliaments and executives occupy a highly privileged space in the public-policy-making process. This is because uniquely TDs, MPs and Ministers enjoy democratic legitimacy. The people elect members to sit in a national parliament. In the European model, parliament chooses the executive. This executive enjoys a mandate from the people to implement certain policy proposals debated during the preceding general election. This executive remains in office only for as long as it retains the confidence of the Dáil or parliament. Parliament may dismiss the executive via a censure or no confidence

---

5   Heywood, 1992: 282.
6   MacPherson, 1988: 78.
7   Held, 1993: 23.

motion. In fact, liberal democracy in its classical guise assigns real power to the parliamentary branch, contending as it does that 'Government merely does the bidding of Parliament'.[8] Thus, public policy outcomes are determined by parliament and implemented by an executive branch.

On the other hand, within political science it is taken as axiomatic that actors other than elected politicians make public policy. Unsurprisingly, different theories have offered competing perspectives. Thus, the elitist perspective holds that:

> Beneath the façade of democratic politics a social and economic elite will actually be found running things.[9]

Similarly, according to the classical Marxist perspective, liberal rights and a widening franchise are deemed a façade. As such, the liberal bourgeoisie state is an instrument of the ruling class.[10] Policy preferences will thus reflect the interests of the ruling class. Under both the elitist and Marxist frameworks power is concentrated in the hands of a few rather than widely dispersed.

These positions contrast with the classical pluralist framework (informed by liberal democratic assumptions), which favours interest groups and the electoral process. According to this framework, power is widely dispersed rather than concentrated. As Peters observes:

> The actors involved generally agree on the rules of the game, especially the rule that elections are the principal means of determining policy.[11]

---

8   Gallagher, Laver and Mair, 2001: 68.
9   Dahl, 1961: 6.
10 Laski, 1927: 123–137.
11 Peters, 1996: 50.

Pluralism in its classical form holds that all interest groups have an opportunity to determine policy outcomes in a relevant sphere. In this sense, the playing pitch is level. Thus, the pluralist state:

> ... will produce policies roughly responsive to public desires, and no single set of interests will dominate.[12]

However, later pluralist accounts acknowledge the importance of asymmetrical power relationships:

> Some interests systematically lose in the policy process; others habitually win.[13]

Marxist and elitist theories, to mention but two, thus challenge the core assumptions of liberal democracy. Even in ostensibly democratic polities, the policy preferences of capital or elites may prevail. Classical pluralism, on the other hand, approximates quite closely to liberal democratic assumptions. Rather than acting as individuals, citizens act collectively through the medium of organisations. In this sense, groups act 'as surrogates for individuals'.[14] Policy outcomes will therefore closely resemble the preferences of individual citizens. Neo-classical approaches, whilst acknowledging spheres of concentrated power, do not hold to the elitist contention that a ruling elite exercises power. Interest groups and professional politicians remain the central actors.

However, the assumptions of liberal democracy still resonate strongly with citizens. Citizens hold politicians responsible for

---

12 Cigler and Loomis, 1998: 4.
13 *Ibid.*
14 Greenwald, 1977: 305.

public policy outcomes. Ultimately, citizens may throw the rascals out. Much of everyday political discourse and media narrative is informed by these assumptions. Apart from discourse within academia, these assumptions tend not to be challenged by citizens. In fact, they are all-pervasive during general elections, which are after all liberal democracy's chief legitimating mechanism. Parliamentarians likewise tend to operate within this framework. The parliamentary mindset is strongly conditioned by the doctrine of the separation of powers, which places parliaments and executives at its decisional centre.[15]

In the eyes of citizens, parliamentary government is held responsible for public policy decisions. However, it seems that modern parliamentary government has little or no input into a vast range of public policy decisions. Is parliamentary government being held responsible for decisions over which it has no say? The post-parliamentary governance model points towards an affirmative answer. This appears to be a case of responsibility without power. Potentially the legitimacy of liberal democracy is damaged because of a:

> …frustrating and delegitimising gap between representative democracy's responsibility and its lack of structural capability and control.[16]

It seems that the normative underpinnings of Western liberal democracy are undermined because there is an ever-widening gap between *de facto* political conditions (multiple power centres) and the expectations of citizens (informed by liberal democratic assumptions).

---

15 Boothroyd, 2000; Hague, 2000; Major, 2000.
16 Andersen and Burns, 1996: 243.

Contemporary politics, it seems, is characterised by highly fluid multiple power centres. Contrary to classical liberal democratic assumptions, contemporary parliamentary government enjoys a diminishing capacity to influence, let alone determine, public policy outcomes. However, party elites and citizens are not taking cognisance of the emerging realities of 21st-century politics. Elite and voter attitudes on public policy formation continue to be informed by state-centric liberal democratic assumptions. Citizens expect parliaments to deliver public policy outcomes. More importantly, citizens hold parliaments responsible for the delivery/non-delivery of public policy outcomes whilst at the same time parliaments cannot actually deliver such outcomes. Thus, there is a gap between *de facto* political conditions and the normative expectations of citizens. **Parliaments are** thereby held responsible for outcomes over which they have diminishing control. Parliamentary government is based on a mythical normative foundation.

In the light of these apparent new realities, I suggest that both political elites and citizens ought to readjust their normative orientations. The myths and fictions of the liberal democratic framework should be illuminated. In particular, citizens and elites need to adjust their normative horizons in respect of parliaments. Parliaments can no longer be held democratically responsible for an increasing array of public policy outcomes. Readjusting the normative orientations of citizens and elites will not prove to be an easy task. This liberal democratic mythical normative base is deeply embedded in the mindsets of citizens and elites alike. The party political system relies largely on the liberal democratic account of public-policy-making processes.

If parliaments are not to become redundant entities, there is an onus on practitioners and theoreticians to craft new roles, taking cognisance of contemporary political conditions. Parliaments are imbued with a strong democratic heritage. Although, they are in effect the vehicles of democratic legitimacy, their *raison d'être* must change. Parliaments can play a new democratic role under the conditions of contemporary politics.

In her retirement statement to the House of Commons, Speaker Betty Boothroyd stated that parliament 'is the chief forum of the nation – today, tomorrow and, I hope, for ever'.[17] Speaker Boothroyd's description of parliament as a forum is apt. In fact, she may have arrived closer to the future essence of parliaments than she realised. I speculate that parliaments' primary future role may well be as a democratic 'forum' in the contemporary public sphere. Parliaments would be returning to their etymological roots as fora of deliberation rather than power.

CATEGORISING PARLIAMENTS

Having analysed the scholarship on change/transformation (globalisation, risk society and multi-level governance), post-parliamentary governance, parliamentary decline and liberal democracy, an important matter of categorisation arises. How can the position of parliaments under conditions of early 21st-century politics be most accurately described? I argue that there are three possibilities: parliamentary government, post-parliamentary governance or parliamentary governance. Firstly, that the present era is one of *parliamentary government* can be rejected as in the context of modern governance to suggest that the tenets of classical parliamentarism still prevail is an utterly counter-factual exercise which flies in the face of

---

17 Boothroyd, 2000.

existing political realities. In fact, as suggested earlier, with the possible exception of a brief pre-democratic period in 19th-century Britain, it is highly improbable that such a classical era ever exited beyond the realms of political theory and philosophy.

Secondly, the current era may indeed be a *post-parliamentary* one. Parliaments either count for little or perhaps not at all. Actors such as interest groups and experts are crowding out parliaments. Parliaments are unable to cope with the complexities of contemporary political conditions. Parliament is thus just one of an array of many 'posts' in contemporary political life.

Thirdly, the current era may be one of *parliamentary governance*. In other words, parliaments are participants rather than mere observers in contemporary governance processes. This position does not question many of the key assumptions associated with 21st-century governance processes. It does, however, contend that parliament is a player on what is admittedly a complex and transformed playing pitch. Sure there are an ever-increasing number of players on the pitch. But it is a player not a passive spectator. It is holding its own in not being overwhelmed.

I believe that liberal democracy's explanatory power and normative orientations regarding the politics of public policy-making are largely redundant in the context of early 21st-century political conditions. In particular, liberal democracy affords an excessively privileged explanatory and normative role to parliaments. Furthermore, parliaments can be either categorised as institutions of post-parliamentary governance, parliamentary government or parliamentary governance. This threefold classification moves beyond an oppositional dualistic choice between parliamentary government and post-parliamentary governance.

5

DEMOCRATIC POLITICS

Democracy is a much contested concept. Fundamentally, though, it is a matter of making social outcomes systematically responsive to the settled preferences of all affected parties. Voting is the classic mechanism for ensuring systematic responsiveness of that sort.[1]

Elitism, the claim the few alone ought to enjoy the prerogatives of political power in light of their special knowledge of the Good, has an extensive genealogy, a family tree to which virtually every age has contributed a branch.[2]

According to the ideal of deliberative democracy, political power must proceed on the basis of a free public reasoning among equals.[3]

In this chapter I concentrate on deliberative democratic theory and its partner, public sphere theory. Contrasting the ideal of deliberative democracy with the world of everyday competitive electoral politics, this chapter lays vital theoretical groundwork for the remainder of the book. It should be clearly understood at the outset that the model of deliberative democracy presented in this chapter is counterfactual or

---

1 Goodin, 2003: 1.
2 Gundersen, 2000: 5.
3 D'Entreves, 2002: 21.

ideal typical, meaning that it does not exist in political reality. Readers might enquire what the possible value of this exercise is; after all, it would be all too easy to dismiss it as utopian and useless. Young, however, rescues us from such charges by reminding us that ideal types:

> ... allow thinkers and actors to take a distance from reality in order to criticise it and imagine possibilities for something better.[4]

I proceed in the spirit of Young with the firm intention of ultimately making this counterfactual exercise relevant to Dáil Éireann operating under the real world conditions of early 21st-century politics. Public sphere theory is explained in the second half of this chapter.

Stoker defines democratic politics as 'the tough process of squeezing collective decisions out of multiple and competing interests and opinions'.[5] The challenge democracy faces, therefore, is not so much arriving at decisions which accurately reflect the *will* of the people, but rather the *wills* of the people. As such, in any democracy there will be a diverse range of contesting views and preferences held by individuals and groups. Channelling these divergent views and preferences into collectively binding outcomes is essentially the very essence of politics. Contemporary electoral democracy interprets this process as a competition between political parties to achieve a majority from the voting public. Voting, whether in elections or plebiscites, is the central mechanism used to determine majority decisions. Electoral democracy closely resembles what democratic theorists call the aggregative model. This model understands democracy as one in which:

---

4 Young, 2002: 10.
5 Stoker, 2006: 1.

Competing for the majority's vote is the essence of the exercise, and the challenge for democratic theorists as they conceive it is to come up with the right rules to govern the contest.[6]

In essence, electoral democracy is a competitive process and public policy outcomes are a reflection of numerical strength. Politicians usually vie in an adversarial fashion for the votes of citizens. Frequently, those seeking political office engage in cat and mouse games of strategic action. Political shrewdness suffocates openness and genuine discussion:

> In order to stay in office, politicians act like entrepreneurs and brokers, looking for formulas that satisfy as many, and alienate as few, interests as possible.[7]

According to Young, those who subscribe to an aggregative understanding of politics:

> … believe that democratic politics is nothing other than a competition between private interests and preferences.[8]

However, deliberative democratic theory offers an alternative to the foregoing account. Operating from radically different assumptions, it invites us to see democratic politics as more than a mere strategy-driven competition for votes. This model of democracy places the concepts of discourse, reason, inclusiveness, consensus and the common or public good at its normative centre.

---

6 Shapiro, 2003: 3.
7 Mansbridge, 1980: 17.
8 Young, 2002: 22.

In a deliberative democracy, all members of the political community affected by a decision arrive at collective decisions through the medium of deliberation. And in making decisions, participants embark upon a *reasoned* quest for the common good, thereby transcending self-regarding behaviour. Deliberative democrats therefore eschew democratic practices which rely on power, deception or any kind of coercion. To make a political process accord to deliberative democratic criteria it must be both *deliberative* and *democratic*. Deliberative processes may therefore be undemocratic and democratic processes can obviously be non-deliberative. Thus, a democratic outcome arrived at whimsically or in the heat of an intensely emotional moment is flawed. Likewise, exclusionary deliberative processes which seek to ensure that public policy outcomes reflect the preferences of privileged elites only are self-evidently undemocratic.

In overall terms, an ideal typical deliberative democratic setting may be said to possess five key characteristics. Firstly, participants affected or about to be affected by a particular outcome or decision are entitled to participate. No participant is denied a voice and the claims of all participants are listened to respectfully. This openness enhances the legitimacy of decisions because participants:

> ... who lose out in the resolution of competing claims are more likely to accept the decision when it is adopted after careful consideration of the relevant merits of competing moral claims for resources.[9]

Secondly, the private interests of participants are parked. Participants behave in a transparent and open manner. The common or public good prevails over selfish interests. Young highlights this aspect of deliberative democracy:

---

9 Freeman, 2000: 383.

> Instead of reasoning from the point of view of the private utility maximiser through public deliberation, citizens transform their preferences according to public-minded ends, and reason together about the nature of those ends and the best means to realise them.[10]

Thirdly, all participants may express their views without fearing sanctions, formal or informal. It is therefore a free discursive space for participants. Freedom is interpreted in much wider terms than in classical liberal democratic understandings. Whilst freedom of speech in the formal sense is a necessary pre-condition, it is not sufficient. Informal societal barriers such as class and gender are incompatible with an ideal typical deliberative democratic setting.

Fourthly, participants behave rationally and reasonably. Models of deliberative democracy position reason and rationality at their normative core, thereby seeking to diminish and displace the emotional sphere. As a reasoned discursive space, deliberative democratic settings frown upon extra-rational forces such as emotions, faith, tradition, myths and superstition. The emphasis is on 'public reasons in the give and take of free and open dialogue'.[11] Participants assert and interrogate their reasons openly. Outcomes are therefore arrived at based on reasoned deliberation.

Fifthly, decisions are arrived at discursively. By discursively I mean that monological understandings of acquiring reason and learning are transcended. A deliberative democratic setting can therefore be described as dialogical and inter-subjective.[12] It can be distinguished from processes such as meditation, inner reflection or what Goodin and Niemeyer term

---

10 Young, 1997a: 61.
11 Bohman, 1996: 7.
12 Venturelli, 1998: 23; Pennington, 2003: 723.

discussion 'in each person's own imagination'.[13] Dewey, for example, takes a decidedly discursive/dialogical approach to knowledge. For Dewey, knowledge is intrinsically inter-subjective and public as:

> Knowledge cooped up in a private consciousness is a myth, and knowledge of social phenomena is peculiarly dependent upon dissemination, for only by distribution can such knowledge be obtained and tested.[14]

A deliberative democratic setting also facilitates a reflective, potentially transformative, process for self and others. As a dialogical process, it compels participants to examine their assumptions, outlooks and orientations. Socially embedded, taken for granted assumptions are revised or abandoned. Where self encounters others who are different, deeply held cultural convictions are probed and examined.

The following conditions facilitate deliberative democratic settings. The discursive space must be open and free. All hierarchies (gender, class, religion, status and prestige) are parked. The absence of power relations is a precondition of an ideal deliberative democratic setting. Discursive relations, therefore, prevail. In this respect, the best argument, rather than the superior power of certain participants, determines outcomes and decisions, as 'Under such conditions, the only remaining authority is that of a good argument'.[15] Neither are decisions arrived at based on superior numerical strength but rather by 'determining which proposals the collective agrees are supported by the best reasons'.[16]

---

13   Goodin and Niemeyer, 2003: 627.
14   Dewey, 1927: 176-177.
15   Dryzek, 1990: 15.
16   Young, 2002: 23.

Force, coercion and power are anathema to this deliberative democratic setting. Consequently, the discursive process is both consensual and voluntary. Discourse proceeds rationally with issues approached in a dispassionate way. Trust and honesty being essential prerequisites, participants may not therefore hide their real intentions.

There are barriers to deliberative democracy. As Jonas observes, 'Few would argue that the distinction between deliberation and self-interested calculation is not a real one'.[17] Strategic, calculating and self-interested behaviours are insurmountable barriers to a deliberative democratic setting. Rather than deliberating, members play a discursive game of poker. Cunning and opportunistic behaviour, rather than discursive quality, determines outcomes and decisions. Rhetoric and sophistry are further barriers to pure speech since they manipulate speech thereby distorting ultimate truth. Thus, rather than assessing rationally the merits and demerits of a contribution, members are swayed by how an argument is presented. Presentation and performance, rather than content, become the determining factors. Like contemporary public relations, rhetoric is considered a shallow and superficial exercise designed to conceal rather than reveal.

Finally, deliberation, discussion and bargaining should be distinguished. In discursive terms, deliberation conjures up the notion of a careful, studied, dispassionate and reflective consideration of issues. As Fearon explains, outcomes and decisions are reached carefully and seriously, not whimsically. Arguments and counter-arguments are addressed and weighed-up rationally. Thus, spur of the moment decisions made in heated and highly charged emotional atmospheres fall foul of the deliberative ideal. Discussion, on the other hand, is a generic term for both deliberative and non-deliberative discursive

---

17 Jonas, 1984: 40.

processes. Discussion need not necessarily be cool, calm and studied.[18] Bargaining occupies the furthermost distance from the deliberative democratic ideal type. Conceptually, it is at the opposite end of the spectrum to deliberative practices. Bargaining (or negotiating) epitomises the idea of strategic and calculating behaviour by self-interested actors.

The public sphere is one of two key theories utilised here. A normative partner of deliberative democracy, it is nevertheless more concrete in its theoretical dispensation. To appreciate this point, it must be understood that the idea of the public sphere can be interpreted in both normative and empirical terms.[19]

It will be recalled from chapter one that the public sphere was taken to be a communicative and discursive space, an arena in which actors, individual and collective, state and civil society, debate and discuss a vast diversity of issues before an observing, judging and evaluating audience. Writing on the Habermasian concept of the public sphere, Fraser says:

> It designates a theatre in modern societies in which political participation is enacted through the medium of talk. It is the space in which citizens deliberate about their common affairs, and hence an institutionalised arena of discursive action. This arena is conceptually distinct from the state; it is a site for the production and circulation of discourses that can in principle be critical of the state. The public sphere in Habermas' sense is also conceptually distinct from the official economy; it is not an arena of market relations but rather one of discursive relations, a theatre for debating and deliberating rather than for buying and selling.[20]

---

18 Fearon, 1999: 63.
19 Fraser, 2007: 7.
20 Fraser, 1992: 111.

Crucially, issues are 'played out' in front of a critical public. Habermas emphasises that the 'public audience possesses final authority' to make judgments on contrasting positions,[21] adding that:

> In complex societies it is an intermediary structure between the political system and the private sectors of the lifeworld.[22]

The contemporary public sphere is generally a mediated communicative and deliberative space. State and civil society actors discuss, debate and propagate issues through various media such as newspapers, television and other electronic communications.

The literature on the public sphere makes an important distinction between strong and weak publics.[23] As Lewandowski explains, strong publics possess both institutional and deliberative power. Weak publics, on the other hand, possess deliberative power only. Thus, weak 'publics do not make policy and do not write laws'.[24] Habermas explains that the 'weak public is the vehicle of public opinion'.[25] Weak publics, therefore, exercise influence, not power. Strong publics include the institutions of parliamentary government, which possess the capacity to make collectively binding decisions. According to Habermas:

> The flow between public opinion formation, institutionalised elections and legislative decisions is meant to guarantee that influence and communicative power is transformed through legislation into administrative power.[26]

---

21 Habermas, 1996: 364.
22 *Ibid.*: 73.
23 Fraser, 1992; Ericksen and Fossum, 2002; Lewandowski, 2003.
24 Lewandowski, 2003: 125.
25 Habermas, 1996: 302.
26 *Ibid.*: 299.

Thus, the state apparatus exercises two types of power. Parliamentary government exercises communicative power whilst the bureaucratic complex exercises administrative power. Non-state actors exercise influence which can potentially be transformed into binding decisions by the state apparatus. Habermas contends that:

> Deliberative politics thus lives off the interplay of democratically institutionalised will formation and informal opinion formation.[27]

The history of the public sphere has been one of expanding pluralism in two respects. Firstly, there has been a vast increase in the number of participating and observing actors. Elite and privileged membership in the early historical period was accompanied by a trend leading eventually towards mass membership in the contemporary public sphere. Membership of the contemporary public sphere is, therefore, not confined to historically privileged actors such as church officials, feudal barons, enlightenment intellectuals or the 19th-century middle class. Secondly, ontological diversity has eroded the previous authority of dogma and a singular worldview. These broad trends were evident during the public sphere's historical infancy. Thus, it was during the Renaissance and the Reformation that the Roman Catholic Church lost its ontological monopoly. The irreversible split in Christendom smashed existing religious orthodoxy resulting in sharply competing interpretations of scriptures. An emerging free intelligentsia provided competing interpretations of the social and political worlds. The intellectual stranglehold of pre-Reformation Christianity had been broken.

Similarly, during the Enlightenment reason and faith provided deeply conflicting and, for the most part, irreconcilable interpretations

---

27 *Ibid*.: 308.

of reality. However, it is during recent transformations in the contemporary public sphere that these trends have accelerated at a hitherto unprecedented pace. The term 'hyper pluralism' is employed to describe this pattern of the public sphere's exponential growth, rapid growth not only in respect of membership but also in respect of diverse worldviews.

Transformations in the contemporary public sphere commenced in the 1960s and 1970s, coinciding with the communications revolution. As the 20th century closed, it was clear that a qualitatively different public sphere to its 19th-century liberal predecessor was emerging. The communications revolution, particularly the rapid advance of computer technology in the 1990s, in no small way accounts for this transformation. Similarly, the emergence of new social movements in the 1960s and 1970s increased and diversified the public sphere's membership. Strydom stresses the plurality of the contemporary public sphere:

> Due to an influx of participants who themselves are heterogeneous, the public sphere became more pluralistic and democratic.[28]

Reference should also be made to Habermas' 'core-periphery' model of the public sphere.[29] As Strydom explains, the model has three dimensions. The first dimension is the core consisting of the formal decision-making organs of state, executive, legislative, courts and bureaucracy. The second is the inner periphery consisting of bodies exercising delegated state functions. The third is the outer periphery consisting of civil society and the interface between public bodies and

---

28 Strydom, 2002a: 107.
29 Habermas, 1996.

private organisations. Habermas' core-periphery model should not be understood in static, staid or rigid terms. On the contrary, the model clearly illuminates the dynamic and fluid nature of the contemporary public sphere. It holds that power shifts from the core to the periphery when the public sphere is in a state of agitation. In such circumstances, civil society may exercise influence over the core. However, when the public sphere is at rest, the core takes precedence.[30]

This account of an ideal deliberative democratic community obviously sets the normative bar very high. For theorists dissatisfied with existing democratic arrangements in which power relations and manipulative political behaviour are taken for granted, deliberative democracy offers a compelling and very attractive alternative. Public sphere theory as an innovative but feasible real world role will be sketched later for Dáil Éireann under contemporary political conditions. However, for the moment I continue on the ideal typical journey.

---

30 Strydom, 2002a: 112–113.

6

AN IDEAL TYPICAL PARLIAMENT

The process of reaching a decision will also be a process whereby initial preferences are transformed to take account of the views of others.[1]

The norms of deliberation, finally, privilege speech that is dispassionate and disembodied. They tend to presuppose an opposition between mind and body, reason and emotion. They tend falsely to identify objectivity with calm and absence of emotional expression. Thus expressions of anger, hurt and passionate concern discount the claims and reasons they accompany.[2]

Knowledge cooped up in a private consciousness is a myth, and knowledge of social phenomena is peculiarly dependent upon dissemination, for only by distribution can such knowledge be obtained and tested.[3]

My aim in this chapter is to sketch an idealised parliament, informed by the tenets of deliberative democratic theory, to outline and analyse the key characteristics of *an idealised model*. I conclude by deriving a key norm from the ideal model.

---

1   Miller, 1993: 75.
2   Young, 1997a: 64.
3   Dewey, 1927: 176–177.

Under my idealised model the institutions of parliamentary government are at the polity's decisional centre. Parliament is not a peripheral actor in the polity, but, rather, possesses both decision-making capacity and responsibility. As such, parliament is responsible for decisions over which it exercises control. Parliament puts innovative structures and mechanisms in place, which take cognisance of the transformed and ever dynamic conditions of 21st-century governance.

Parliament does not retrospectively rubber-stamp supranational processes. Rather, it has the opportunity to shape legislative/policy outcomes prospectively. Policy networks and social partnership type arrangements are channelled through parliament. Decision-making is not concentrated in the executive branch. Parliamentary responsibility is accompanied by decision-making capacity. Parliament acts autonomously of the executive. It is therefore not simply an extension of the executive.

In contemporary parliamentary settings power, rather than discursive relations, prevails. Executives occupy a highly privileged space within parliamentary chambers. Numerical strength (majority voting) determines outcomes. The whipped system ensures that members do not exercise a truly free vote. Ideologically divided chambers prevent the emergence of true discourse. Entrenched party positions ensure that participants do not change their minds because of superior argument.

Rhetoric and passion are the normal discursive instruments. Dispassionate deliberation is frowned upon, particularly in adversarial models such as in Ireland. Governments and oppositions play a strategic game of power. Hiding its true intentions, each side tries to inflict the maximum political damage upon the other. In an era of public relations, much posturing is done for the television news. The term 'sound bite' has entered the vernacular.

The composition of parliaments reflects societal stratification. With few exceptions, the majority of members are middle-class, professional males. Within parliaments, those incapable of rhetorical flourishes are at a distinct disadvantage. It would be difficult to argue that the exigencies of the common good are always a core feature of parliamentary life. It is hard not to conclude that contemporary parliamentary politics is a very long way removed from a deliberative democratic setting.

Ideal typically, the executive does not enjoy an automatic majority. The discursive process is both consensual and voluntary. As such, the parliamentary whipping system associated with the Irish and Westminster model is prohibited. Discourse proceeds rationally and it follows that issues are approached in a dispassionate way. Trust and honesty are essential prerequisites. Participants do not hide their real intentions.

PARLIAMENT AS A LEGISLATIVE ASSEMBLY

A common criticism of contemporary parliaments is that they are not genuine legislative assemblies. Unlike the United States Congress, parliaments do not make laws independently of the executive. In Ireland the Executive sponsors virtually all legislation; private members' bills rarely make it on to the statute books. Because the legislative agenda of the Executive tends to prevail, parliaments are accused of being mere legislative rubber-stamps. Whilst opposition amendments may be accepted, ministers remain in a position to push home their legislative advantage. Ultimately, legislation can be rushed through parliaments at speed without proper discussion. This so called 'guillotine procedure' is a powerful instrument available to ministers.

Parliaments enjoy an independent law-making capacity. Bills are passed based on discursive merit (informed by the exigencies of the common good), rather than their origin on the executive or opposition benches. Therefore, all bills have an equal chance of becoming law. Only in the rarest circumstances (emergency bills) can legislation be rushed through parliament. Thus, for ordinary bills, guillotine mechanisms are prohibited. An orderly legislative timetable is agreed to at the beginning of each session. Any remaining bills are not rushed through at the end of the session. Rather, the session is either extended or bills are held back until the following session. Standing Orders afford no special speaking or procedural privileges to particular members. Discursively, parliament is a level playing field. All stages of a bill are dealt with in plenary sessions with all members participating fully. With the exception of emergency legislation, responsibility is not delegated to committees for any stage of a bill.

EXECUTIVE ACCOUNTABILITY

Ideally, parliament holds the executive to account. Parliament is neither a bystander in the political process nor a mere instrument of the executive. Accountability occurs in both its *ex-post* and *ex-ante* forms. *Ex-post*, or retrospective, accountability occurs when parliaments seek explanations from executives after decisions are made. Thus, ministers come before parliaments justifying past actions or recently made decisions. *Ex-ante*, or prospective, accountability provides for meaningful parliamentary input before decisions are made. Ministers come before parliament explaining and justifying proposals. Parliament can thus shape decisions at the decision-making phase. The Danish Parliament's EC Committee is a good example of *ex-ante* accountability. This Committee has the power to 'give a negotiating mandate to Ministers in Brussels'.[4] The Committee does not confine its remit to questioning Ministers after decisions are made. On the contrary, it sends Ministers to Brussels with a clear mandate from members.

What are the desired outcomes of strong accountability in the ideal typical parliament? Firstly, ministers reveal fully, swiftly and frankly all relevant facts and information. A culture of transparency, rather than secrecy, pervades the accountability process. Regarding disclosure of information, ministers adopt a maximalist rather than a minimalist approach. Ministers share information willingly and voluntarily instead of under circumstances of parliamentary duress. Point-scoring, long-winded irrelevant replies and outright avoidance of questions are prohibited. The opposition probes ministers with a view to getting maximum information rather than party political advantage. In spheres where *ex-ante* accountability applies, ministers adhere to instructions given by parliament. Breach or deviation from instructions results in executive resignation.

Secondly, accountability mechanisms at all times seek to promote and enhance the common good of the polity. Mechanisms are not employed to protect or promote vested interests. Rather, the general interests of the polity take precedence. As such, accountability mechanisms seek to expose breaches of the common good. Where ministers behave as self-interested actors, sanctions are imposed.

Everyday practical party politics is in many respects antithetical to the notion of the common good. Party politics can be interpreted as a strategic and competitive 'game' where the exigencies of the common good are neglected or ignored. Parliamentary accountability

---

4 Moxon Browne, 1996: 81.

mechanisms can quite easily become the tools of strategic party political games. The emphasis is on point scoring at 'Question Time' rather than eliciting from ministers or officials whether the polity's common good has been advanced by executive action or inaction. Party politics is indeed innately strategic. Placing the common good at the normative centre of accountability instruments can, therefore, be regarded as an insurmountable obstacle. However, later I will demonstrate that Dáil Éireann possesses the capacity (in the real world) to act as a normative vehicle for the common good via the contemporary public sphere.

Thirdly, the polity's democratic legitimacy is enhanced. Authoritative and binding decisions, which are made by the executive, are subject to genuine democratic scrutiny. Authoritative decisions in the polity are largely made by the democratically elected institutions of parliamentary government. As binding decisions for the polity are not in the main made in non-parliamentary settings, the challenges of democratic legitimacy are reduced. Multiple and fluid *decisional* centres do not exist. This is not to imply the absence of private spaces such as civil society. It does, however, mean that these spaces do not make authoritative decisions for the polity. Civil society inputs its policy preferences. A crucial 'mechanism' available to civil society in this regard is the public sphere.

CONSTITUENCY REPRESENTATION

Members of parliament possess a dual role. Firstly, they are elected by constituents to represent local interests. Secondly, they are national actors contributing *inter alia* to public policy outcomes. There can be an obvious tension between both roles. Is a member's first duty to constituents who have sent him/her to parliament? Or does the member owe an overriding allegiance to society as a whole rather than to one component? Is the member a delegate bound by constituency instructions? Is the member a trustee bound by reasoned debate in parliament? How should our ideal typical parliamentarian behave if a conflict arises between local and national interests?

These are hardly novel questions. In his famous address to the electors of Bristol in 1784, philosopher and politician Edmund Burke contended that the MP's first duty is to the general good of the polity 'not local purposes, not local prejudices'.[5] MPs are not constituency delegates bound by constituency instruction.[6] Rather, they are members of a genuinely deliberative assembly, bound by reasoned debate, and not prisoners of particularistic and localised interests.

Ideal typically, members of parliament represent the common good. If there is a conflict between constituency interests and the general good of society, the latter prevails. Thus, parliamentarians do not behave as delegates who operate in accordance with constituency instructions. Instead of representing the interests of constituencies, members rise above localist and particularistic pressures. Members attending parliament and operating in accordance with deliberative norms seek to promote the common good.

EMOTIONS

Deliberative democrats position reason and rationality at their normative core, diminishing if not displacing the emotional sphere. Emotional forces are frowned upon and discouraged. However, I contend that models of deliberative democracy should incorporate

---

5   Burke [1784], 1999.
6   Judge, 1999: 13.

the emotional sphere of the human condition. Young recognises the importance of the emotional sphere in discursive settings.[7] Her analysis is particularly insightful:

> The norms of deliberation, finally, privilege speech that is dispassionate and disembodied. They tend to presuppose an opposition between mind and body, reason and emotion. They tend falsely to identify objectivity with calm and absence of emotional expression. Thus expressions of anger, hurt and passionate concern discount the claims and reasons they accompany.[8]

Young is surely correct to point out that, under certain models of deliberative democracy, objectivity is synonymous with emotionless and placid discourse, and that deliberative democrats should *not* disavow reasons that are accompanied by emotion. To do so places a core feature of the human condition beyond the deliberative democratic model's normative reach.

Young correctly focuses on the emotions of hurt and anger. Is it proper to expect individuals or groups that have been psychologically injured with perhaps life-long repercussions, to be calm, dispassionate and self-possessed? Are victims of violence and abuse expected to share their hurts and anxieties in a detached and logical way? Are we as witnesses expected to respond to their suffering in a detached and cold fashion? Young is rightly critical of the expulsion of passion by some models of deliberative democracy. It is, therefore, necessary to adopt deliberative norms which 'move the heart and engage the imagination'.[9]

---

7 Young, 1997a, 2002.
8 *Ibid.* 2002: 64–65.
9 *Ibid.*: 63.

The norms of calm and dispassionate deliberation may also have the undesirable effect of placing socially and economically marginalised groups at a significant discursive disadvantage. Young highlights how social movements intentionally reject deliberative norms and practices. Rejecting, in particular, political processes based on reasoned discourse, consensus and compromise, social activists relying on oppositional tactics (sit-ins, street demonstrations, boycotts) as deliberative practices are exploited by elites to perpetuate existing power relationships. Young proceeds to argue that settings which are genuinely discursive in the deliberative sense may mask disguised power relationships. She further contends that these deliberative settings rely on certain premises and taken for granted assumptions which serve to protect, entrench and reproduce the status quo. She describes these deliberative processes as ones of hegemonic discourse or systematically distorted communication.[10]

Strydom makes the important point that spaces of social interaction (including discursive spaces) are relational rather than individualist. As such, the skills and abilities which different actors bring to them 'can socially be expected to vary considerably'.[11] This social variance means that those from marginalised socio-economic backgrounds may be placed at a disproportionate disadvantage. For example, referring to gender relations, Hudson argues that women suffer a discursive disadvantage because concepts of rationality are shaped by 'male ideals of the priority of reason over emotion, the value of self-control, detachment and impartiality'.[12]

Rules, procedures and Standing Orders designed to run meetings

---

10 *Ibid.*, 2001: 670–690.
11 Strydom, 2002b: 126.
12 Hudson, 2003: 117.

tend to be very formal, complex and perhaps even rigid. It is, of course, true that rules and procedures are *prima facie* designed to bring structure and organisation to meetings. Nevertheless, meetings may intimidate or even silence some participants. The educated and those accustomed to public speaking have clear advantages in these situations. The language of agendas, motions, minutes, points of order and amendments, on the other hand, may have a suppressive impact on participants from poor and uneducated backgrounds. Young asserts correctly that those from deprived and disadvantaged backgrounds frequently:

> ... feel intimidated by the argument requirements and the formality and rules of parliamentary procedure, so they do not speak, or speak only in a way that those in charge find 'disruptive'.[13]

It is difficult to imagine any discursive setting proceeding because of pure reason and rationality. Indeed, as much of life is concerned with emotional hurts and needs, the absence of an emotional sphere would prove very detrimental to the discursive process. Whilst, classically, reason and emotion are seen as irreconcilable enemies, this need not be the case. Human beings, after all, are both rational and emotional actors.

An ideal typical parliament incorporates the emotional sphere of human behaviour. Members of parliament behave sympathetically and empathetically. They do not divorce themselves from the emotional sphere. Sympathetic parliamentarians feel for the plights and dilemmas of their fellow citizens. Empathetic parliamentarians try to understand and relate to the pain and distress of their fellow citizens.

---

13   Young, 1997a: 64.

Empathetic parliamentarians are obliged to ask the following questions: How would I cope if placed in the particular situation? What can I do to increase my understanding of this situation? Are there any experiences in my life that I can draw from which would increase my capacity to relate to distressed fellow citizens? The empathetic parliamentarian, therefore, does more than feel the suffering of others. Whilst this is a crucial initial step in any empathetic exercise, it is insufficient. The empathetic parliamentarian goes a step further and seeks to understand and relate to the experiences of others.

Ideal typically, parliamentarians are not obliged to make decisions in the heat of an individual moment or a collective moment for society as a whole. Distance between emotional moments and decision-making is encouraged. But when making collective decisions, parliamentarians are not permitted to make law and policies on a purely rational basis. Thus, if parliament has listened to the painful experiences of distressed others as part of a consultation process with civil society, there is a clear onus on parliamentarians to ensure that reasoned and *sensitive* decisions are arrived at. Parliamentarians are thus obliged to respond in a meaningful way to the totality of the human condition. Rationality and reason provide partial understanding of the human condition. Therefore, parliamentarians cannot rely solely on rational speech, which is composed of 'assertions and giving sober reasons for them, with the logical connections among them clearly spelled out'.[14]

This approach invites political theorists to move beyond dualistic analysis. Antagonistic opposites are open to at least partial reconciliation. Young advocates moving beyond sterile and fruitless

---

14 Young, 1997a: 70.

antagonisms by reconciling reason and emotion. In doing so, she arrives at a more inclusive set of deliberative norms.

Endorsing this approach, Fraser contends that the philosophy has long been divided into two groups, namely separationists and conversationalists, with Fraser a member of the latter group. The separationists eschew consensus, arrive at antagonistic outcomes and conclusions, see differences as unbridgeable, and demand that individuals take sides. Conversationalists see differences as reconcilable and advocate dialogic understandings. Attempting to rise above ontological and epistemological dichotomies, entrenched positions are frowned upon. The goal of integrating ostensibly hostile concepts and theories drives those of a conversationalist persuasion.[15]

RHETORIC

Speech, language and debate are essential political tools. Political historians frequently rely on great orations, speeches and debates to capture defining times. Wordsmiths such as speechwriters help the politician convey his/her messages, policy positions, hopes, ambitions and visions. Rhetoric provides the scholar with a window through which to explore key political concepts. The changing nature of political concepts can thus be traced over time through the medium of rhetoric. Politics implies struggle. These struggles manifest themselves in many different arenas such as parliament, the media and civil society. Ultimately, political struggle may manifest itself in war and violence. Political actors struggle over the meaning of concepts. In public debates, they offer conflicting and competing perspectives. They struggle to get public approval for their particular

---

15 Fraser, 2004: 125–126.

perspectives. As such, rhetoric provides political actors with the communication tools to acquire public approval. Rhetoric may be defined as:

> The art or discipline that deals with the use of discourse, either spoken or written, to inform or persuade or motivate an audience, whether that audience is made up of one person or a group of persons.[16]

Classically, the Ancients understood rhetoric as the act of oratory. Its remit concerned spoken, not written, discourses. Eloquent public speakers could win an audience over to their position. However, the printing revolution of the 15th century broadened rhetoric's scope to include the written as well as verbal discourses. As such, the invention of the printing press in Mainz circa 1450 radically altered the meaning and ambit of rhetorical studies. Henceforth, rhetoricians would seek to apply classical maxims to pamphlets, treatises and books. However, rhetoric in both its written and spoken guises shared a key characteristic: namely that the discursive act's central objective was to persuade an audience.

Classical rhetoric appeals to three different facets of the human condition. Firstly, it appeals to the rational facet or *logus*. The rhetorician hopes to persuade his/her audience based on reason and understanding. Secondly, it appeals to the emotional facet or *pathos*. The rhetorician is aware that human beings enjoy free will. By appealing to the audience's emotions and passions, the rhetorician's intention is to sway free will in a particular direction. Thirdly, classical rhetoric appeals to the ethical facet or *ethos*. In this situation, the character and standing of the rhetorician is a crucial factor. It is hoped that the

---

16 Corbett and Connors, 1999: 1.

good character of the rhetorician will generate a persuasive effect on the audience.

Three kinds of persuasive discourse are recognised in classical rhetoric; namely deliberative, forensic and epideictic. The deliberative approach refers to matters of public affairs and politics as understood by classical Athenians. The orientation is futuristic. Rhetoricians may appeal for changes in institutional structures or policy positions. The forensic, or legal, approach is primarily associated with courtroom and judicial settings. The emphasis is on the rhetorician defending past actions rather than advocating future changes. The epideictic, or ceremonial, approach tends to honour past events of significant importance and its purpose seems to be one of inspiring citizens as such an approach may help to create unifying myths around the polity.[17]

From a deliberative democratic perspective, one key central objection can be raised towards the employment of rhetoric. Rhetoric distorts and conceals truth. It is merely a strategic device used to achieve objectives by stealth. Thus, in contemporary political campaigns rhetoric is deployed to denigrate opponents and avoid factual analysis. An interesting example of how rhetoric is used politically is the contemporary United States. Many commentators argue that there are few significant policy differences between Republican and Democratic administrations. The United States suffers from an 'extraordinarily narrow spectrum of political discourse'.[18] As such, rhetoric is used by elites in both parties to generate superficial policy divisions. Mainstream ideas, which do not disturb the status quo, dominate the public sphere.

---

17 *Ibid.*: 1–26.
18 Chomsky, 2003: 119.

Another case is contemporary Britain where the traditional Left has tended to be thoroughly disenchanted with 'third way' politics.[19] In fact, the phrase 'Old Labour' is frequently used to either describe or deride adherents of the classical post-Second World War social democratic model. In this regard, Blairite Britain adopted the Conservative rhetoric of welfare dependence. As such, it is possible to argue that party politics in the UK is converging on the centre. Assuming this centre space is crowded, rhetoric becomes crucially important if only as a differentiating tool. Therefore, rhetoric seems to be incompatible with the ideals of a deliberative democratic community.

But can the use of rhetoric be justified? Aristotle defends rhetoric as a political device, making a clear distinction between forensic and deliberative rhetoric. As explained above, forensic rhetoric is the essential tool of a courtroom lawyer, with its emphasis being on delivery, theatre and showmanship. The lawyer's sole concern is to get the best possible hearing and outcome for his/her client. When analysing rhetoric, Aristotle contends that scholars tended to confuse forensic rhetoric with its relation: deliberative rhetoric. Aristotle interprets deliberative rhetoric in a much more favourable light. Deliberative rhetoric, which is the province of legislators, is deemed a noble activity which seeks to mediate between private interests and the common good. Hence, deliberative rhetoric is not simply a tool of strategic self-interested actors.[20]

Young also defends the use of rhetoric in certain circumstances. Moving beyond deliberative democracy's excessive emphasis on rationality, Young advocates communicative democracy. Unlike

---

19 Callnicos, 2000.
20 Nichols, 1987: 657–677.

deliberative democracy, communicative democracy does not favour rationality and literal speech. Young, for example, values narrative and figurative language as a dimension of communicative democracy.[21] Rhetoric also clearly incorporates the emotional space. Parliamentarians will frequently be obliged to highlight the 'mood' of the nation. This cannot always be done in a calm, sober and dispassionate way. Rhetoric may be an indispensable communicative tool in instances where parliamentarians need to convey emotions to their audience.

It can also be argued that great rhetorical moments may capture the mood of an era. Who would dismiss Robert Emmet's speech from the dock, Lincoln's Gettysburg Address, Winston Churchill's wartime orations, Martin Luther King's 'I Have a Dream' Washington address, Nelson Mandela's passionate plea from the courtroom dock, Geoffrey Howe and Robin Cook's Commons resignation speeches and Jimmy Carter's Nobel Peace Prize acceptance speech?

DISCURSIVE ACCOUNTABILITY

Many of the idealised functions of parliament discussed in this chapter are quite clearly incompatible with the conditions of 21st-century politics. For example, it is unrealistic to advocate that parliament ought to be at the polity's decisional centre as modern polities are characterised by multiple and fluid decisional sites. Thus, the idea that parliament ought to be the polity's chief policy-making and legislative space is totally at variance with contemporary political realities. Similarly, it is difficult to imagine an eventuality whereby the parliamentary process is devoid of power and strategic considerations.

---

21 Young 2002: 52–80.

Should I therefore give up on my quest to map out a role for Dáil Éireann which is shaped by the theoretical and conceptual underpinnings of an ideal typical parliament? The answer is clearly in the negative as I can achieve this through the key norm of discursive accountability which is derived from the parliament just sketched. So what is the meaning of discursive accountability? It means that actors are required to provide reasons publicly for decisions made or not made against the benchmark of polity's common good. Dáil Éireann provides a democratic and public forum where a range of actors would give reasons for decisions made.

In a departure from ideal typical deliberative norms, discursive accountability is not, however, equated with rational/dispassionate discourse. Reasons may be accompanied by passion and rhetoric. Discursive accountability, therefore, coincides with Young's communicative ideal which incorporates emotions and passions, rather than the deliberative ideal which favours dispassionate discourse. Communicative and deliberative ideals can therefore be clearly distinguished. It is my contention that Young's ideal is more socially and politically inclusive and transferable to real world settings. The communicative ideal therefore encourages us to strive for *approximate* ideal communication settings.

7

Separation of Powers and Resources

When I entered the House, there were ten members to each typist. The typist who worked for me used an Underwood typewriter and had to use a brush to clean the letter 't' which otherwise appeared on the page as 'I'.[1]

Significant progress was made in 2006 towards achieving the long-term ambition of making the Irish Parliament a world-class Parliament of which we can all be proud.[2]

Some contend that too much is expected of members of Congress. How can elected generalists render intelligent judgments on the dizzyingly complex problems of governance?[3]

A press release issued by the Oireachtas Public Relations Office dated 26 February 2002 announced a major parliamentary reform programme. Stating that the reforms are the product of over two years' work by the Dáil Reform Committee, it describes the package as 'historic and comprehensive'. In their scope, the reforms are said to amount to 'the most far-reaching reforms of the Dáil since the

---

1 Connolly, 1996.
2 O'Hanlon and Kiely, quoted in Houses of the Oireachtas Commission 2007.
3 Davidson and Oleszek, 2000: 417.

foundation of the State'. Among the reforms mentioned in the release are: electronic voting in the Dáil, enhanced monitoring of European Union legislative proposals, reform of Dáil question time and the establishment of an independent Oireachtas Commission.

To describe the reform package as the most significant since the State's foundation is indeed a bold claim. Can the language be dismissed as mere public relations' hype designed to get good copy in the following day's newspapers? Or is there actually some substance to the claims made? This chapter and the subsequent three chapters address a core concern of this book: Is the contemporary Dáil Éireann a displaced institution, or is it attempting to change with the times as the above press release implies?

SEPARATION OF POWERS

The doctrine of the separation of powers occupies a central space in western political theory and practice. The doctrine holds that political power should not be concentrated in any one individual or organ of government. Concentrations of political power, it is contended, undermine liberty and lead to tyrannical government. Therefore, political power should be divided among three separate organs of government, namely executive, legislative and judicial. Theoretically, each organ is meant to act as a check on the other. This section will focus exclusively on the relationship between the Republic of Ireland's lower legislative chamber (Dáil Éireann) and executive branch (Cabinet). Virtually all democratic polities adopt versions of this doctrine in their constitutional architecture. Whilst the doctrine has its origins in a pre-democratic age, it has become synonymous with democratic government. In particular, academics, parliamentarians and public commentators bemoan the arrival of over-mighty executives and the apparent subservience of legislatures. In this regard the All-Party Oireachtas Committee on the Constitution refers to 'the tendency of democratic Government to gather power into their own hands to the detriment of Parliament'.[4] The literature assigns Dáil Éireann a subservient role. Typical is Farrell's assertion that:

> The Government can effectively control the legislature as long as its party support remains solid.[5]

In these circumstances it may be particularly difficult for the Opposition to discharge its parliamentary obligations. This was evident when then Opposition Chief Whip and future Taoiseach, Bertie Ahern, raised an issue on the Order of Business. The Chief Whip was looking for notice of pending legislation, thereby affording his Front Bench time to make preparations before legislation reached the floor of the House. However, it seems that even this basic facility was being denied to them. His words during Dáil exchanges not surprisingly have an air of frustration about them:

> For a number of weeks past I have been endeavouring to ascertain what legislation will be taken this side of the summer recess so that I could inform our Front Bench spokesmen of what they should be researching and what is coming up for debate. But I do not have any idea.[6]

Deemed a creature of the executive branch, the Dáil's constitutional independence operates purely at a *de jure* level. A former TD, Party Leader and Minister put the position eloquently:

---

4 All-Party Oireachtas Committee on the Constitution, 2002: 11.
5 Farrell, 1994: 74.
6 Ahern, 1984.

In parliamentary and political theory, the parliamentary institution has always been the superior one. In this country, the parliamentary institution is by far the inferior ... It is becoming progressively more inferior as the power and strength of the Executive dominates.[7]

An important milestone in the evolving relationship between Parliament and the Executive in Ireland's case was the Parliamentary Inquiry into DIRT (Deposit Interest Retention Tax) which resulted in two reports (1999, 2001). A Sub-Committee of Dáil Éireann's Public Accounts Committee carried out the inquiry. Whilst the investigation *per se* is outside the ambit of this book, it should be stated that the inquiry explored allegations of widespread tax evasion facilitated by the banking sector. From this chapter's perspective, the reports' observations on the separation of powers are particularly salient.

Dáil Éireann's apparent subservience to the Executive was strongly criticised by the Sub-Committee. Explicitly invoking a separation of powers discourse, the Sub-Committee moved beyond a purely descriptive approach. It argued that:

Accountability to the Oireachtas is weakened further by a lack of clear boundaries between Parliament and Government.[8]

The Sub-Committee cited one very significant breach of the boundary. It conducted a wide-ranging inquiry into DIRT tax evasion and several actors, including the Department of Finance, were among those under investigation. However, it was the Department of Finance which was

---

7 O'Malley, 1996.
8 Parliamentary Inquiry into DIRT, 1999: 181.

financing the Committee's inquiry.[9] As the inquiry proceeded and when the Committee needed supplementary funding it was the Department of Finance which made the funding decisions! Obviously, it would have been impossible for the Committee to proceed in the absence of proper financial resources. Yet the Committee was, theoretically at least, a 'prisoner' of one of the bodies it was investigating. It is little wonder that these circumstances provoked the Sub-Committee to state:

> This is but one example of a totally unacceptable subjugation of Parliament to Government when one of Parliament's fundamental roles is to hold Government to account.[10]

The Sub-Committee also makes a clear connection between parliamentary independence and counter-corruption measures. This is an important point as allegations of widespread political corruption burst onto the Irish political stage from the mid-1990s onwards. Whilst the case of political corruption in the Irish polity is complex, it is hard to disagree with the Sub-Committee's assertion:

> A vigorously active and independent Parliament with the powers to investigate matters of serious public importance will ensure that the systemic abuses and breakdown of good Government highlighted by this Inquiry, the Tribunals and other inquiries, make it much less likely that it will happen again.[11]

Perhaps the most significant development to impact on the relationship between Dáil Éireann and the Executive is the establishment of an

---

9   *Ibid.*

10 *Ibid.*

11 Parliamentary Inquiry into DIRT, 2001: 92.

independent Commission to run the Houses of the Oireachtas. The origins of this development can be traced to the reports of the Public Accounts Committee. It is my contention that this Commission is by far the Sub-Committee's most important legacy. The Commission was established by the Houses of the Oireachtas Commission Act (2003) and began operating on 1 January 2004. It consists of eleven members including the Chairs of the Dáil and Seanad, the Clerk of the Dáil (who is also Secretary General of the Commission), a nominee of the Minister for Finance and four TDs and three Senators nominated by their respective houses. Essentially the Commission manages and administers the day-to-day affairs of the Oireachtas. Its key function is an administrative one: organising the secretarial facilities for members. The Commission is entitled to represent both Houses in legal proceedings. In this regard, it should be observed that a further key recommendation of the Sub-Committee was that the Houses of the Oireachtas should have autonomous legal representation.

The Minister for Finance, however, retains important functions under the 2003 Act. Crucially, it is the Minister and not the Commission who determines allowances and expenses (including attached conditions) for members and staff alike. Whilst the Commission makes informal recommendations to the Minister on matters related to allowances and expenses, the Minister remains the sole statutory authority in this sphere. Self-evidently this situation violates the separation of powers.

Nevertheless, arising from the establishment of the Commission the contemporary Dáil has an enhanced capacity to shape its own preferred future direction. Under the 2003 Act, the Commission is obliged to report on its activities and draw up its future plans. The constituent legislation for the Commission provides for a specific grant payable from the Central Fund to meet the expenses of the

Commission. An amending Act in 2006 made similar provisions for the years 2007–2009. The 2003 Act is thus very empowering in its overall orientation. It is firmly within the remit of the Commission to prioritise key objectives.

The Commission met thirteen times during 2007. It has two key Sub-Committees: Finance, which considers quarterly financial reports and the Audit Committee, which supervises internal financial controls.[12] Adopting a corporate approach to its management, it operates on the basis of strategic plans, business plans and work programmes. In this regard, it has adopted a strategic plan entitled *Excellence in Parliamentary Service* for the years 2007–2009:

> The Plan sets out an ambitious vision of a world-class Parliament, enabled by excellences in parliamentary services. We have concentrated our efforts during the past year in moving closer to making this vision a reality. The Plan contains clear purpose, mission, vision and value statements which commit us to a service-delivery ethos.[13]

The plan's four key strategic commitments are: serving sittings, serving members, promoting Parliament and delivering better management. The overall management approach adopted by the Commission is one of dynamism and achieving target-driven and measurable deliverables.

Therefore, for the first time in its history, the Dáil is adopting long-term strategic objectives rather than relying on a short-term ad hoc approach. Such autonomy, I contend, is proving crucial to the House's direction as it copes with the complex dynamics of 21st-century politics.

---

12 Houses of the Oireachtas, 2008: 35.
13 *Ibid.*: 32.

RESOURCES

Compared to their predecessors, contemporary TDs live in a pressure-cooker environment. There are more media outlets, including television, newspapers and local radio. Constituency work occupies a huge proportion of a TD's time. With the advent of a strong committee system, TDs face increased parliamentary duties. Apart from postal inquiries, TDs are on the Dáil e-mail and are expected to be available via mobile phone. Proceedings in the chamber and at committee are televised. Contemporary TDs face multi-faceted demands and must be capable of performing in an environment where time and deadlines are important. It is my contention that, as full-time professionals, they need adequate resources to do an effective job.

In a foreword to the Deloitte and Touche Report, the then Leas-Cheann Comhairle, Dr Rory O'Hanlon, made a telling observation:

> In short, we have a seriously under-resourced parliamentary system. The Houses of Parliament have one legal officer and three researchers for 226 members; insufficient staff to fully service our Committee system, and a level of personal staff support for Deputies and Senators which necessitates help from family members and volunteers.[14]

An extreme historical example of the consequences of under-resourcing was highlighted in the Second Stage Debate on the Oireachtas (Allowances to Members) Bill (1962). According to the contributor, one member had actually been forced to resign his membership of Dáil Éireann because he simply could not afford the costs involved. The contributor provides a colourful account of the reasons underlying the resigning member's decision:

---

14 Deloitte and Touche, 2002.

Look at the case of the former Deputy John Murphy who had to do the unheard of thing of resigning his membership of this House. He had to resign, because he could not afford to continue here. If he wanted to drink a pint, he had to hide in the hallway of the pub in case there was somebody he could not avoid and for whom he would have to buy a drink. He rented a hall for the unemployed but he was not able to pay the few bob for it and the hall had to go.[15]

And when typists were provided for TDs for the first time in the 1970s, it was on a shared basis which was most unsatisfactory. One Deputy describes what it was like when he first arrived in the Dáil during this period:

When I entered the House, there were ten members to each typist. The typist who worked for me used an Underwood typewriter and had to use a brush to clean the letter 't' which otherwise appeared on the page as 'T'.[16]

Whilst contemporary members are fortunately not compelled to share these frustrating experiences, complaints from Deputies that the Dáil is under-resourced were until recently quite common in Irish politics.[17]

Historically, Dáil Éireann has been significantly under-resourced. Upon reading and listening to accounts of its early years one wonders how it functioned at all.[18] There were no proper office facilities, let alone secretarial and administrative back-up. Free post was not provided and research support was unheard of. Even the official Opposition

---

15 Sherwin, 1962.
16 Connolly, 1996.
17 Deloitte and Touche, 2002.
18 Manning, 2000; Pattison, 2002, 2004.

Front Bench was denied basic facilities. The Dáil was clearly run on an amateur basis. Many members had outside interests and were effectively part-time parliamentarians, thus ensuring that the days of a fully professionalised Parliament had yet to arrive.

As early as 1 April 1919, just two months after the Dáil was founded, Deputies could hardly be accused of extravagance. A motion regarding the payment of Deputies' travel expenses generated intense debate before agreement was eventually reached that Deputies be provided with a third-class return train fare plus a fifteen shilling per day maintenance allowance. One Deputy had put forth an amendment proposing:

> ... that Constituencies be asked to maintain their Deputies so as to enable them to attend meetings of Dáil Éireann.[19]

It should be added that extravagance also appeared to have been denied to the Executive. According to the 1937 Committee of Inquiry into Ministerial and Other Salaries, the entire Executive had three official cars at its disposal. The inquiry discovered that because of heavy demands the cars fell into bad repair and consequently, between 1924 and 1927, Ministers actually used their own cars.[20]

By 1929, attitudes to providing resources had not changed. *A Report of the Joint Committee on the Remit of Ministers and the Allowances of Members of the Oireachtas* adopted a conservative position on the Leader of the Opposition's resource needs:

> It realises that the amount of work which the Leader of the Opposition or of any large party continuously in Opposition has to perform to

---

19 *Dáil Éireann: Minutes of Proceedings*, 1919: 31.
20 Committee of Inquiry into Ministerial and Other Salaries, 1937: 58.

enable him to deal adequately with the various matters which come before the legislature is exceedingly heavy and all the more so by the reason of the fact that he has not access to technical advisers, nor the use of an official executive staff such as are at the service of Ministers.[21]

However, despite acknowledging the heavy workload of the Leader of the Opposition, the Committee of Inquiry did not provide any special allowance to help him discharge his parliamentary functions. The Leader of the Opposition would have to wait a further eight years before such an allowance was granted. Similarly, this 1929 report did not recommend free postage to members. The report did acknowledge the necessity of free public travel for members. But once members arrived in Leinster House they were left to their own devices.

Former Ceann Comhairle, Seamus Pattison, provides a first-hand account of Dáil Éireann's resource deficiencies in the 1960s. Arriving in Kildare Street on 11 October 1961 for the new Dáil's first day, he faced a situation where essentially members had no back-up. Members had no secretaries, all letters had to be handwritten and, since they did not have office space, any correspondence was dealt with on a bench or desk, assuming one was available. In the Party offices up to ten members at a time would seek desk space. There was one phone in this office which members could use for Dublin calls only. Calls to the constituency necessitated the member going to a coin-paying kiosk in Leinster House. Members were assigned a small locker and, as there was no free postage, members incurred the cost from their own finances. The Leinster House complex was considerably smaller in those days. Seamus Pattison and his 1961 contemporaries enjoyed

---

21 *Report of the Joint Committee on the Remit of Ministers and the Allowances of Members of the Oireachtas*, 1929: ix.

none of the generous allowances of their 2009 counterparts. The travel allowance amounted to a shilling a mile.[22]

Manning's account mirrors that of Pattison:

> There were no offices, secretaries, telephone or postal facilities. Members worked from the single room assigned to each party. Even party leaders did not have rooms; Dillon, as a Vice-President, shared an office with Cosgrave at Fine Gael party headquarters.[23]

As Manning explains, the then Leader of the Opposition, James Dillon, had 'no secretarial or other back-up provided to him or his party colleagues'.[24] In fact, Dillon's entire Leinster House staff appears to have amounted to one typist, which the meagre Opposition Leader's allowance barely covered. Manning does emphasise that government was much simpler in those days and the parliamentarians had a much lighter workload than their contemporaries as they did not have to contend with two significant pressures, namely, high volumes of constituency work and media relations.[25] Adding that parliamentary life was very low key, Manning states that:

> There was no such thing as investigative journalism, no lobby system, no over-mighty columnists, no opinion-formers beyond politicians themselves. In that pre-television age, most politicians could travel the country without being recognised.[26]

It was not until December 1962 that an attempt was made to move

---

22 Pattison, 2002, 2004; O'Connor and O'Halloran, 2008: 85–88.
23 Manning, 2000: 110.
24 *Ibid.*: 330.
25 *Ibid.*: 111–112.
26 *Ibid.*: 111.

beyond this archaic approach. By virtue of the 1962 Oireachtas (Allowances to Members) Act, the first semblance of a proper parliamentary allowances system appeared. Members received three privileges. Firstly, they would be provided with an overnight hotel allowance. This was targeted at rural members who hitherto had to pay their own hotel expenses. Secondly, limited free post was granted. However, in a highly restrictive move, letters had to be franked in the Leinster House Post Office. Thus, members were precluded from posting letters in their constituencies. Thirdly, members could henceforth make free telephone calls from Leinster House. No telephone allowance was provided for work at constituency level. Whilst the overall thrust of the 1962 Act could by contemporary terms be described as very conservative, it nevertheless established important precedents and future generations would build upon the base. It was a vast improvement on the previous (1938) Act which grudgingly provided limited travel allowances to members. The Second Stage debate on the 1962 Act, which took place on 6 December, offers a fascinating insight into the attitudes of Deputies on the matter of allowances and expenses. In his contribution, the then Minister for Finance, James Ryan, contended:

> The duties of a Deputy are always increasing, while his occupation is officially regarded as part-time, it is not feasible for many Deputies to engage in occupations or supplement their incomes from any source of employment.[27]

One TD observed the emerging trends:

> It has now become commonplace for Deputies, particularly from country areas, to receive letters from their correspondents about

---

27 Ryan, 1962.

every phase of life. They are not restricted entirely to Public Bills and Legislation going through here. Every phase of life is concerned.[28]

Comparatively speaking, however, the Dáil might not have been exceptional. For example, until the 1960s the British House of Commons also suffered from a lack of resources and basic facilities. Many MPs were part-timers, had no offices and kept most of their material in one assigned locker.[29] Speaking during a 1958 House of Commons debate, Labour MP Tony Benn provided the following account:

> Each of us has only one place private to ourselves, a locker which is so small it will not take the ordinary briefcase to be locked away. We have no access to a telephone unless we make the endless, senseless tramp around the corridors, waiting outside the kiosks, with our papers, waiting to telephone … We cannot even communicate freely with each other. There is no general pigeonhole where one can put messages for a member.[30]

Another former Labour MP's description of the 1960s when he entered as a new member coincides with these accounts. Frequently, Harold Walker used to handwrite his correspondence on a tiny desk in the anteroom of the Commons. Essentially, Walker and his contemporaries ran a DIY operation once they arrived in Westminster.[31]

Writing on the 1960s/1970s period, it is little wonder therefore that Norton observed:

---

28 Sweetman, 1962.
29 Norton, 1994: 15–16.
30 Quoted in Crick, 1965.
31 Walker, 2000, 2001, 2002.

Whilst Parliament retained its late-19th-century character, public policy-making underwent a virtual transformation.[32]

And in Ireland, many members in a 1996 debate on Dáil reform highlighted the then resource deficits. Tommy Broughan gave a newcomer's perspective complaining that the Dáil had retained a 19th-century approach to conducting its business:

> On the question of resources I must inform the House that I share an office with two other Deputies, our secretarial staff, on occasion visiting staff from the Labour Party.[33]

Michael Ring also offered a newcomer's perspective:

> During the summer recess, a member of another Parliament visited me. I was embarrassed to bring him into my office where the only equipment is a telephone. I do not have a fax or a photocopier and my secretary was working in my constituency office. When he asked me how many researchers I had I told him I was not a Minister and only had a secretary who has an enormous amount of work to do in my constituency office.[34]

As late as 1999 the Dáil Committee of Public Accounts commented in its report on DIRT tax evasion that:

> Oireachtas procedures, practices and resources have not kept pace with the expansion of our economy and the modernisation of our society. Additional resources and staffing are required to ensure true accountability, which would minimise the number of extra-parliamentary inquiries in the future.[35]

---

32 Norton, 1994: 16.
33 Broughan, 1996.
34 Ring, 1996.
35 Parliamentary Inquiry into DIRT, 1999: 180.

It needs to be emphasised that there is a direct and logical link between effective parliamentary scrutiny and sufficient resources. Both are two sides of the same coin because in the absence of proper resources Parliament is handicapped. Or to put it more blatantly, accountability costs money. In other words, increased accountability is not a resource-neutral phenomenon. As the Committee of Public Accounts suggested, the modernisation of Ireland's society and economy in the 1990s meant that the Dáil was in catch-up mode both resource-wise and procedurally. According to the Clerk of the Dáil, Kieran Coughlan, as quoted in the Committee's second report of 2001, Dáil Éireann suffered in comparative cross-country terms from a severe resource deficit.[36]

Matters have, however, progressed. In this regard, the most comprehensive and up-to-date review on resources available to both Houses of the Oireachtas is the Deloitte and Touche Report which was conducted over a six-month period from July to December 2001. Published on 11 March 2002, it constitutes the single most important review of Oireachtas resources. Indeed, the report can rightly be categorised as an important moment in Dáil Éireann's history, constituting as it did an emerging mood for change and reform. In fact, the report states that the resource analysis was taking place in the context of a coherent drive for parliamentary reform.[37]

The report's examination was conducted under the following headings: Research Supports, Secretarial Supports for both Constituency and Dáil, Supports Provided to Oireachtas Committees, Supports Provided to Investigative Inquiries by Parliamentary Committees, Procedural Service Supports, Office Service Reports,

---

36   *Ibid.*: 2001: 91.
37   Deloitte and Touche, 2002: 6.

Information Technology Supports, Public Relations Supports and Members' Entitlements Supports. Methodologically, the report adopted a comparative (cross-country) perspective. The Parliaments/ Assemblies of the United Kingdom, Scotland, Wales, Northern Ireland, Denmark, Australia, New Zealand and Germany were examined. The methodology included a combination of desk research and actual visits to a selection of the Parliaments. One hundred and six of Dáil Éireann's 166 TDs replied to a questionnaire circulated by the consultants and interviews were conducted with key actors such as TDs, secretarial assistants, Dáil officials and trade union representatives.

Its findings reveal a multitude of resource deficiencies. Whilst over 88% of members availed of research support, half described the service as poor. Given that at the time of the report's publication the Oireachtas library only employed three researchers, such dissatisfaction is hardly surprising. Three researchers could not adequately service the research needs of 226 parliamentarians. In comparative EU terms, the Irish Parliament was clearly at the bottom of the league on the library research staff measure. In this regard, it even came in behind three regional Assemblies: Wales: 4 library research staff, Northern Ireland: 19 library research staff and Scotland: 22 library research staff.[38]

Another key area explored was secretarial support. In the report's secretarial support index, the Irish Parliament scored badly. In terms of research support, it again scored worse than the three regional Assemblies of Scotland, Wales and Northern Ireland.[39] It appeared that secretarial assistants were stretched to the limit as many of them were working fifty hours a week and at weekends. Observing one

38 *Ibid.*: 16.
39 *Ibid.*: 27–28.

member's office, a Deloitte and Touche researcher discovered that daily phone calls demanded 400 follow-up responses per month.

It is also apparent from the report that information technology for TDs' offices was very inadequate. Dissatisfaction was also expressed at response rates from the information technology desk. And over 70% of members stated that they required information technology support at constituency level. Combining the sections on secretarial and information technology supports, it is clear as of December 2001 that there was much room for improvement in TDs' administrative facilities.

There are much more positive findings in that section of the report which deals with administrative back-up to Oireachtas Committees. In fact, only 14% of survey respondents rated internal secretarial assistance to Committees as poor. However, respondents were much more critical regarding internal research facilities and the lack of external supports to members.[40] One frustrated member was quoted as saying:

> For the Committees to function properly, members must have access to fast and thoroughly researched material – I just can't do it myself.[41]

Another stated that supports were 'totally geared towards the chair'.[42] The support offered to parliamentary inquiries also gets some positive commentary. Thus, 75% of members rated the provision of secretarial and legal supports as either good or excellent.[43] However, there is a view that:

---

40 *Ibid.*: 32.
41 *Ibid.*: 33.
42 *Ibid.*
43 *Ibid.*: 35.

The resourcing of inquiries has been met at the expense of other work of the Houses of the Oireachtas.[44]

Nevertheless, the overall tone of members who participated in parliamentary inquiries veers towards the positive. The report made a number of recommendations to address the resource deficits. Two of the recommendations are worth emphasising. Firstly, it recommended that a dedicated research unit of twenty-five staff be established within the Oireachtas library. Secondly, in respect of secretarial support it simply suggested that each TD be assigned two staff, an increase of one. This recommendation has been implemented.

In overall terms, the accommodation, budgetary and staffing situation has improved enormously. Deputies no longer share offices with other members. And, where members have a secretary based in Leinster House, a separate office is provided in most but not all cases. As staff levels increase, accommodation pressures remain and may very well increase. The days of primitive accommodation conditions are, however, consigned to historical memory.

For the period 2007–2009 both Houses of the Oireachtas were allocated a budget of just under €400,000,000. Seven hundred and eighty-eight staff were on the Houses of the Oireachtas payroll.[45] As of December 2008, members received a host of allowances plus a basic salary of €100,000 (see Appendix 1). In fact, the issue of salaries, pensions and allowances for members is one of the perennial 'hot potatoes' of Irish politics.[46] Many citizens contend that members are overpaid and receive too many generous allowances. It is probably no exaggeration to state that some citizens adopt a very hostile stance on

---

44 *Ibid.*
45 Houses of the Oireachtas Commission, 2008: 34.
46 Brennan and McDonagh, 2008; Hunt, 2009; Whelan, 2009.

this question. The 'gravy train' argument is deeply ingrained in the Irish political psyche. There is undoubtedly merit in their argument, one which incidentally resonates more with citizens in times of economic recession. That is not to say that a 'tabloid' approach to this issue is to be recommended. The reality is that members require allowances which enable them to *discharge their parliamentary obligations whether at national or constituency level.* But allowances should not be used as a vehicle for making tax-free income on top of an already generous salary, which is almost three times the average industrial wage. Equally, one has to question a situation where members' incomes are so far in excess of the average industrial wage.

There was a widely publicised controversy surrounding Mayo TD Beverley Flynn. It emerged in January 2009 that Deputy Flynn, who had been re-admitted to the Fianna Fáil Party following previous expulsion, continued to draw a special independent members' parliamentary allowance of €41,000 per annum. In an editorial called 'Beverley Flynn Crosses the Line' *The Irish Times* put it bluntly:

> If Beverley Flynn lacks the moral compass to behave in an ethical fashion then Taoiseach Brian Cowen has a duty to remove her from membership of Fianna Fáil. At a time when public confidence in Government is at an all-time low and people are desperately seeking a restoration of standards in public life, her determination to draw the untaxed allowances of an independent TD while enjoying the full benefits of Fianna Fáil membership cannot be tolerated.[47]

Deputy Flynn eventually gave up her allowance following a telephone conversation with the Taoiseach. However, it is probably reasonable to conclude that this incident acted as a catalyst for broader reform.

---

47 Editorial, *The Irish Times*, 2009a.

Moves to bring more transparency to the system of parliamentary allowances were made throughout 2009.

There is an increasing emphasis on providing good quality research support to members. Thus, during 2007 the library and research service completed 2,058 queries. All new members were assigned a library liaison officer after the 2007 general election. In the contemporary Leinster House there is a strong emphasis on training for both members and staff. Thus, 641 people participated in training seminars during 2007. A wide range of courses was offered, including constituent database management, media skills, presentational skills, effective writing skills, parliamentary procedures, time management, ICT and BlackBerry use. Information technology has become a key feature of parliamentary life in Leinster House. A dedicated ICT unit exists to service the needs of both houses. An information technology help desk located in Leinster House is supported by field staff in thirty-four locations and an electronic version of the Dáil's daily schedule is e-mailed to members.[48] The following quote from the 2007 Annual Report of the Houses of the Oireachtas Commission demonstrates the extent to which the contemporary Dáil Éireann is embracing information technology:

> Digital dictation facilities which enable members to transcribe memos, correspondence etc. into a handheld device which, when cradled, automatically routes an electronic sound file of their dictation to their secretarial staff (based in Leinster House or a remote location) via the Oireachtas computer network. Staff can process dictation without any transition delay.[49]

---

48 Houses of the Oireachtas Commission, 2008: 42–43.
49 *Ibid.*: 44.

Resource-wise Dáil Éireann has made significant progress. Until the late 1980s, the House suffered serious resource deficiencies, making it nigh impossible to carve out a meaningful role for itself in the polity. Even into the 1990s, Deputies such as Michael Ring and Tommy Broughan were still expressing dissatisfaction.[50] On the other hand, Dáil Éireann in the early 21st century is a place where training seminars, e-mails, BlackBerrys and digital dictation are taken-for-granted services. It could hardly be more different than the world described by Seamus Pattison and Maurice Manning. A young politics student would thus find it hard to believe that one of the most useful innovations of Pattison's era was the duplicate notebook.

Under the separation of powers category, there is evidence of a shift from the Executive towards the Legislature. Subtle changes are occurring which suggest that Dáil Éireann is asserting its presence within the political system. Like its counterparts in other jurisdictions, this once staid and static assembly is indeed changing with the times. The single most important development in this regard is the establishment of an independent Commission for both Houses. The House's *de jure* independence has been given a *de facto* boost. The importance of the House's new legal independence is an important step in this regard. Financially, though, the determination of allowances and expenses for members should not be a matter for the Minister for Finance. This is something that both Houses should address as a matter of urgency.

---

50 Ring and Broughan, 1996.

8

FIDDLING ABOUT WITH DÁIL ÉIREANN'S STANDING ORDERS

The Order of Business is not as it should be. At times we act in an unethical and unprofessional manner and have made the Chair's job impossible on most mornings.[1]

I do solemnly declare that I will duly and faithfully and to the best of my knowledge and ability, exercise the office of Ceann Comhairle (Leas-Cheann Comhairle) of Dáil Éireann without fear or favour, apply the rules as laid down by this House in an impartial and fair manner, maintain order and uphold the rights and privileges of members in accordance with the Constitution and the Standing Orders of Dáil Éireann.[2]

The Dáil shall go into Committee whenever it reaches business on the Order Paper which is to be considered in Committee.[3]

Dáil Éireann's internal business both plenary and committee is governed by a set of rules termed Standing Orders. Evolving throughout the Dáil's history, these Standing Orders are an important

---

1 FitzGerald, 1996.
2 Dáil Éireann, Standing Orders 8 and 9, 2002.
3 Dáil Éireann, Standing Order 74, 2002.

but hitherto largely unused research source for political scientists. The Standing Orders have been amended fifty times since 1926. Over a fifty-seven-year period from 1926–1983, they were amended nineteen times. Over a thirty-year period from 1953–1983, they were amended a mere nine times. However, between 1983 and 2004, a period of twenty-one years, the Standing Orders were amended a total of thirty-one times. Twenty-nine of these are very recent editions originating in the 1990s, a decade of significant change for the Dáil's internal procedures and rules. However, it would be unwise to come to a definitive conclusion based on how many times the Standing Orders have been changed.

Whilst this quantitative indicator is important, it nevertheless is suggestive of the pace of, rather than the nature of, change. The more challenging question concerns the nature of the changes. Will O'Malley's assertion during a Dáil debate on parliamentary reform that 'Fiddling around with the detail of Standing Orders will not create accountability' be proven correct?[4] This chapter compares the 2002 Standing Orders to those of 1974. The Dáil is run based on 171 Standing Orders. I will select a sample of Standing Orders for illustrative purposes and for their particular relevance to the current discussion.

LEADERS' QUESTION TIME AND THE ORDER OF BUSINESS

Standing Order 26 is important as it contains the rules governing the Dáil's Order Paper. The Order Paper contains the Dáil's Order of Business or agenda. This Standing Order today is substantially different to its 1974 equivalent. In particular, there is a new Order

---

4 O'Malley, 1996.

THE DÁIL IN THE 21ST CENTURY

called 26A which significantly departs from previous practice. Termed Leaders' Questions, Standing Order 26A provides that every Tuesday and Wednesday the Leaders in Opposition are entitled to ask one initial question each, plus one supplementary question of the Taoiseach. Crucially, no advance notice of the question is provided to the Taoiseach. The Leaders in Opposition simply rise in their places and put the questions to the Taoiseach. Whilst the Taoiseach and his/her officials will most probably be in a position to predict most questions, it, nevertheless, does require some nimble parliamentary footwork on the Taoiseach's part. Hitherto, the Standing Orders of the House had always insisted on advance notice for all questions. This even applied to Private Notice questions, which allow for the asking of urgent questions at relatively short notice. In this regard, Standing Order 26A is a truly innovative move.

For the duration of the 29th Dáil, a total of twenty-one minutes was allocated to this exercise which was divided evenly between the Leaders of Fine Gael, the Labour Party and the Technical Group. The Technical Group consisted of Sinn Féin, the Green Party, independents and the sole Socialist Party TD. This disparate group was a procedural flag of convenience which was formed to ensure its members received enhanced speaking rights under Dáil Standing Orders. However, with the advent of the 2007 general election results which saw the Green Party enter Government and the depletion of independents, the Technical Group disappeared. This left a situation where only the leaders of Fine Gael and the Labour Party were entitled to ask questions.

The addition of Leaders' Question Time evolved partly in response to ongoing problems with how the Dáil dealt with the Order of Business. From the early 1980s onwards, the Order of Business became a mini question time. By the 1990s, it frequently constituted the main daily parliamentary battle between Government and Opposition. The Opposition would seek to raise topical issues, which they could not otherwise raise. Of course, this was never the function of the Order of Business. In particular, occupants of the Chair began to allow Party Leaders to comment on Northern Ireland atrocities during the Order of Business. This practice was totally at variance with Standing Orders but nevertheless, over time, a convention emerged and the variety of issues increased, as did the number of contributing speakers.[5]

Speaking in a 1996 Dáil debate, Brian Fitzgerald commented that:

> The Order of Business is not as it should be. At times we act in an unethical and unprofessional manner and have made the Chair's job impossible on most mornings.[6]

The Order of Business is meant to discuss the business of the Dáil. Standing Order 26 is the relevant Order and is based on a printed Order Paper circulated to all members – the Taoiseach announces Government business and the order in which it shall be taken in the House. The 1974 Standing Orders made no provision for Opposition involvement in the Order of Business. By 2002, the Standing Orders provided that any member may ask a question on the Order of Business. Similarly, what matters may be raised on the Order of Business are outlined. These include business or legislation promised within or outside the House, as well as circulation of bills and questions relating to secondary legislation. One unwelcome change is that the Government Chief Whip or a member of the Government *may* stand

---

5 O'Connor and O'Halloran, 2008: 114.
6 FitzGerald, 1996.

in for the Taoiseach on Tuesdays and Wednesdays. On Thursdays, the Standing Orders provide that the Government Chief Whip *shall* take the Order of Business. This new situation means that the Taoiseach is obliged to spend less time in the House than previously.

ADJOURNMENT ON MATTERS OF PUBLIC INTEREST

Standing Order 31 has been the source of much comment throughout its existence. It provides for the adjournment of the House on a specific and important matter of public interest requiring urgent consideration. It is designed to allow for the suspension of normal business. Its predecessor (Standing Order 29) was criticised in a 1972 report on Dáil reform, which states that between 1932 and 1971, a period of forty years, business had been suspended only thirteen times. Incredibly, the previous time business was suspended was in 1947. Thus, the Ceann Comhairle had not granted a debate under this Standing Order in almost a quarter of a century. By 1996, things had not improved. Then Opposition TD Willie O'Dea made the following comment:

> It seems it is little more than a parliamentary ornament shown to visitors to the House. It has little or no effect in practice. Because the word 'urgent' is rigidly and narrowly interpreted Standing Order 30 is used consistently to avoid discussing matters of topical importance which are being discussed in the media. It seems they can be discussed everywhere but in this House.[7]

The wording of this Standing Order remains substantially unchanged and just as restrictive as previous versions. In the decade 1990 to 2000,

---

7 O'Dea, 1996.

eight debates were permitted under this Standing Order. No debates were allowed in 1991, 1992, 1995, 1996 and 1997.[8] Thus, it appears that the restrictive interpretation by the Ceann Comhairle has not changed significantly either.

QUESTION TIME

Question time is an essential parliamentary tool. Accordingly, rules and procedures dealing with question time are an important guide as to how any parliament conducts this aspect of its affairs. The use of parliamentary questions 'has exploded in recent years'.[9] A look at earlier decades highlights the dramatic increase in the number of questions asked. For the mid-1930s, just over 1,000 questions per year were asked. This figure had risen to 24,000 a year for the period 2001–2003.[10]

Standing Orders 32 to 41 set down the rules for question time. The 2002 Standing Orders are substantially different to those of 1974. Most interestingly, the Standing Orders of 2002 recognise the existence of Shadow Cabinets or Opposition Front Benches within the Irish parliamentary structure. By the use of a new devise called 'questions nominated for priority' (Standing Order 38), the Opposition spokespersons enjoy a special status during oral questions to relevant Ministers. These spokespersons are afforded the opportunity to put down five questions amongst them. They are also afforded priority with regard to supplementary questions arising from the Priority Questions, which appear on the Order Paper. Priority Questions

---

8   Statistics provided by the Leas-Cheann Comhairle's Office, 2005.
9   Murphy, 2006: 439.
10   Gallagher, 2005: 228.

to Ministers (other than the Taoiseach) appear first on the Order Paper. The Standing Orders seek to eliminate long-winded replies by allowing a maximum of six minutes per Priority Question. The Minister's initial reply cannot exceed two minutes.

Another difference in how contemporary practice differs to that of 1974 is that each Minister currently has a specific day for question time. However, in 1974 the entire Cabinet appeared in the chamber together for question time and, starting with the most senior Minister, questions would be asked of all Ministers. With the sheer volume of questions put down by current members such a system would be unworkable.

RULES OF DEBATE

Standing Orders 44 to 64 determine the Rules of Debate in the House. The Rules of Debate have not proven immune to change. Number 47 is a new Standing Order. It allows for the speaker in possession to give way to another member. This Standing Order was presumably introduced with the intention of injecting more spontaneity into debates. The often-stated complaint about Dáil debates is that they tend to consist of a series of self-contained, scripted monologues. This Standing Order replicates a long-standing practice in the British House of Commons which positively encourages cut and thrust debate. However, the Dáil Standing Order is much more restrictive; thus, as general rule, interventions are only permitted towards the end of a speech. Similarly, the intervening speaker is allowed a maximum speaking time of thirty seconds. It is highly unlikely that this Standing Order will enhance Dáil debating standards to any significant extent.

Debating deficiencies in the House go much deeper than

interventions.[11] According to former Ceann Comhairle Seamus Pattison, practices have changed significantly since the 1960s. Firstly, scripted speeches were (and technically remain), with the exception of ministerial statements, strictly forbidden. Members had to make non-scripted speeches possibly with only the aid of a few speaking notes permitted. Quoting from documents was generally frowned upon. According to Pattison, most current members rely on scripts. During his time in the Chair, it became clear to him that some members were reading their speeches for the first time in the Chamber. These speeches may have been prepared by party officials and handed to the member on the way to the Chamber. This practice effectively kills debate, as the member in possession is not replying spontaneously to previous speakers. In Pattison's early years he would typically arrive in the Chamber with pen and paper in hand. While listening to other speeches, he would pen a few notes. He and his contemporaries were thus engaging with each other rather than acting out self-contained monological exercises.

Under the Westminster model the Speaker takes precedence in the Chamber and as such controls parliamentary debates. In particular, it falls to the Chair to select speakers. Thus, discretion lies with the Chair. This has always been the intention under Dáil Standing Orders, including number 44 from 2002. However, the practice is entirely different. In reality, the party whips determine the speaking order in the House. In fact, the Ceann Comhairle is provided with the speaking list on his/her monitor in the Chamber. This *de facto* kills the Chair's discretion. Because of this practice a TD can judge his/her arrival in the Chamber within five minutes of the preceding speaker concluding his/her speech. Thus, the member arrives, waits

---

11 O'Connor and O'Halloran, 2008.

five minutes, is called from the list by the Ceann Comhairle, makes a speech and leaves. The effects of this practice are manifestly clear: no debate in the real sense can take place in the Chamber because members are not listening to each other. This situation and the practice of making scripted speeches ensure that proper debates do not take place in the Dáil Chamber.

VOTING

The traditional way of dealing with voting divisions in the Dáil was archaic and very time-consuming. Members had to physically walk through the yes or no lobbies in the aisles. Tellers were appointed to count the votes. The Ceann Comhairle then announced the vote to assembled members. Yet another new Standing Order, namely number 69, dispenses with this voting method save in certain limited circumstances. The Standing Order provides that votes may be conducted by electronic means. The new system is very simple: members press a button on their seats. The vote is illuminated on a video screen over the chamber and the Ceann Comhairle makes the formal announcement. Efficient and modern, the new approach demonstrates that the House is indeed moving with the times. If the Opposition wishes to frustrate the Government by trooping through the lobbies in the traditional way that option is still open, provided twenty members rise in support from their seats.

RESTRICTIONS ON DEBATE

Standing Orders 56 and 58 are also new. Both indicate awareness that during debates the House has responsibilities to non-members. Standing Order 56 restricts debate where matters are *sub judice*. It appears to be a sensible measure designed to protect the legal rights of citizens and the independence of the courts. Standing Order 58 is particularly lengthy, consisting of nine sections and numerous sub-sections. Complex in its design, it seeks to prevent members from making defamatory utterances. Breach of this Standing Order is a serious matter constituting a *prima facie* breach of parliamentary privilege. The Ceann Comhairle has wide-ranging powers to deal with members who breach this Standing Order. In certain circumstances the Ceann Comhairle may compel a member to make a personal statement to the House in which he/she fully withdraws the defamatory utterance. A person outside the house who believes he/she has been defamed can raise the matter with the Ceann Comhairle in the form of a written submission. This is an important addition as members enjoy absolute privilege whilst speaking in the House. As such injured citizens are deprived of their constitutional right to protect their reputation in a court of civil law.

However, the Standing Order is questionable in some respects. Defamation is a complex legal matter. A branch of the law of torts, it is far from easy to be precise about its scope and application. To be succinct, is the House straying into a complex legal domain? Equally, the Standing Order defies the doctrine of absolute parliamentary privilege. After all what is deemed defamation today because of the non-existence of evidence to prove it, may be deemed non-defamatory when new evidence comes to light. A case in point was the strong suspicion of widespread political corruption in Ireland during the 1980s. However, it is only in recent years that the evidence is coming to light. TDs need scope to alert the public in a responsible way to certain matters. In so doing this may necessitate falling foul of what would be civil law standards in a non-parliamentary setting.

COMMITTEES

The 1974 Standing Orders make few references to Committees. This is hardly surprising as the only Committee of consequence was the long-standing Public Accounts Committee. If the student of politics needed convincing that Dáil Éireann is not standing still he/she only has to compare the 1974 and 2002 Standing Orders. Where in 1974 sparse reference is made to Committees, the 2002 document dedicates 26 Standing Orders to Dáil Committees. In fact, the Standing Orders on the functioning of Committees constitute the largest single section in the 2002 document. Barely meriting a mention in 1974, the age of Committees has truly arrived in Dáil Éireann. This is because for most of its history the whole House has discharged Committee affairs. This was made clear as early as 1947.[12]

The powers conferred on Select Committees are listed in Standing Order 81. The powers consist of taking evidence, oral and written, inviting and taking written submissions from interested parties, appointing sub-committees, recommending new/amending legislation, requiring attendance of a Government Minister in certain circumstances to discuss policy/legislative matters, requiring attendance of principal office holders of state bodies in certain matters, engaging specialist/technical advice and undertaking travel. Standing Order 98 provides further evidence of the enhanced role committees are enjoying within Dáil Éireann. This Standing Order establishes a Working Group of Committee Chairmen. It provides a forum in which all Committee Chairs can discuss and make recommendations on matters of mutual interest.

Another new addition is the Joint Committee on Broadcasting

---

12 Malone, 1947.

and Parliamentary Information. Radio and television coverage of Dáil sittings, both plenary and Committee, are an accepted feature of Irish parliamentary life. Some of the more important occasions are frequently afforded live television coverage by Radio Telefís Éireann, the national broadcasting service. For example, Leaders' Questions are usually covered live on Wednesday mornings. Both radio and television produce a recorded programme on daily proceedings in Dáil Éireann. This Joint Committee has responsibility for overseeing radio and television coverage. It sets the rules as to what the cameras can and cannot show during proceedings.

However, the Committee has much broader responsibilities. During 2002 both Houses established an Information and Public Relations Service, headed by a Public Relations Officer. Among its responsibilities are increasing public awareness of the work carried out by both Houses. The Joint Committee is responsible for monitoring the activities of and suggesting improvements to the Information and Public Relations Service.

Standing Order 156 deals with the powers and functions of the Committee of Public Accounts. Like all Committees, it enjoys new powers regarding travel and the hiring of consultants.

INDEPENDENCE OF THE CEANN COMHAIRLE AND LEAS-CHEANN COMHAIRLE

New Dáil Standing Orders 8 and 9, whilst minor in procedural terms, nevertheless represent a change in the House's collective mindset. The effect of both Standing Orders is to enhance the standing and independence of both the Ceann Comhairle and Leas-Cheann Comhairle. On taking the Chair for the first time after their elections, both office-holders make a declaration before the House:

I do solemnly declare that I will duly and faithfully and to the best of my knowledge and ability, exercise the office of Ceann Comhairle (Leas-Cheann Comhairle) of Dáil Éireann without fear or favour, apply the rules as laid down by this House in an impartial and fair manner, maintain order and uphold the rights and privileges of members in accordance with the Constitution and the Standing Orders of Dáil Éireann.

In the Westminster model, the Speaker is charged with protecting members' rights and the position of Parliament generally. In sharp contradistinction to the United States model, the Westminster Speaker is strictly non-partisan and very independent of the executive branch. Indeed the Speaker is obliged to defend the House from improper encroachment by the Executive. Ireland inherited this aspect of the Westminster model. House Standing Orders specifically exclude Ministers from seeking election to the Chair. Respecting the separation of powers, the Chair must be drawn from the pool of TDs who do not hold ministerial posts. The declaration strengthens the constitutional independence of the Chair and Deputy Chair.

As can be seen, the twenty–eight year period between 1974 and 2002 has witnessed a remarkable transformation in how Dáil Éireann conducts its business. Putting the two sets of Standing Orders side by side, it is safe to say the 2002 document bears only minimal resemblance to the 1974 document. Over the period in question, the House has not merely been 'fiddling' with its rules,[13] rather it has created many new rules and changed the procedural orientation of the House. The changes have been many and varied.

---

13 O'Malley, 1996.

Two stand out as particularly significant, namely the setting up of a strong Committee system and Leaders' Questions. Considering that until the 1980s a Committee of the whole House dealt with legislation, the change is quite staggering. Much of the House's important business is currently conducted in Committee rather than in the Chamber. Mirroring similar trends in other legislatures, Dáil Éireann is anything but static. Similarly, the addition of Leaders' Questions corrects a long-standing anomaly in the House's procedures: its inability to discuss topical matters. The fact that this can be done without giving prior notice of questions to the Ceann Comhairle provides the Opposition with an advantage. Other changes may not be as dramatic but they are nevertheless significant.

The Order of Business has been a much more inclusive affair, depriving Taoisigh of their former monopoly. Special Committees on Dáil Reform and for Committee Chairs may not be radical developments, but they are indicative of a nascent trend: the Dáil is acquiring a more independent collective identity. Beyond the fray of adversarial and divisive Chamber politics, and away from the glare of publicity, non-partisan politics is shaping a new identity for Dáil Éireann.

Desmond O'Malley was correct to argue that fiddling about with Standing Orders will not create accountability. However, generating real change in Standing Orders clearly has the capacity to improve accountability. This is particularly true of Executive accountability to Parliament. But it is also true of providing a space in which civil society works through rather than bypasses Parliament. Dáil Éireann has clearly been the beneficiary of many of the changes examined in this section. In this sense, there is evidence of a shift in the power equilibrium.

9

European Union and Civil Society

In applying for membership, therefore, we are using our sovereignty in order to achieve greater sovereignty.[1]

If the third amendment is adopted the Oireachtas which up till now has been the supreme law-making body in the country and is directly responsible to the electorate will be handing over to the EEC and its institutions the power to legislate in future in ways which will not even be known at the time of adoption. Such a surrender of sovereignty has to be guarded against and has to be legitimately circumscribed within such a bill.[2]

The evidence suggests that the Dáil is acquiring a more autonomous identity. Whilst it is competing in a crowded political arena it is not being crowded out. In this chapter and the one which follows it I focus on what might be termed exogenous influences, namely European Union, civil society, social partnership and expert sovereignty.

Ireland became a member of the European Economic Community (EEC) on 1 January 1973. Having signed the Treaty of Accession on 22 January 1972, membership of the EEC required a constitutional referendum, which was held in May 1972. On a turnout of 71%, 83%

---

1 Lynch, 1971.
2 Desmond, 1971.

of voters approved of membership. Membership necessitated a radical transformation of Ireland's Constitution, including the abandonment of its state-centric notions of sovereignty. Henceforth, both elites and citizens would adopt a pragmatic approach to membership.

Subsequent to the electorate's approval to enter the EEC, the incorporation of Community law into domestic law was achieved through the European Communities Act (1972). Speaking during the Dáil debate on this crucial piece of legislation, Deputies Tully and Ryan highlighted the extent to which, in their view, Irish parliamentary sovereignty had been eroded by the 'yes' vote some months earlier. Both members clearly realised that a new political game had arrived in town. Whilst the language of both members may certainly be described as colourful, the rhetorical flourishes should not detract from the salience of the contributions:

> While some people are talking about a glorified London County Council for the north of Ireland it does appear as if we could have a glorified Mayo or Clare County Council running the State here. It would be a sad day if that happened and we should not allow our national Parliament to be downgraded to County Council status.[3]

> A vow of chastity does not require an operation to create sterility in order to implement the vow but this House and the Seanad are being asked to render the Parliament utterly sterile in relation to a vast and growing field of legislation and Ministerial and Governmental decisions which go far beyond the obligations of the treaties establishing the European Communities.[4]

On reading the literature on Dáil Éireann both pre- and post-accession

---

3 Tully, 1972.
4 Ryan, 1972.

to the EEC, it would be tempting to opine that in any event Ireland's Lower House of Parliament never amounted to much more than a County Council chamber. Was it not an impotent institution in the first event? In reality power was exercised by the Cabinet with the Dáil enjoying a purely nominal role.

This being the case, what were the members complaining of? One can only assume that they possessed quite a legal-centric view of the national Parliament. Adopting this framework, membership of the EEC constituted a radical transformation in the constitutional standing of Parliament. The 1972 bill before the House gave unprecedented power to the Executive in the legislative sphere. Post-1972, Irish parliamentarians were living in a different constitutional world. Adherents of a classical Westphalian approach would henceforth be living in a constitutional fairyland. Speaking during the same debate as Deputies Tully and Ryan, the then Taoiseach Jack Lynch was quite frank about the obligations of membership:

> There is a certain loss of freedom of action involved here. This, I think, is fully appreciated by Members of this House and by the people … The treaties establishing the Communities assign certain powers of decision to the Community institutions. As a consequence, there are corresponding limitations of freedom of action at the national level, limitations which relate however only to the economic, commercial and related social matters covered by the treaties.[5]

This corresponded with earlier views which he expressed during the 1971 debate on the Third Amendment to the Constitution Bill. Speaking in the House on 9 December 1971, Lynch was adhering to the pooling of sovereignty view. Small-scale open polities such as

---

5 Lynch, 1972.

Ireland would only achieve real sovereignty by combining with others in collective enterprises such as the Community:

> In applying for membership, therefore, we are using our sovereignty in order to achieve greater sovereignty.[6]

It is difficult to overstate the historical significance of Ireland's entry into the European Economic Community in 1973. Constitutionally, membership amounted to a revolution. In particular, it involved a head-on assault on the Constitution's state-centric understanding of sovereignty. What is remarkable about this development is the ease with which most party elites in Leinster House accepted this new situation considering the historical baggage of the political system at that time. In a political system where the rhetoric of nationalism and of independence were all-pervasive, one has to ask why the clothes of a new emperor were embraced with such incredible ease. The answer to this question is reasonably straightforward: economic considerations were of central importance. Membership, it was believed, would help Ireland become a modern and vibrant free-market economy.

In his analysis of the Government's 1972 White Paper, *The Accession of Ireland to the European Communities,* Lee emphasises these economic considerations. Conceding that jobs would be lost in traditional sectors such as textiles, the Government contended that these losses would be outweighed by the advantages associated with increased foreign investment and access to the Common Market. The benefits to agriculture were emphasised. The Common Agricultural Policy, it was argued, would generate a 150% growth in Irish farm incomes. Adherents to an undiluted Westphalian approach to

---

6 Lynch, 1971.

political and economic sovereignty were given short shrift.[7] It seems that parading the green flag of Irish nationalism became unacceptable, at least in this sphere of Irish politics. Economic generation took precedence over green rhetoric.

As evident in the Dáil debates surrounding the Treaty of Accession, it is ironic that it was the internationalist Labour Party who had most difficulty in discarding the clothes of Westphalia. Typical were Labour Party TD Barry Desmond's assertions during the 1971 debate on amending the Constitution:

> If the third amendment is adopted the Oireachtas which up till now has been the supreme law-making body in the country and is directly responsible to the electorate will be handing over to the EEC and its institutions the power to legislate in future in ways which will not even be known at the time of adoption. Such a surrender of sovereignty has to be guarded against and has to be legitimately circumscribed within such a bill.[8]

On the other hand, Fianna Fáil, the party of nationalist Ireland, recognised the emerging new realities of mid-20th-century economics.

What is equally remarkable, but hardly surprising, is that the role which Dáil Éireann might play in future arrangements merited only a cursory examination by the then Government. This is reflected in the very weak parliamentary scrutiny procedures which were established originally. Again, given that Ireland's economy was so weak at the time of accession, the Government might be forgiven for focusing on economic growth and prosperity. It would be thirty years before

7 Lee, 1993: 461–465.
8 Desmond, 1971.

the matter of parliamentary scrutiny of European Union legislation would be revisited in a meaningful way. By that point, Ireland had become a model of economic growth and development.

ACCESSION TO THE EUROPEAN ECONOMIC COMMUNITY AND MEMBERSHIP OF THE EUROPEAN UNION

I will now focus on whether Dáil Éireann has adapted to the complexities of contemporary European Union governance. I will ask whether adequate scrutiny measures were put in place by Dáil Éireann or whether the Executive was given *carte blanche*. I will also ask whether membership of the EEC/EU either improved or diminished the role of Dáil Éireann within the political system. Included in this section will be an assessment of parliamentary accountability procedures established in 1972 and 1973. Also, the rhetoric and legislation in the aftermath of the first Nice referendum held during 2001 will be explored.

In a number of pre-accession Government documents, the matter of Dáil Éireann's future constitutional role hardly merits a mention, let alone detailed examination. Two documents stand out in this regard. The 1961 *White Paper on the European Economic Community* reads more like an introductory text on EU politics rather than a Government document meant to generate discussion. Providing elementary information rather than political analysis, this document skims over the constitutional implications of EEC membership. It does not refer to, let alone analyse, the parliamentary implications of EEC membership. Even the section of the document which deals with the approximation of Irish laws to Community laws is silent on the role of Parliament in what would be in reality a new constitutional framework. The 1961 White Paper would most certainly not conform to our contemporary understanding of what constitutes a White Paper.

The document seems to be more concerned with the economic implications of future membership. It is particularly concerned as to whether Britain will become a member. Irish membership is ruled out should Britain remain a non-member. It also examines issues such as quantitative restrictions and free movement of goods, persons, services and capital. The Common Agricultural Policy is dealt with quite extensively. However, the overall impression the reader gets from the document is that it is technical and explanatory rather than political and analytical. It may not be an exaggeration to describe the document as apolitical.

What explanations can we offer for the near total absence of political analysis? Firstly, the date the document was laid before the Houses of the Oireachtas may offer a partial clue. It would not be until the late 1960s that a package of cases explicitly recognising the embryonic Community's *political* and economic character would be decided. By 1970, such was the Community's legal architecture that the political implications of membership could not be open to any doubt. However, in 1961 it might not have been unreasonable to categorise the Community as a common market with few implications for state sovereignty.

Secondly, it must be remembered that the Government would have had few, if any, experts on Community law and politics available to it. It would be well into the 1970s before a pool of such scholars emerged. Lawyers of the 1960s must have found this new creature peculiar: the founding treaties alone would have stretched the legal horizons of any lawyer trained only in the Irish Common Law tradition.

Thirdly, this was the Government's first foray into Community politics and it was most likely starting from a *tabula rasa*. Thus, as with all exercises of historical analysis, present-day scholars need to be careful not to make rash judgments. The 1961 document was merely a document of its time. As such, the authors may simply not have understood the broader political implications, including the profound impact of EEC membership on Irish parliamentary life. However, the nearer we come to 1972 the less sympathetic we ought to be to the three caveats above. One would expect the Governments of those years to be better informed than their 1960s predecessors.

One may find a degree of comfort for these propositions in a statement by the then Taoiseach to Community Ministers.[9] The implications of membership for Irish agriculture and industry are Seán Lemass' predominant concern. The political implications of membership for Ireland are barely addressed. However, Lemass' attitude to Europe is very clear when he states that 'Ireland belongs to Europe by history, tradition and sentiment no less than by geography'.[10] The entire tone of his speech is very pro-Europe. This is not a man who was embracing the project in a half-hearted way. On the contrary, the tone is one of commitment and enthusiasm. Even ten years before Ireland became a member the rhetorical tone is non-state-centric. Non-state-centric perspectives would attach little normative importance to national parliaments.

What are we to make of Lemass' 1962 speech? Perhaps the easiest explanation is to state that it was audience-centric rhetoric: an effort by an applicant country to impress adjudicators. It must also be borne in mind that Lemass is usually described as a pragmatist. He tends to be credited with Ireland's break from failed protectionist economics. As one who had fought in the War of Independence (1919–21), he would have been entitled to wave the green flag of a sovereign independent Irish Republic. But Lemass had been a member of every Fianna Fáil Government since 1932. His pragmatic streak forced him to conclude

---

9 Lemass, 1962.
10 *Ibid.*: 58.

that failed policies had to be replaced as a matter of some urgency with fresh and innovative approaches to economic development. Given the depth of the economic crisis Ireland experienced in the 1950s, his position is understandable. Additionally, he would have been sufficiently astute to foresee that membership of the EEC might release Ireland from its excessive dependence on the United Kingdom market.

Jumping forward to a 1972 Department of Foreign Affairs document further muddies the waters. *Into Europe: Ireland and the EEC* clearly acknowledges that the Community is more than an economic club. In fact, it has a specific section which examines 'The Political Implications of Membership'. However, the document is cautious on the question of political union. Its tone is decidedly state-centric and inter-governmental. It rejects the notion that Ireland will lose sovereignty by virtue of membership. In a phrase that would become part of the Community's future vernacular, the document states that sovereignty will be 'pooled'.[11]

Ten years after Lemass' 1962 speech Ireland was preparing for entry into the EEC. By 1972, the EEC was firmly established. A common market in goods, persons, services and capital was operational in the six founding member states. The Community's institutions were up and running and the European Court of Justice had clearly established a federal legal corpus. The EEC's first enlargement (Ireland, United Kingdom and Denmark) could be deemed a success.

The European Communities Act (1972) paved the way for Ireland's entry into the EEC on 1 January 1973. It will be recalled that this is the Act which excited much colourful language from Deputies Tully and Ryan. A very short Act consisting of six sections, it seeks to put in place the parliamentary mechanisms whereby EEC law is 'domesticated' into

---

11 Department of Foreign Affairs, 1972: 13.

national law. Section 2 of the Act goes directly to the issue at hand. In straightforward, unambiguous language, Community law, past and future, becomes part of Irish law:

> From the 1st day of January, 1973, the treaties governing the European Communities and the existing and future acts adopted by the institutions of those communities shall be binding on the State and shall be part of the domestic law thereof under the conditions laid down in those treaties.

This provision would have flowed logically from the referendum passed by voters in 1972. The people assented to membership of a supranational entity which brings with it an obligation to incorporate the laws agreed by this supranational collectivity. The next step is to decide how the law should be incorporated. Section 3 (1) and (2), which deal with the 'how' question, proved very controversial during its passage through the Dáil. It reads as follows:

> A Minister of State may make regulations for enabling Section 2 of this Act to have full effect (3.1).
> Regulations under this section may contain such incidental, supplementary and consequential provisions as appear to the Minister making the regulations to be necessary for the purpose of the regulations (3.2).

Heavily criticised at the time, it was contended that this section of the 1972 Act gave unfettered discretion to Ministers to bypass the legislature. It could be deemed an exercise in Executive usurpation of the Legislature. Rather than being afforded an opportunity to contribute to EEC legislation at proposal stage, Parliament was granted retrospective powers only. It should be understood that this power was granted to the Dáil in its plenary guise because the 1972 Act did not establish a Committee which might examine Community legislation in a more nuanced way than would be possible in full through plenary sessions. Consequently, something approximating to parliamentary farce occurred with the passage of the 1973 European Communities (Confirmation of Regulations) Act. The Confirmation Act was meant to be an annual event whereby Parliament retrospectively approved all Community incorporated regulations during the preceding year. As matters transpired, the 1973 Confirmation Act was to be the first and final Act of its kind. Thus, it is the only Confirmation Act on the statute books. The Act in its entirety consisted of two sections, namely:

1 The several regulations mentioned in column (2) of the Schedule to this Act, and made under the European Communities Act, 1972, are hereby confirmed.
2 This Act may be cited as the European Communities (Confirmation of Regulations) Act, 1973.

The relevant regulations were simply attached to the schedule. It did not matter whether there were thirty, fifty or two hundred regulations. All regulations were retrospectively passed *en bloc*. Hardly surprisingly the exercise was a shambles, as even the most well-briefed members could hardly handle the complexities of regulation *en masse*. In an era when members suffered severe resource deficits, they faced an impossible task. According to MacMahon and Murphy, the texts of regulations were often not available.[12] Robinson states that members ended up 'confirming blindly regulations'.[13] So unsatisfactory did the operation of the original 1972 Act prove that it was amended a year later by the European Communities (Amendment) Act (1973).

---

12 MacMahon and Murphy, 1989: 273.
13 Robinson, 1979: 1.

The 1973 Amendment Act adopted a different approach. It established the Joint Committee on the Secondary Legislation of the European Communities. Under the Act, Community legislation is given immediate statutory effect. The ambit of the Committee is retrospective. Section 1 (2) (a) thus reads:

> If the Joint Committee on the Secondary Legislation of the European Communities recommends to the Houses of the Oireachtas that any regulations under this Act be annulled and a resolution annulling the regulations is passed by both such Houses within one year after the regulations are made, the regulation shall be annulled accordingly and shall cease to have statutory effect, but without prejudice to the validity of anything previously done hereunder.

This then hardly constitutes an improvement on the 1972 Act. Both the Committee and the House have no input at the proposal stage of Community legislation. In fact, in strict legal terms, the 1973 Amendment Act gives both Houses a diminished role. Community legislation under the 1972 Act lapsed automatically in the absence of proper confirmation procedures. However, the 1973 Amendment Act merely granted *discretionary* powers of subsequent annulment to both Houses. In any event, only on one occasion up to 1977 did the Committee recommend annulment.[14] However, the Amendment Act did at least establish a Joint Committee to examine, albeit retrospectively, Community legislation. It must be remembered that in the early 1970s the practice of Standing Dáil Committees had yet to take root. 'Committees of the Whole House' examined the Committee stages of most bills. In that sense, the Joint Committee could be categorised as an innovation.

---

14 Robinson, 1979: 15.

How then did this Committee perform? Robinson provides a comprehensive interrogation of the Committee's performance. A reading of her account makes clear that the Committee faced many obstacles; insufficient staff and lack of interest by Ministers are cited as two significant barriers to effective scrutiny by the Committee.[15] Yet the Committee appears to have been very hard-working. In fact, between 1974 and 1977 it produced fifty-nine reports. Incredibly, 'not one of the fifty-nine reports was in fact debated'.[16] The overall impression formed is one of a hard-working Committee being virtually immobilised by systemic barriers and apathy. A speech by the then Taoiseach, Jack Lynch, during the passage of the 1972 European Communities Act through Dáil Éireann is quite revealing. Lynch was non-committal on the potential role of a Oireachtas Joint Committee:

> However, even in member States, which have such arrangements, we understand that considerable difficulties have arisen for the Parliamentary Committees in dealing with the large mass of Community documentation and in distinguishing the more important policy documents from the essentially technical proposals.[17]

Speaking in the pre-Committee era, Lynch's speech typifies low-level cultural resistance to a system which was thus far alien to Irish parliamentary democracy.

One can readily imagine that Committee members must have been frustrated at the fact that not one of their fifty-nine reports was debated in either the Dáil or Seanad. It is little wonder that in its fifty-fifth report the Committee concluded that:

---

15 *Ibid.*: 17–20.
16 *Ibid.*: 20.
17 Lynch, 1972.

The process by which Community law is produced cannot in the Joint Committee's view be described as democratic.[18]

Robinson herself concludes that there was:

> ... a serious lack of adequate political involvement in the scrutinising of European Community decision-making.[19]

What of the constitutional obligation on the Government to account for its actions before Dáil Éireann? Given that Ministers would be *ex officio* members of the Council of Ministers, this is of course a crucial point. Ministers could use the supranational plane to bypass parliamentary accountability. Whilst it is true that Ministers would be accountable in the normal way through question time and debates, one would nevertheless expect that extra accountability mechanisms would be put in place. The only such mechanism is contained in Section 5 of the 1972 Act (not amended by the 1973 Act). Section 5 simply states:

> The Government shall make a report twice yearly to each House of the Oireachtas on developments in the European Communities.

Robinson contends that parliamentary debates on these bi-annual reports were very unsatisfactory.[20]

It is clear that Dáil Éireann coped badly during the early years of accession. Under statute, Ministers were provided with a virtual blank cheque on Community legislation. No adequate parliamentary

---

18 Robinson, 1979: 9.
19 *Ibid.*: 39.
20 *Ibid.*: 12.

mechanisms were put in place to compensate for the privileged role Ministers enjoyed at Community level. Sovereignty may indeed have been pooled but among executives rather than parliamentarians.

Of course, Dáil Éireann of the early 1970s was gravely deficient in several respects. Leinster House was a virtual resource desert, Standing Orders favoured the Executive and the Committee system was for a future era. By 1973, Ireland had enjoyed almost two decades of uninterrupted single-party rule which shifted power from Parliament to the Executive. Innovative or radical thinking was not a prominent feature of Irish life at the time and parliamentary life reflected this conservatism. The era when international travel became commonplace for parliamentarians had yet to arrive. Members of the Dáil, therefore, were not exposed to comparative experiences. These factors generated an Executive-centred culture. There is a clear sense that the House had yet to acquire an autonomous institutional identity. I argue that membership of the EEC aggravated an already bad situation for the Dáil. There was a shift in political reality for a Parliament that was neither culturally nor pragmatically ready for it.

Pre-accession members could at least point to *de jure* declarations in the Constitution. Legally, members could rightfully claim that sole and exclusive power to make laws resided with them. Members could properly assert that the Cabinet was constitutionally bound to account for all of its Executive functions to Dáil Éireann.

In so far as Community decisions were concerned, these constitutional doctrines shifted in a very fundamental way. *De facto* parliamentary practices had always put members of the Dáil at a tremendous disadvantage. Accession removed much of the constitutional clothing from members. In 1973 the EEC operated within relatively limited fields. However, from the mid-1980s onwards the Community acquired a new forward momentum, ensuring that a growing number of spheres would come within their ambit. With the exception of core areas, such as foreign and security policy, the emerging Union's supranational reach knew few boundaries.

How did Dáil Éireann react to the new forward momentum at European level? By now it is evident that counter-intuitively Dáil Éireann, far from being staid, was proving to be quite a dynamic institution. The following question arises: Will this pattern of change and adaptation apply to the sphere of EU governance in the early 21st century? It should be noted that contemporary circumstances are quite propitious for the Dáil. National parliaments are seen as important spaces to redress the EU's democratic deficit.[21] In fact, the Lisbon Treaty affords a key role to national parliaments. Henceforth, national parliaments as a collective entity can force a review of legislative proposals in certain circumstances. Similarly, there is a specific protocol on the role of national parliaments attached to the Treaty of Amsterdam. Signatories to the Treaty call for:

> … greater involvement of national Parliaments in the activities of the European Union and to enhance their ability to express their views on matters which may be of particular interest to them (paragraph 2 of protocol).

Part two of the protocol formally recognises COSAC, the Conference of European Affairs Committees. Calls for greater national parliamentary involvement is primarily a response to arguments that there is a strong sense of disconnection between Europe and its citizens. It is hoped that national parliaments may play a constructive role in bridging that gap. In Ireland's case it should also be noted that a specialist

---

21 Newman, 2005.

European Affairs Committee was established in 1997. Between 1993 and 1997 European Affairs came within the remit of the Foreign Affairs Committee.[22] However, by 1997, the Houses of the Oireachtas obviously recognised that European Union Affairs demanded the specialist attention of a single Parliamentary Committee.

In Ireland's case, political leaders were provided with a very specific incentive to improve Dáil scrutiny of Union decisions, namely the defeat in the first referendum on the Nice Treaty (Nice 1) during 2001. The result, which undermined Ireland's European credentials sharply, focused the minds of domestic elites. Elites faced criticism from prominent figures, such as former Attorney General John Rogers, to the effect that integration was generating significant democratic deficits.[23]

Irish politicians responded to the popular pressures after the Nice Treaty's defeat. As it became clear at an early stage that ratification of the Treaty would be resubmitted to the people, it was important to address issues around accountability. In response, the Labour Party introduced a private member's bill during 2001 which ultimately became the European Union Scrutiny Act (2002). The purpose of the Act is to enhance parliamentary scrutiny of Union legislation. During the course of the report stage, then Minister of State Tom Kitt was upbeat in his assessment of the bill, stating that it 'gives Ireland one of the most advanced systems of parliamentary oversight in the EU'. Sinn Féin TD Aengus Ó Snodaigh disagreed, saying that it provided 'inadequate limitations on ministerial discretion, which is a major contributor to the democratic deficit'. Fine Gael TD Jim O'Keeffe argued that when enacted the bill would reduce the democratic deficit.[24]

---

22 Falkner and Laffan, 2005: 214–215.
23 Rogers, 2001.
24 O'Keeffe, 2002.

The key provisions are contained in Section 2 of the European Scrutiny Act (2002):

As soon as practicable after a proposed measure is presented by the Commission of the European Communities, or initiated by a Member State, as the case may be, the Minister shall cause a copy of the text concerned to be laid before each House of the Oireachtas together with a statement of the Minister outlining the content, purpose and likely implications for Ireland of the proposed measure and including such other information as he or she considers appropriate. [S. 2 (1)]

The Minister shall have regard to any recommendations made to him or her from time to time by either or both Houses of the Oireachtas or by a Committee of either or both such Houses in relation to the proposed measures. [S. 2 (2)]

Subsections (1) and (2) shall not apply, if in the opinion of the Minister, there is insufficient time for the carrying out of the procedures aforesaid and the performance of the functions of the Houses of the Oireachtas in relation to the text aforesaid. [S.2 (3)]

Where, pursuant to subsection (3), a text of a proposed measure has not been laid before each House of the Oireachtas and the measure concerned is adopted by an institution of the European Communities, the Minister shall cause a copy of the text of the measure to be laid before both houses of the Oireachtas together with a statement outlining the implications for Ireland of the measure and the circumstances of its adoption and including such other information as he or she deems appropriate. [S.2 (4)]

Every Minister of the Government shall make a report to each House of the Oireachtas not less than twice yearly in relation to measures, proposed measures and other developments in relation to the European Communities and the European Union in relation to which he or she performs functions. [S.2 (5)]

The Act clearly puts an onus on the relevant Minister to bring proposed measures before each House. Similarly, the Minister is obliged to provide what amounts to a political analysis of the measure.

Henceforth, all Government Departments would have a legal duty of disclosure towards both Houses of the Oireachtas. Ministers and officials need to be alert to the new system. For officials who may have become accustomed to dealing with Parliament in a perfunctory way, the new system is likely to prove a culture shock. The language of Section 2 (1) might have afforded less leeway to Ministers. For example, what does 'as soon as practicable mean'? Why only attach other information which the Minister deems 'appropriate'?

Section 2 (2) could be judged as excessively Minister-centred. The Minister is certainly obliged to take recommendations of both Houses into account. But self-evidently, recommendations are not binding on the Minister. For a classically executive-centred political system, binding instructions would be too much too soon.

Section 3 (3) deserves to be judged harshly. Firstly, Ministers are effectively provided with a means of avoiding their responsibilities. It provides for a ministerial exit strategy from Sections 2 (1) and 2 (2). It might be counter-argued that such an exit strategy is required in certain *limited* circumstances. Thus, if a Minister legitimately does not have sufficient time to abide by Sections 1 and 2, it seems reasonable to legislate for such an eventuality. However, Sub-section 3 appears to provide a ministerial *carte blanche*. The Minister is afforded total discretion when it comes to deciding if there is insufficient time available. There is no check on this aspect of ministerial discretion within the Act so there is scope for ministerial abuse. In this regard Sub-section 4 is a very weak response. It merely provides that, where the Minister has deemed that he/she has insufficient time, he/she must lay before each House of the Oireachtas the adopted measure accompanied by a statement outlining the implications. There is not even an onus on the Minister to retrospectively explain his/her actions.

From the perspective of proper democratic accountability, three possibilities ought to be considered. Firstly, the section, it could be argued, ought to be deleted. Ministers should not be provided with an 'out' in any circumstance. Secondly, if an exit strategy is deemed appropriate it should not be based on undiluted ministerial discretion. Rather, a Committee or Sub-Committee of both Houses should come to a conclusion with the Minister. Thirdly, both the Committee and the Minister should report back to both Houses with explanations. In any case, it should be clear that the unfettered ministerial discretion provided for in the Act is democratically unacceptable.

Sub-section 5 is certainly an improvement on the 1973 Act, which called for twice-yearly reports by the Government as a collective entity to each House of the Oireachtas. On the other hand, the 2002 Act places a statutory responsibility on *all* Ministers to report at least twice yearly to each House on matters within their remit, including adopted measures, proposed measures and general developments.

Is the 2002 Act an improvement on its predecessors? Consisting of six sections, the Act is quite short. However, its orientation is very different to the 1970s' statutes. It is clearly prospective rather than retrospective. Its purpose is to give the Oireachtas input at the proposal stage of EU legislation through the Joint Committee on European Affairs. Rather than the Dáil being presented with a *fait accompli*, it has an input into the decision-making process, so notwithstanding the criticisms of the 2002 Act in preceding paragraphs, it is clearly a vast improvement on its predecessors.

The 2002 Act makes it difficult for Ministers to bypass Parliament. Its central thrust is a form of prospective accountability. Admittedly, it is a weak form of prospective accountability, weak in so far as the hands of Ministers are in no way tied. Ministers cannot be instructed to vote or negotiate in a certain way. Rather, Ministers are obliged to take the expressed views of Parliament into account. Nevertheless, each House enters the legislative fray at the proposal not at the retrospective stage. In the context of an executive-centred Irish parliamentary culture, this is a significant development. Parliament is not afforded a mere rubber-stamping role. Potentially, therefore, the Act allows great scope to Parliament.

It should be noted that the Committee's scrutinising functions are not confined to measures such as regulations, directives and decisions. The Committee may also consider matters related to asylum and immigration and Common Foreign and Security Policy measures. Undeniably, this is a considerable advancement as these policy spheres have tended to be highly inter-governmental in character. It is quite a concession to permit parliamentary scrutiny of this category of proposed measures. However, given that Irish neutrality and an evolving Union military sphere were highlighted as concerns during Nice 1, the Government's hand was forced on this matter.

But how is the Act being implemented on a practical basis? It will be remembered that the political system's first attempt at parliamentary scrutiny was an abysmal failure. The Joint Committee on the Secondary Legislation of the European Communities operated in testing circumstances, being treated with something approaching contempt by Ministers. The Committee struggled to find an effective role. However, the parliamentary circumstances operating during the period of the 29th Dáil (2002–2007) were radically different from those of the mid-1970s. Firstly, a previous culture of parliamentary quiescence was being challenged by an embryonic culture of parliamentary assertiveness. Secondly, the national parliaments have been 'discovered' by European elites. Deemed key democratic actors, the parliaments are likely to play a more important role in the EU's future governance. Because of the Union's quest to challenge perceptions of elitism and remoteness, national parliaments including Dáil Éireann are in vogue. When making a judgment on the implementation of the 2002 Act, these changed circumstances must be taken into account.

FROM LAW TO PRACTICE

For the duration of the 29th Dáil (2002–2007) the tedious task of monitoring EU legislative proposals fell to the European Union Scrutiny Sub-Committee, which examined all proposed measures, including regulations and directives. On perusing the fifth report of the Joint Committee on European Affairs Sub-Committee on European Scrutiny 2007 (1 January to 4 April), I was struck by the fact that a Sub-Committee of seven members was expected to deal with a huge volume of proposals. Between October 2002 and April 2007, it met no less than 80 times and examined 2,183 proposals. In fact, the Sub-Committee considered 179 documents at its four meetings held during the period 1 January to 4 April.[25]

But it is not just a matter of volume and size. The range and complexity of legislative proposals facing members also becomes evident. It seems that expert advice would have been needed for many of the proposals. Initially, therefore, there is an impression of potential overload for Committee members. Even allowing for the fact that the Committee organised its affairs in a meticulous way, the reader must inevitably query whether members had the capacity to adequately scrutinise a huge volume and wide range of matters. My strong impression is that the emphasis on complexity in the post-parliamentary governance model is very salient.

---

25   Fifth Report on the Operation of the European Union (Scrutiny) Act, 2007:
       2.

What categories of documents did the Sub-Committee examine? A further examination of the fifth report yields the following results. The first category to be considered covers the Union's three classical legislative instruments, namely regulations, directives and decisions. For example, during the period 1 January to 4 April 2007 fifty-two regulations, forty-seven decisions and forty-two directives were examined. Secondly, six green papers and one budgetary document were examined. Thirdly, sixteen Common Foreign and Security Policy measures and one Title IV (policing, visa and asylum) measure were examined. Fourthly, fifteen so-called early warning notes were considered. These notes inform the Committee that the Union may be imposing anti-dumping duties on non-member states where flooding of the European market with excessively cheap goods occurs.[26]

How did the Sub-Committee examine these documents during the 29th Dáil? Initially, the Sub-Committee received copies of proposals accompanied by information and assessment notes from Government Departments. The Department of Foreign Affairs had overall responsibility for coordinating the responses of all lead Government Departments. In scrutinising EU legislative proposals, the Sub-Committee divided measures into three different categories, namely proposals where the Sub-Committee considered no further scrutiny is necessary, proposals where further scrutiny is necessary and which were accordingly referred to the relevant Sectoral Committee and finally adopted proposals. According to the Sub-Committee's fifth report, 18% of documents (391 out of 2,183) were referred to Sectoral Committees for further scrutiny between 2002 and 2007.[27]

---

26 *Ibid.*: 4.
27 *Ibid.*: 3.

The referral of certain proposals to Sectoral Committees was not an option available to this Committee's predecessors in the early 1970s. The expertise of each Sectoral Committee can therefore be availed of now. The Sub-Committee had to make judgments as to the merits of certain proposals. Proposals of a routine nature and those with few implications for Ireland obviously deserved less consideration than more controversial measures. The former can therefore be assigned to the 'no further scrutiny necessary' category.

Measures Referred to Sectoral Committee for Further Scrutiny by the EU Scrutiny Sub-Committee at its meeting of 12 October 2006

COM (2006) 397   Proposal for a Directive of the European Parliament and of the Council on environmental quality standards in the field of water policy and amending Directive 2000/60/EEC.

COM (2006) 423   Proposal for a Regulation of the European Parliament and of the Council establishing a common authorisation procedure for food additives, food enzymes and food flavourings.

COM (2006) 425   Proposal for a Regulation of the European Parliament and of the Council on food enzymes and amending Council Directive 83/417/EEC, Council Regulation (EC) No. 1493/1999, Directive 2000/13/EC and Council Directive 2001/112/EC.

COM (2006) 427   Proposal for a Regulation of the European Parliament and of the Council on flavourings and certain food ingredients with flavouring properties for use in and on foods and amending Council Regulation (EEC) No. 1576/89, Council Regulation (EEC) No. 1601/91, Regulation (EC) No. 2232/96 and Directive 2000/13/EC.

COM (2006) 428   Proposal for a Regulation of the European Parliament and of the Council on food additives.

COM (2006) 468   Proposal for a Council framework decision on the European supervision order in pre-trial procedures between Member States of the European Union.

COM (2006) 536   Amendment to Council Directive 91/414/EEC Annex 1, to include flusilazole in the list of active substances which may be included in plant protection products.

COM (2006) 537   Amendment to Council Directive 91/414/EEC Annex 1, to include methamidophos in the list of active substances which may be included in plant protection products.

COM (2006) 538   Amendment to Council Directive 91/414/EEC Annex 1, to include fenarimol in the list of active substances which may be included in plant protection products.

COM (2006) 539   Amendment to Council Directive 91/414/EEC Annex 1, to include dinocap in the list of active substances which may be included in plant protection products.

COM (2006) 540   Amendment to Council Directive 91/414/EEC Annex 1, to include procymidone in the list of active substances which may be included in plant protection products.

COM (2006) 541   Amendment to Council Directive 91/414/EEC Annex 1, to include carbendazim in the list of active substances which may be included in plant protection products.[28]

In overall terms, because of the approach adopted by this Committee, it is clear that scrutiny of Union legislation during the 29th Dáil was a marked improvement in historical terms. This is particularly the case if one considers the totally casual approach adopted by the Dáil in the 1970s.

---

28 www.oireachtas.ie/viewdoc.asp?DocID=6512&CatID=74

Bypassing or Working through Dáil Éireann?

On 21 July 2004, the Joint Committee on Justice, Equality, Defence and Women's Rights launched its report on the criminal justice system. On reading the Chair's (Seán Ardagh, TD) speech to the assembled media, it is interesting to note that he acknowledged the important contribution made by groups and individuals to the process.[29] A number of observations can be made on the Chair's address. Firstly, a central aim of the Committee was to generate public debate on how the criminal justice system might be reformed. Inviting representatives of civil society to participate in the Committee's review process would aid this objective's achievement. The Committee is thus looking outwards and not suffering from parliamentary insularity. Secondly, the Committee held a press conference to launch its report. In this context the Oireachtas Public Relations Office issued the Chair's address as a press release. The address was printed on Committee headed notepaper. All these details can be discovered on a very sophisticated and information-rich Oireachtas website. It appears that Committees are becoming more professional in their approach. Engaging proactively with groups, it seems, is part of this pattern of professionalisation. As late as the 1960s, organisations hardly affected parliamentary life as Parliamentary Committees and a proactive lobbying system were not features of those years. (In contrast, no less than nineteen Joint Committees were established by the 30th Dáil and 23rd Seanad: see Appendix 3.) Moreover, a press statement issued by a parliamentary public relations office would scarcely have been envisaged by politicians of that era – it was a different parliamentary world.[30]

---

29 Ardagh, 2004.
30 Pattison, 2002, 2004.

The anecdotal evidence strongly suggests that the contemporary Dáil has become a hive of interest-group activity. A vibrant Committee system seems to have facilitated the mobilisation of interest groups. Committees have become an important site for groups. More solid evidence is available from the Houses of the Oireachtas Commission's annual reports. During the years 2005, 2006 and 2007, 1,290 Committee meetings were held and 332 reports were issued.[31] And for the years 2004, 2005 and 2006, a total of 3,731 witnesses gave evidence to Oireachtas Committees.[32] Thus, an average of 1,240 witnesses gave evidence per annum so it seems that Committees have indeed become an important site for groups and organisations.

Each House of the Oireachtas has power under its Standing Orders (rules) to form Committees for specific purposes. There are four types of Committees – Standing, Select, Joint and Special (rare):

Standing Committees – Standing Orders provide for the automatic creation of such Committees in a new Dáil or Seanad, e.g. Committee of Public Accounts, Joint Committee on Consolidation Bills.
Select Committees – Comprise membership of one House only, whether Dáil or Seanad.
Joint Committees – Comprise Select Committees from both Houses sitting and voting together under common Orders of Reference.
Special Committees – Established for the sole purpose of considering a specific bill.[33]

---

31 Houses of the Oireachtas Commission, 2008: 16.
32 Houses of the Oireachtas Commission, 2007: 14.
33 www.oireachtas.ie/ViewDoc.asp?fn=/documents/leaflet/comm. htm&CatID=102&m=k

What is the *modus operandi* of the interaction between Committees and civil society? Firstly, it should be understood that Committees are proactively engaging with civil society. Submissions are sought in response to proposed legislation or, more generally, a topic of public concern. Having examined the written submissions a selection of the groups will be invited to make oral presentations before the full Committee and having made their oral presentations, group spokespersons are questioned by Committee members. At the conclusion of these public hearings the Rappoteur, on the Committee's behalf, draws up a report. When a report is produced it is laid before each House for its consideration. Apart from being formally invited to make oral and/or written submissions by the Committees, groups may take the initiative by contacting the relevant Rappoteur seeking permission to make a public presentation.

The criminal justice system is never far off the political agenda. The then Garda Síochána Bill was examined by the Joint Committee on Justice, Equality, Defence and Women's Rights during March 2005. After advertising for submissions in the national media, it held a series of public presentations with a focus on community policing over a period of five days. A diverse range of groups gave their views on the topic of community policing generally and the Joint Policing Committees in particular.

An examination of the Committee debates demonstrates the extent to which a vast array of groups mobilised around the issue of community policing. The following groups made presentations: National Council on Aging, National Crime Council, Victim Support, National Consultative Committee on Racism and Interculturalism, Irish Senior Citizens Parliament, Lord Mayor's Commission, Community Alert, General Council of County Councils, County and City Managers' Association, Association of Municipal Authorities of Ireland, Local Authority Members' Association, Consortium of European Counsellors, Rialto Community Network, Cabra Community Policing Forum, North Inner City Drug Task Force, Finglas Cabra Drugs Task Force, Tallaght Drugs Task Force, Irish Council for Civil Liberties, General Council of County Councils and the Northern Ireland Policing Board represented by Denis Bradley.[34]

Two interesting questions arise. Firstly, what factors have led to the emergence of relationships between Committees and civil society? Secondly, how are the relationships best described? The Committee system is currently well established in Dáil Éireann. Equally, organisations of all hues engage in the lobbying process. It would therefore be surprising if groups were not exploiting this new political site. Both Parliament and civil society have become more professional. Voluntary-run organisations now employ full-time staff. Committees are acquiring more resources. Crucially, I argue, Committees are becoming autonomous and institutionalised. There is an overlap in the interests of Parliament in its Committee guise and the representatives of civil society. The Committee system obviously presents organisations with a useful lobbying platform: groups can promote their policy agendas, not only to Committee members but also to the broader community. In a situation where Ministers may be proving unresponsive, the Committee system provides groups with a non-executive political space. If the gates in Merrion Street are closed, why not avail of the open gates in Kildare Street? An alternative point of political leverage is thereby available to groups.

Apart from the formal parliamentary space which Committees provide, informal processes cannot be overlooked. It is not unusual to discover that Opposition Committee members are also their party's

34 Committee Debates, 2005, 22–23 March. See www.oireachtas.ie.

spokespersons in Dáil Éireann. Groups are therefore provided with an opportunity to press their cases with Opposition spokespersons outside of the Committee hearing room. The same applies to Government Committee members. Government Deputies, for example, hold most Committee chairs. This may provide an indirect path to the Minister's office. In overall terms, whilst the formal presentation to the Committee is a crucial space in its own right, the informal contacts and networks may prove equally crucial. By mingling and networking with Deputies in the informal spaces, groups may further progress their policy goals. Equally, a day in Leinster House may generate future contacts.

Developing a relationship with civil society also benefits the Committee system. In what has been hitherto an executive-centred political system, the Committee system is acting as an important space for Dáil Éireann, cementing, perhaps for the first time, a parliamentary identity. More to the point, Committees are actively forging this identity. Committees are not passively waiting for groups to initiate relationships, rather they are proactively engaging with civil society by inviting groups to make written and oral submissions.

Likewise, Committees are publicising their efforts, including the launching of consultation processes and reports. Engaging with civil society enhances the legitimacy of the Committee system. Committees can rightfully argue that they are facilitating a dialogue with civil society and the process of publicly consulting with groups makes for a more inclusive and transparent parliamentary system. The processes also bring Ministers into the parliamentary arena perhaps more often than they would wish. Similarly, civil servants frequently appear before Committees. Bureaucratic veils of secrecy are thus burst open as Ministers and civil servants are forced to explain and justify their positions.

The net effect is that Committees need groups as much as groups need Committees. Their relationship is mutually beneficial and interdependent. I characterise the relationship as being symbiotic in nature; rather than behaving as antagonistic actors (antibiotically) the Committee and representatives of civil society are 'locked' into a reciprocal relationship.

So is civil society bypassing or working through Dáil Éireann? In Ireland as in all Western polities, groups clearly employ multi-faceted strategies to achieve their objectives. Operating in several different spaces either simultaneously or concurrently, modern governance demands complex approaches.

Civil society clearly contributes to the policy-making process: either by articulating grievances or engaging in strategies of collective mobilisation and action, groups force their agendas on to the political stage. Engaging in power politics, groups may actually generate policy or administrative change and, as such, groups are key actors in the complex web that constitutes early 21st-century governance. However, it is an entirely different proposition to suggest that we live in an era of governance that 'tends increasingly to be on of organisations, by organisations for organisations'.[35] Groups (non-governmental organisations and social movements) are certainly in the political ascendant, but not to the extent that other actors are dominated and excluded.

It is equally the case that a sceptical eye should also be cast upon the process. A sceptic might argue that the process of ongoing dialogue with civil society could be described as mere window-dressing. In reality, the dialogical process is nominal and superficial. Committee meetings are only talking shops which do not shape the policy process. The process gives the impression that a genuine dialogical process is occurring. And does the process generate public involvement? It can hardly be assumed that all groups that make submissions and appear before

---

35 Andersen and Burns, 1996: 229.

Committees have a wider democratic base. Similarly, Committees are partisan forums and the allocation of Chairs and other positions is a decidedly partisan process. Chairmanship of a Committee is frequently perceived as political compensation for those who were not rewarded with Ministerial office. Nevertheless, it is impossible to deny that a new dynamic is evolving between Dáil Éireann and civil society.

Groups, far from bypassing Dáil Éireann, are in reality working through it. The emergence of a strong Committee system has facilitated this. Parliamentarians are not throwing in the 'political towel', rather, Irish parliamentarians are carving out an increasingly defined space in the political system. By engaging proactively with Committees, groups recognise this reality. I reject that aspect of the post-parliamentary governance model which favours the role of civil society to the exclusion of parliamentary settings. In contemporary Ireland, Dáil Éireann, particularly in its Committee guise, has become an important forum for civil society.

Are political processes crowding out Dáil Éireann? In the case of European Union governance and civil society, Dáil Éireann is far from being crowded out; rather it is asserting itself as an institution in both spheres. This is particularly the case with regard to civil society as Dáil Éireann is becoming an increasingly important site for groups via the Committee system. Progress in the European Union sphere is very impressive. In strict legal terms, the European Union Scrutiny Act (2002) is a critical improvement on its 1970s predecessors. In fact, the 2002 Act marks the first occasion that Dáil Éireann has taken its task of monitoring Union legislation seriously. And the Act's implementation during the twenty-ninth Dáil via the Sub-Committee on European Scrutiny marked a significant improvement from earlier periods when members of Dáil Éireann adopted a purely nominal approach.

10

SOCIAL PARTNERSHIP
AND EXPERT SOVEREIGNTY

The sole and exclusive power of making laws for the State is hereby vested in the Oireachtas: no other legislative authority has power to make laws for the State.[1]

The fundamental issue is that it is the duty and responsibility of our politicians to face up to the appalling nature of the economic crisis and to govern with the common good as their fundamental concern. Politicians are elected to govern; social partners are not.[2]

It is also seen to be undemocratic in elevating the influence of interest groups in economic policy-making over that of the elected Parliament. This has been an important strand of commentary on the Irish experience; but as social partnership seemed to prove its economic worth as the 1990s proceeded, this view was pressed less forcefully.[3]

In this chapter I explore Dáil Éireann's role in two domains: social partnership and the appointment of consultants and working groups by Government Departments. I will ask whether Dáil Éireann is a

---

1 Article 15.2.1 of the 1937 Irish Constitution.
2 Collins, 2008.
3 Roche and Cradden, 2003: 74.

spectator or participant in these spheres. A key concern is whether both processes suffer from a democratic deficit. The social partnership process will be divided into four phases: pre-negotiation, negotiation, agreement and implementation.

DÁIL ÉIREANN AS A SPECTATOR OR PARTICIPANT?

The social partnership model has been the key component of Irish public policy-making since the 1990s, although as previously noted it remains unclear whether it will survive the recession. Credited with generating economic recovery, it has few detractors within established political parties; on the contrary, for many its virtues are indisputable. Whilst aspects of the model have been criticised in some quarters, few commentators challenge its usefulness. Rather, certain outcomes and processes are criticised. For example, it could be argued that the equality agenda has not received sufficient attention within the framework. But, there has been little debate and public commentary on the democratic underpinnings of social partnership. Given that it shapes the polity's public policy direction this should be of concern to democratic theorists and practitioners alike. If the process does indeed suffer from a democratic deficit, a means of democratising it must be considered.

In the pre-negotiation phase, the partners set out their optimum positions. Often using the media to 'sell their stall', it is likely that their demands at this early stage are deliberately inflated. Thus, employers, unions, Government Ministers and community groups attempt to take the high moral ground. In reality, however, this stage of the project, as with later stages, is imbued with strategic self-orientating considerations. Bottom-line positions emerge as the formal negotiations evolve. Dáil Éireann does not play any meaningful role at this stage. Apart from a few random parliamentary questions, the social partners shape the parameters of emerging negotiations. On the other hand, the Executive enjoys a highly privileged position at this point.

The negotiations proper are conducted behind closed doors in Government Buildings. Away from the public and media gaze, public policy is negotiated non-transparently. Citizens observe the comings and goings of the social partners on television whilst inside a strategic game of poker is played as each side seeks to maximise its gains. The Taoiseach and senior Ministers chair and direct the negotiations, which can be both tortuous and protracted. Dáil Éireann is excluded from this part of the process. Public policy is determined without reference to Dáil Éireann. At the negotiation's conclusion a formal agreement is publicly announced. Again, Dáil Éireann plays no part as the Taoiseach and Ministers occupy a privileged role.

The process of implementing and monitoring agreements is becoming increasingly institutionalised. Under Sustaining Progress (2003–2005), the sixth social partnership agreement, a special steering group consisting of partners and Government representatives was established and charged with responsibility for managing and implementing agreements. Similarly, quarterly plenary meetings are held in which all the main players are afforded an opportunity to test each agreement's implementation. Apart from these formal mechanisms, the Taoiseach and Ministers have regular bilateral meetings with the social partners. The views of groups which may have withdrawn from the process are still sought. However, the pattern of Dáil Éireann's exclusion continues. It has not been afforded any role in the emerging machinery.

The Dáil depends on conventional parliamentary mechanisms to ascertain to what extent the Executive is adhering to commitments made under each agreement. One such mechanism is Taoiseach's question time. Under this format, the Taoiseach faces a total of ninety minutes of oral questioning from members per week (forty-five minutes on Tuesday and on Wednesday). In accordance with standard parliamentary procedures, formal advance notice of questions must be provided to the Taoiseach and members are entitled to ask supplementary questions.

Taoiseach's question time is a very unsatisfactory mechanism for several reasons. Firstly, the Ceann Comhairle is reluctant to allow the Taoiseach to be confronted on detailed matters of policy and frequently interrupts questioners because they stray from Standing Orders. Questioners are invariably invited to put specific questions to the line Minister. Secondly, because of time limits, questioners tend not to get the opportunity to put enough supplementary questions. Thirdly, the real game takes place elsewhere. It is only at the post-negotiations stage, via parliamentary questions, that the Lower House is afforded any role, a role which could only be described as purely nominal. What is most surprising is that no special parliamentary mechanisms have been put in place to ensure the elected Lower House is involved in a meaningful way during all phases of the negotiations. More surprisingly, members do not appear to be demanding an enhanced parliamentary role in this key area.

Speaking on social partnership during question time on Wednesday 6 February 1991 the then Taoiseach, Charles Haughey, made it clear that as Chief Executive he envisaged a very limited rubber-stamping role for Dáil Éireann:

> There are countless occasions on which a Government as the Executive negotiates with different persons, bodies, agencies and then brings that negotiation here for confirmation.[4]

---

4 Haughey, 1991.

The then Leader of the Opposition, John Bruton, held very different views on the issue. He posed the following question during Taoiseach's question time:

> Would he agree that it is not desirable from the point of the sovereignty of Parliament that Parliament should be presented with a *fait accompli* which has been agreed outside this House in respect of which we would have no choice but to either accept *in toto* or reject it *in toto*?[5]

Bruton advocated that the social partnership process should be subjected to 'the best available democratic input'. During the same question time, his Front Bench colleague Deputy Jim Mitchell described social partnership as 'a third House of Parliament'.[6] It should be noted, however, that when Deputy Bruton became Taoiseach in 1994 the *modus operandi* of social partnership remained substantially unchanged for his period in office.

It is time to return to my core question: Is Dáil Éireann a participant or spectator in the social partnership process? Clearly, it is more accurately described as a spectator as it does not enjoy any meaningful say in the four phases of the process. Indeed, it is remarkable that the Dáil has not been more aggressive in promoting a more proactive role for itself. Considering the Dáil has no democratic input, social partnership suffers from weak democratic underpinnings.

To date, social partnership has been judged on an instrumental basis. Delivering the goods, rather than how the goods ought to be delivered, has been the main concern. This has allowed the executive

---

5   Bruton, 1991.
6   Mitchell, 1991.

branch to occupy centre stage, whilst Parliament is at best a spectator and at worst an outsider. How this situation might be remedied will be addressed in the next chapter.

EXPERT SOVEREIGNTY? WORKING GROUPS AND CONSULTANTS' REPORTS

The volume and complexity of contemporary policy demands that politicians receive expert advice. It would be completely impractical to expect politicians and their aides to acquire a command of all complex issues. It will be recalled that the post-parliamentary governance model places a strong emphasis on the centrality of experts in contemporary politics: 'Expert sovereignty tends to prevail over popular sovereignty'.[7] Whilst the concept of expert sovereignty may exaggerate the point somewhat, few would deny the crucial role experts play in contemporary politics. Irish politics is not exceptional in this regard, but this situation has implications for a political system's democratic life. Working away from the public gaze, experts and consultants are influencing policy outcomes. Concerns around transparency and accountability arise. Cost issues are also relevant as public monies should be spent prudently.

I examine the role outside experts play in advising Government Departments on certain policy matters but do not focus on personally appointed advisors who counsel Ministers on a day to day basis. I will ask: How widespread is the use of consultants, experts and working groups? What kinds of issues are examined and reported on? Are expert and consultants' reports really that expensive? An analysis of three parliamentary answers put down for written reply received by

---

7 Andersen and Burns, 1996: 229.

Deputy Joan Burton (Dublin West) on 6 October 2009 will help us gauge trends (see Appendix 2).

What observations can be gleamed from the reply provided by the Minister for Foreign Affairs? A combined total of forty-two experts and consultants' reports were commissioned by the Department of Foreign Affairs during 2008. Total costs amounted to €1,073,495. The cost factor could therefore hardly be described as insignificant, particularly when one considers that these figures only represent a one-year time period for one out of fifteen government departments. Looking through the list it is obvious that a wide range of topics were examined including health, education and agricultural matters. The list admirably demonstrates the complexities of foreign policy sphere and tends to support the assertion that the presence and influence of experts and specialists characterise contemporary politics.

Analysing the replies from the Ministers for the Environment and Social Affairs, the combined amount of working groups established by the two departments during 2008 amounts to forty-four. It is also worth noting that the combined costs for both departments came to €1,235,112. The highest consultancy fees for any one working group came to €368,573. The diverse range of topics considered by the groups is very apparent. The complexity and breadth of modern governance is once again illuminated.

Andersen and Burns alert us to an important feature of 21st-century governance. Whilst it is difficult to measure the precise influence which consultants and working groups possess, it would be foolish to deny the importance of these actors. This assertion is strengthened if a further reality is considered: the data presented in this section deals with consultants/experts commissioned by the *State*. However, non-governmental actors are also likely to be quite prolific in this regard. Consultants and experts are feeding into the policy-making process through private as well as public channels.

Whilst they are not nearly as important as social partnership in public policy terms, they should not be lightly dismissed. Apart from the fact that public money is involved, there is the further issue of democratic accountability and transparency. There is also the fact that the reports of consultants and working groups are likely to be important agenda setters and as their deliberations are held away from the public gaze, this is a matter of serious concern. Considering the apparent importance of consultants and working groups in modern Irish politics, a key question arises: To what extent (if any) does Dáil Éireann monitor and scrutinise their activities? The answer is that consultants and working groups are free from meaningful parliamentary input and oversight. The process of appointing and monitoring consultants operates in a 'Parliament-free zone'. Operating outside of the Dáil, these actors have escaped its reach. To remedy this situation, an injection of transparency is required and I will examine possible measures in the next chapter.

The Dáil's spectator status in social partnership gives cause for democratic concern. The current institutional mechanisms for social partnership afford a purely nominal role to Dáil Éireann. Similarly, so-called 'expert sovereignty' has implications for the democratic process. It is in these spheres, social partnership and 'expert sovereignty' that Dáil Éireann most closely resembles Andersen and Burns' post-parliamentary governance model.

Dáil Éireann as an Advocate for the Common Good?

Schumpter compared the political competition for votes to the operation of the (economic) market; voters like consumers choose between the policies (products) offered by competing political entrepreneurs and the parties regulate the competition like trade associations in the economic sphere.[1]

Civic virtue is a fragile growth in societies divided by differences of the market, which reinforce a self-image of society as a bundle of consumers, each with their separate interests. Contemporary liberal democracy seems to bear out the nightmare scenario of de Tocqueville, with his picture of an excessively individualised society of people indifferent to the fate of their fellow citizens.[2]

The mass population engages in uncritical consumption of news and products, while elites use their rational-critical skills for behind closed doors activities and exclusionary debate.[3]

My central task in this chapter is to map out a novel but achievable democratic role for Dáil Éireann in the conditions of 21st-century

---

1 Pateman, 1970: 3.
2 Schwartzmantel, 2003: 143.
3 Stromer-Galley, 2003: 727.

politics. A core concern of this book is that contemporary parliaments are deemed responsible by citizens for a vast array and huge volume of decisions made by non-parliamentary actors. In chapter six a logical and straightforward solution to this dilemma was offered: place parliament at the polity's decisional centre. This may be a good example of where logic is rendered the foe of feasibility. It is, therefore, necessary to reassess the connection between decision-making and parliamentary responsibility.

Under conditions of modern parliamentary governance, a more nuanced form of parliamentary responsibility is required. Parliament should obviously be directly responsible for the decisions it makes. This is not to say parliament makes or indeed should make all the decisions. However, political decisions should not be beyond the reach of parliamentary scrutiny and accountability. As such, parliament should be at the accountability centre of the political system rather than at its decisional centre. Where parliament fails to exercise its accountability obligations, citizens could properly criticise such inaction.

The key to enhancing Dáil Éireann's democratic role is to extend the reach of parliamentary accountability. This can be achieved by extending the norm of discursive accountability into a prescribed role for Dáil Éireann. As explained previously, in this scenario, Dáil Éireann would provide a democratic and public forum where a range of actors would justify decisions made or not made. My preferred forum is the contemporary public sphere. Parliament could compel other actors to give reasons for their actions and decisions in the public sphere. When holding such actors to account Parliament will always be probing as to whether they acted in the public interest (common good). The public is then in a position to reach conclusions on the matters under discursive consideration.

Taking the concept of discursive accountability a little further, the following question was posed in chapter six: What are the desired outcomes of strong Executive accountability to Parliament? The answer is that there are two desired outcomes. Firstly, Ministers reveal fully, swiftly and frankly all relevant facts and information. A culture of transparency pervades the accountability process. Regarding disclosure of information, Ministers adopt a maximalist rather than a minimalist approach. Secondly, accountability mechanisms at all times seek to promote and enhance the common good. Mechanisms are not employed to protect or promote vested-interests. These desired outcomes could be extended to actors other than Ministers. The social partners, civil servants, civil society, experts and working groups are obvious examples. Maximalist understandings of ministerial accountability to the Dáil are thus extended to other important decisional spheres.

By employing the concept of discursive accountability in the public sphere, parliaments are provided with an opportunity to reach and receive the approval of the public. The democratic potential of the public sphere is highlighted in the deliberative democratic model:

> Participants in the democratic process offer proposals, for how best to solve problems or legitimate needs, and so on, and they present arguments through which they aim to persuade others to accept their proposals. Democratic process is primarily a discussion of problems, conflicts, and claims of need or interest. Through dialogue others test and challenge these proposals and arguments. Because they have not stood up to dialogic examination, the deliberating public rejects or refines some proposals.[4]

---

4 Young, 2002: 22–23.

In short, the public sphere is a potentially empowering democratic and political space. Given that there is evidence to suggest that contemporary polities are undergoing processes of radical transformation, parliaments ought to be sensitive to fresh approaches on how to generate debate, highlight/absorb issues, and perhaps shape and influence outcomes. Discursive accountability in the public sphere provides such an avenue.

CONSUMERISM: ERODING THE PUBLIC SPHERE

Whilst the public sphere clearly possesses democratic potential, it faces challenges from certain aspects of contemporary society, most notably consumerism.[5] Encouraging individuals to behave as egotistical self-contained atomistic actors, consumerism is conceptually at variance with any notion of a public. Thus, writing on the United States, Stromer-Galley contends that 'US citizens are private citizens uninterested in coming together to engage public issues'.[6] The author suggests that:

> The mass population engages in uncritical consumption of news and products, while elites use their rational-critical skills for behind closed doors activities and exclusionary debate.[7]

To participate in the public sphere citizens require the skills of civic engagement. However, as market relations become increasingly pervasive, Galston suggests that these skills may be lost. Operating in the privatised sphere of market relations requires different skills, since

5 Habermas, 1989.
6 Stromer-Galley, 2003: 727.
7 *Ibid.*

actors need to be calculating, strategic, competitive and egotistical. In this context, Galston suggests that during the late 20th century the market became more pervasive, thereby reducing opportunities to practise civic non-market skills.[8]

Consumerism therefore must be clearly distinguished from citizenship. Put simply, a citizen is a member of a political community. Central to all citizenship models is the concept of equality, however interpreted. As a member of a community, the citizen is conferred with rights and duties. All citizens are entitled to be treated equally, but it has to be borne in mind that citizenship rights are not necessarily always on an upward trajectory. Since the 9/11 terrorist attacks of 2001, it seems that civil rights are contracting in both the United States and the United Kingdom. One source contends that security concerns are taking precedence over civil liberties.[9]

In modern democratic polities, citizens are generally conferred with a bundle of civil, political, economic and social rights. Civil and political rights are constitutionally enshrined in all liberal democracies. Economic and social rights, which classically manifested themselves through the welfare state, are generally statutory based.

Historically, citizenship has possessed strong exclusionary tendencies.[10] Thus, whilst ancient Athens is cited as an epoch-breaking era of direct democracy, it must be remembered that women, slaves and migrants were excluded from participating in the *Polis* and only resident adult males were conferred with the status of citizenship. Similarly, during the 19th century, elites resisted moves towards universal adult suffrage. Non-property-owning males and women were denied the

---

8 Galston, 2004: 263.
9 Hudson, 2003.
10 Delanty, 1995.

political right to vote for their representatives. It was only after the First World War that political citizenship was extended to all adult members of the political system irrespective of gender or social class.

There is a strong tension between civil and political rights on the one hand and social and economic rights on the other. This is hardly surprising as both sets of rights have different ideological origins. Civil and political rights owe their origins to liberal and democratic traditions respectively. Freedom of expression, assembly and association are the three great classical liberal constitutional rights. On the other hand, universal adult suffrage became the clarion call of 19th-century democrats. By the early 20th century, a marriage of both ideologies resulted in the birth of Western liberal democracy.

Economic and social rights are usually (though not exclusively) considered the ideological property of the social democratic labour movement. Such rights are also associated with welfare liberals such as J.M. Keynes and T.H. Marshall. From the 1940s onwards, social democrats advocated the extension of universal citizenship rights to include those in the social and economic sphere.

Believing that *de facto* citizenship was impossible in the absence of such rights, the welfare state became the vehicle through which social democrats extended the egalitarian impulses of citizenship beyond the civil and political spheres. As such, the welfare state in its social democratic guise possessed significant redistributive tendencies. Participation in the political system, society and economy can only be realised when civil and political rights are complemented with social and economic rights. Outcomes ranging from social exclusion to poverty are probable in the absence of social and economic rights. Citizenship in this holistic sense provides individuals with the opportunity to become full and proactive members of their respective polities, economies and societies.

Citizenship with an associated rights-centred approach is not deeply engrained in Irish political culture. This situation can be traced to various factors, including the near monopoly which the Catholic Church exercised over social policy and the absence of a strong social democratic base. However, the primary barrier to the evolution of a citizenship framework is the fact that a clientelist culture has taken hold in the Irish political system. Individuals have tended to rely very heavily on clientelist/brokerage-type representations to have their grievances addressed. The belief arose that 'a word in a politician's ear' could prove crucial in successfully addressing a grievance. Whilst the clientelist framework has been extensively examined in the Irish political science literature, it has generally focused on how clientelist pressures shape the behaviour of TDs. Clientelism's impact on the evolution or non-evolution of a citizenship framework has been largely neglected.

This clientelist culture has proven to be a significant obstacle for the evolution of a citizenship framework. Rather than asserting their citizenship rights, individuals depended on an elected intermediary to address their grievances. In fact, the essence of a clientelist culture is the evolution of a dyadic, asymmetrical power relationship. Clientelism quite simply erodes the concept of citizenship, particularly for the poor. By personalising grievances, it encourages clients to ignore systemic and structural reasoning.

Since the advent of the so-called Celtic Tiger economy in the mid-1990s, a consumerist model has taken root in Ireland. The consumerist model is the ideological bedfellow of the so-called new public management paradigm. New public management is an approach which seeks to apply market principles to the provision of public goods. Individuals are treated as market consumers rather than as citizens with enforceable rights. The consumerist model is the opposite of a holistic citizenship model, which confers members of the political system with universal rights of access to education, housing and healthcare. Access is guaranteed rather than contingent on ability to pay. Individuals are treated as citizens with rights rather than consumers with purchasing power.

Consumerism's normative base relies on self-regarding rather than other-regarding acts. Thus, consumerism de-emphasises unselfish acts of human agency, such as generalised reciprocity, which Putnam defines as 'the practice of helping others with no expectation of gain'.[11] Consumerism lacks notions of community, solidarity and requirements of social obligation to others. Adopting a shallow and impoverished account of human agency, consumerism treats individuals as self-satisfying, egotistic market actors. In effect, consumerist discourse advocates what one source describes as the privatisation of citizenship.[12]

Consumerism has a long history. This is evident from Macpherson's account of liberal democracy in its early 19th-century guise:

> Its advocacy is based on the assumption that man is an infinite consumer, that his overriding motivation is to maximise the flow of satisfactions, or utilities, to him from society, and that a national society is simply such a collection of individuals.[13]

Writing on the influential 1943 publication *Capitalism, Socialism and Democracy*, Pateman observes that its author Joseph Schumpeter compared electoral politics to the operation of the market. Pateman employs consumerist language to illuminate her argument:

---

11 Putnam, 2000: 505.
12 Somers, 2000: 24.
13 Macpherson, 1988: 43.

Schumpeter compared the political competition for votes to the operation of the (economic) market; voters like consumers choose between the policies (products) offered by competing political entrepreneurs and the parties regulate the competition like trade associations in the economic sphere.[14]

Forty years have elapsed since Pateman wrote her book, but these words are even more relevant today. The language of the market, marketing and public relations has contaminated liberal democracy's most sacrosanct process: electoral politics. In this respect, a market-driven consumerist rhetoric has further eroded notions of the public good. In the very arena where the notion of the public good should be paramount, the market-driven ethos pervades the process. If politics treats electors like consumers, electors may very well behave as consumers.

It appears that a consumerist discourse is establishing firm roots in contemporary Ireland. This is hardly surprising given that a reconstituted 19th-century classical liberalism appeared on the political stage during the last two decades of the 20th century. Reappearing in the guise of Thatcherism and Reaganism in the 1980s, individuals are treated as consumers rather than citizens. Both the rhetoric and policy positions possess a decidedly hard, uncompromising, free market edge. Somers captures this hard edge eloquently:

> Instead, the punitive language of moral degradation, dependency and failed personal behaviour has been resurrected to explain social exclusion and poverty. This is the dark underside of romancing the market and reviling the state; here, the indignities of poverty are but collateral damage in the exigency of ministering first to the ever-expanding demands of stateless cash.[15]

---

14 Pateman, 1970: 3.
15 Somers, 2000: 25.

Notoriously, former British Prime Minister Margaret Thatcher suggested that there was no such thing as society, only a collection of individuals. In this vein, Corrigan suggests that 'consumers are the perfect creatures of capitalism'.[16] It is clear that Ireland has not proved immune from the political influences of the United Kingdom.[17] Currently, consumerism is deeply embedded in Ireland's political system. I argue that there is a particular obligation to challenge the consumerist frame. By shifting to a civic republicanism framework the notion of the common good could be advocated by the Dáil.

My preferred framework for membership of the political community is citizenship, which encompasses social and economic rights and incorporates a republican concept of civic virtue. I reject outright both the consumerist and clientelist frameworks. As previously indicated, both frameworks offer a shallow and impoverished normative account of human agency. Consumerism favours selfish acts to the detriment of other-regarding acts. Through its emphasis on personalism, clientelism disempowers individuals. Both frameworks generate asymmetrical power relationships, particularly for the most vulnerable and marginalised, so both models are incompatible with citizenship.

In its most challenging guise citizenship invites members of the political community to mould a virtuous civic circle which places the common good at its normative centre. Turner's definition of citizenship satisfies key elements of my preferred framework:

> As an ensemble of rights and obligations that determine an individual's access to social and economic resources … his juridic identity is part of

---

16 Corrigan, 1997: 182.
17 Allen, 2000; Lynch, 2001.

a civil society organised around a set of values which we may broadly define as 'civic virtue'.[18]

It is important to emphasise three points. Firstly, citizenship has major implications for an individual's access to economic and social resources. In the absence of economic and social rights, individuals will be hampered in their capacity to access such resources. Many individuals suffer *de facto* class discrimination in Ireland. This is evident for example in the sphere of educational access. Secondly, inequality of access to social and economic resources simultaneously hinders individuals in their role as members of the political community. *De jure* equal members of the political community are *de facto* profoundly unequal. Educational disadvantage, for example, which may range from illiteracy to non-third-level attendance, may hinder individuals in their capacity to access vital information and engage in political dialogue and analysis. Thirdly, citizenship is usually ascribed rather than acquired. An individual at birth becomes a citizen. Thus, there is a very strong onus on the political system to be just in its ascription of an 'ensemble of rights and obligations'.

What of civic virtue? Is it possible for consumerism and civic virtue to happily co-exist? Clearly, it is not acceptable to eliminate private interests. European history has witnessed the horrendous consequences which occur when the collective (Fascism and Communism) smothers and absorbs the private sphere. Freedom perishes. A vibrant private sphere is a necessary condition of a free society but a private sphere cannot be held to be both a necessary and sufficient condition of freedom. On the contrary, a vibrant civic space is an essential prerequisite for a substantive rather than a purely formal understanding of freedom. To

---

18 Turner, 2000: 23.

be succinct, civic virtue cannot flourish when private interests colonise the public good as the public good perishes in such circumstances. Schwarzmantel highlights this point:

> Civic virtue is a fragile growth in societies divided by differences of the market, which reinforce a self-image of society as a bundle of consumers, each with their separate interests. Contemporary liberal democracy seems to bear out the nightmare scenario of de Tocqueville, with his picture of an excessively individualised society of people indifferent to the fate of their fellow citizens.[19]

This has been the trend since the arrival of Thatcherism on the global political stage. Private interests are in the ascendant to the detriment of the public good. Can civic virtue be rescued in this hostile political environment? Philosophically, the answer to this question is yes. Republican concepts possess the potential to release civic virtue from the suffocating embrace of market-driven understandings of politics. Offering an alternative to liberal democratic normative accounts, Schwartzmantel's perspective draws on the republican political theory, which favours the common good or public interest. It is worth stating, though, that there is probably not one coherent theory called republicanism. It is a broad family, derived from different sources and possessing contrasting normative orientations during various historical periods and moments.[20] According to Schwartzmantel, the liberal democratic perspective is deeply flawed as its individualistic and particularistic orientation creates a fragmented political system. This contrasts sharply with the republicanism he advocates because:

---

19   Schwartzmantel, 2003: 143.
20   Isaac, 2005.

Its difference from liberalism resides in that it operates with some concept of a common good or public interest, which is not just the sum total of individual interests.[21]

Schwartzmantel makes it clear that he does not seek the elimination of private interests. What is sought is a pluralistic framework, which creates a citizen identity. Thus, singular notions of identity and extreme forms of collectivism are rejected because of the threat posed to personal freedoms, particularly civil and political rights. The republican concepts of civic virtue and the common good offer a valuable counter-narrative to the individual as a self-regarding, maximising 'market man'.

There is a crucial overlap between civic republican values and the ideal typical standards of a deliberative democratic community. Both perspectives position the common good at their normative centre. Both perspectives hold that consumerism is a threat to the common good. It will be recalled that Habermas and other theorists contend that consumerism is eroding the public sphere as classically understood. Consumerism threatens two aspects of the public sphere. Firstly, it encourages the elevation of self-regarding market relations to the detriment of the common good. Secondly, it encourages the uncritical acceptance of information. This is particularly the case in situations where consumption and the mass media have become so intertwined as to make them inseparable.

TONY BLAIR, TURKISH WORKERS AND A NIGERIAN REFUGEE

Tony Blair resigned as British Prime Minister in June 2007. A key reason for his resignation can be traced to Britain's participation in

---

21 Schwartzmantel, 2003: 8.

the invasion and subsequent occupation of Iraq by the United States. Whilst Blair retained a parliamentary majority, public support for his actions in Iraq evaporated over time. In this regard, it is important to distinguish between a House of Commons majority and the public sphere. Even if the Executive achieves its objectives via majority votes in Parliament, it may subsequently be electorally punished if it defies a strong consensus in the public sphere. Blair operated in a radically different political setting to that of any of his predecessors, namely the contemporary public sphere. This is a crucial point in understanding Blair's demise.

Blair's management of the Iraqi crisis took place at the height of the modern communications revolution. In this respect, he was subject to a level of public scrutiny which none of his predecessors had to contend with. Before Blair, Anthony Eden was the most recent Prime Minister to fall foul of an international crisis. On the other hand, Winston Churchill flourished during war and international crisis. However, unlike Blair, neither Churchill nor Eden were obliged to face live studio debates before sceptical audiences at the conclusion of their parliamentary orations.

In reality, Blair was but one player in an enlarged, ever expanding and, apparently, radicalised public sphere. The activation of the public sphere was made possible by modern communications. Citizens watched debates live in the House of Commons. No sooner had Mr Blair resumed his seat in the Commons than one heard an alternative opinion from an expert on the other side of the globe. Journalists reported live from potential trouble spots. Friends discussed the crisis via emails and text messages. Social movements used the Internet to promote their cause. Leaders such as Blair and peace activists vied with each other for the public ear. They competed with each other in order to persuade the public of the merits of their respective cases.

The situation demonstrated that the public sphere is no mere debating club. Potentially, an excited and agitated public sphere can rein in elites thereby influencing policy outcomes. The public sphere was rarely more agitated than it was at the height of the Iraqi crisis during 2003.

Discursive accountability prevailed both inside and outside the British Parliament. On 18 March 2003, 139 Labour MPs voted against going to war in a Commons vote. The Prime Minister was forced to rely on Conservative MPs to acquire parliamentary approval. The previous day, Robin Cook resigned as Leader of the House of Commons because of his opposition to the pending war. Whilst the invasion of Iraq proceeded as planned on 20 March, Tony Blair was leading a divided country and Parliament.[22]

For politicians to ignore a strong consensus in the public sphere might prove fatal. It should therefore be no surprise that Blair paid the price in the 2005 general election. With a reduced majority in the Commons, Blair's position looked less than secure. As such, it could be argued that discursive accountability, which was played out in highly agitated public spheres (both weak and strong), was ultimately translated into political power at the ballot box. The public sphere exposes all political leaders to a previously unprecedented extent. In particular, it illuminates gaps between political leaders and ordinary citizens.

On Tuesday 8 February, 2005, Socialist Party TD Joe Higgins rose from his seat on the Opposition backbenches in Dáil Éireann to put questions to the Taoiseach during Leaders' Questions. He alleged that Gama Construction was grossly exploiting Turkish workers. In his reply, the Taoiseach kept emphasising that labour law existed to protect all workers. Because Deputy Higgins' question generated

---

22   Cook, 2003; Glover, 2003.

huge media interest, he succeeded in exposing a major scandal which involved the use of international bank accounts in Amsterdam to hide money belonging to the Turkish workers. Apart from a valuable debate in the public sphere, a number of positive outcomes were achieved; for example the Cabinet made an executive decision to increase the number of staff working for the Labour Inspectorate.[23]

The Gama workers' case is an example of exchanges on the floor of Dáil Éireann igniting a debate in the contemporary public sphere. All too often it is stated that Dáil Éireann is bypassed, but in this case the genesis of what ultimately became a major public issue was Leaders' Questions in Dáil Éireann. Discursive accountability was, therefore, of crucial importance. Secondly, it is worth noting that Deputy Higgins was Dáil Éireann's only Socialist Party member. Whilst he was episodically entitled to speaking rights equivalent to Leaders of the Opposition, it is nevertheless a considerable feat for a 'one man show' to generate a national debate. The case illustrates that one member can make a difference. The Dáil as a forum can claim a degree of credit for these outcomes. The case also highlights that power relationships can be transformed via the public sphere. The politically and economically disempowered became discursively empowered. If anything, the standing of the Gama workers was very much in the ascendant whilst that of the company was in free fall.

Exchanges during Leaders' Questions, Tuesday 8 February 2005, on the Gama Workers Controversy:

> **Mr J. Higgins:** Many recent reports in the media have highlighted grievous exploitation of immigrant workers. In the construction

---

23 Dooley, 2005; O'Halloran, 2005.

industry SIPTU officials have found such exploitation. Recently the bricklayers union, BATU, was so concerned that it met the Polish and Lithuanian ambassadors to highlight a gross abuse of their nationals. I wish to raise, in particular, one major scandal of immigrant worker exploitation of massive proportions. There is a major foreign-based multinational construction company employing approximately 10,000 people, 2,000 approximately in this State, which has secured massive local authority and State contracts here. This company imports workers from its home base, who do not speak English, controls their passports and work permits, accommodates them often in company barracks, demands an extent of hours worked that can only be called grotesque and, incredibly, pays unskilled construction workers between €2 and €3 per hour basic pay and skilled workers somewhere over €3 an hour. In short, this is a modern version of bonded labour. The instigator is Turkish-based Gama Construction Ireland Limited.

The national minimum wage is €7 an hour. The registered employment agreement for the lowest paid operative in construction is €12.96 an hour. This case is a national scandal financed by extensive public funding. I call on the Taoiseach to ask the Minister and the Department of Enterprise, Trade and Employment, as a matter of priority, to order an immediate investigation into Gama Construction and its pay and work practices. Will its records be demanded? Will the Taoiseach ensure that interviews are conducted with workers out of the way of company pressure? Will he ensure the Department sees that no worker is victimised as a result of this investigation and if Gama Construction should act to send workers home, a method used by these companies, those workers are sheltered and protected? I will ask SIPTU, to whom the company signed up some of its workers as a cover, to do so. Companies like Gama Construction not only exploit immigrant workers but also undermine wages and conditions for all workers and … they underbid other companies who pay the full rate. This is a serious matter.

The Taoiseach: I reiterate that every worker is entitled to the full protection of the law. The workers referred to by the Deputy are entitled to full legislative protection. The inspectorate of the Department of Enterprise, Trade and Employment can apply the full powers and rigours of the law to inspect the records and investigate any breaches.

I am aware of some other cases where trade unions have asked the Department to investigate and this has been fully carried out. The Deputy has referred to the company by name. The Minister for Enterprise, Trade and Employment is in the House and will raise the matter of inspection with his departmental officials. Legislation to deal with such cases is pending. Any information on the case will be followed up. The key point is that every worker is entitled to the full protection of the law. The minimum rate of pay has been agreed through the Labour Court and employers have an obligation under the law to pay that rate. The inspectorate implements the law and investigates any employer in breach of the law.

Mr J. Higgins: As the Taoiseach stated, the workers have entitlements. However, these workers are vulnerable and afraid. That is why they need the security of knowing that any attempted victimisation will be resisted. I welcome the Taoiseach's undertaking that the Minister for Enterprise, Trade and Employment will take action. We will make every information available to the inspectors. There should be many more than 21 of them, by the way.

This company has done work for local authorities. It built the Ennis and Ballincollig bypasses and was proud of the fact that it completed the work six months ahead of schedule. That is easy when using a bonded labour force working eleven or twelve hours a day with two Sundays off in a month. The company can underbid because of these rates of pay.

I want the Minister to take personal charge along with the Secretary General of the Department because it is a serious allegation. This is not a fly-by-night operation from the boot of a car. This is a major company financed by major State public contracts. I will therefore keep a close eye on it. The rights of immigrant workers are paramount, as are the rights of Irish workers who are undermined by this.

An Ceann Comhairle: I advise the Deputy that it is not appropriate to name a company in the House when it is not here to defend itself.

Mr J. Higgins: It is entirely appropriate because –

An Ceann Comhairle: No, Deputy, it is not. It is a long-standing precedent in this House.

Mr J. Higgins: It takes advantage of its power over vulnerable workers to exploit them. I will not allow that to happen.

An Ceann Comhairle: There can be no argument about it. The Chair has ruled.

The Taoiseach: I do not know if Deputy Higgins or others have made a complaint to the Labour Inspectorate about the particular company. The Minister will raise the matter with the inspectorate. I note the Deputy has said he will make the information available to the inspectorate and this will be helpful. I reiterate that every worker in this country is entitled to the protection of labour law. This has been enforced in many cases. Members may remember a case three years ago where the Department took firm and positive action to uphold the rights of the workers who were from one of the now member states, then an applicant country. The same examination will take place in this case.[24]

Another case is that of Olukunle Eluhanla, a Nigerian refugee studying for his leaving certificate in Palmerstown Community School, Dublin. Apparently well integrated with his classmates, he was only three months away from sitting the State Leaving Certificate Examination of June 2005, when without warning, he was arrested by An Garda Síochána and deported back to Nigeria. The deportation order was signed and approved by the Minister for Justice. As public controversy began to grow, the then Minister, Mr Michael McDowell, remained resolute, refusing to change his mind. Few political commentators could have predicted the episode's eventual outcome.

Olukunle's sixth-year classmates organised a campaign to reverse the Minister's decision. In particular, the campaign stressed that Olukunle should be allowed to complete his Leaving Certificate examination. Arriving at Kildare Street on Wednesday 23 March 2005, the students protested outside Leinster House and the issue became a major media story. The previous evening, Tuesday 22 March, Minister McDowell defended his action during an adjournment debate in Dáil Éireann (see

---

24 www.oireachtas.ie

below). The students' decision to voice their concerns publicly brought support from many sources, including anti-racist groups and the Catholic Church. Feeling the political pressure, on Thursday 24 March, McDowell reversed his decision. Arrangements were put in place to bring the Nigerian student back to Ireland. McDowell was subjected to intense criticism for his handing of the entire episode.[25]

A number of observations can be made. The students recognised that the Dáil was a site from which they could project their message. Discursive accountability was an important feature of the episode. Political astuteness and an awareness of the public sphere characterised their behaviour. It must be emphasised that the students compelled a Minister to change his mind. As such, discursive accountability resulted in a political outcome. The students sought to generate an emotional response from members of Dáil Éireann and the wider political system. Relying on an empathetic response from the public, the students transcended a purely rational approach. The pain of a fellow human being was more important than language alone. Iris Marion Young's concept of communicative language comes to the fore again.

Extract from Dáil Adjournment Debate on Tuesday 22 March 2005 concerning Olukunle Eluhanla:

> **Minister for Justice, Equality and Law Reform (Mr McDowell):** It is important that I preface my remarks by pointing out that it has been the policy of successive Ministers for Justice, Equality and Law Reform not to reveal the personal details of the cases of individual applicants for asylum whose applications are received and treated in confidence. Having said that, I do not wish to shirk the issues Members have raised.

---

25 Cullen, 2005.

Underlying this case are two fundamental principles. First, the cases of asylum seekers who apply for our protection must be fairly and independently examined. Second, a deportation process must be central to the proper running of any immigration and asylum system. The definition of 'refugee' is well known and set out in section 2 of the 1996 Act. In the case of each asylum seeker, the task is to determine whether he or she is deemed to meet the terms of the definition on the basis of all of the information gleaned. I emphasise that all of the information is considered.

Under the Refugee Act 1996, two independent statutory offices were established to consider applications and appeals in respect of refugee status and to make recommendations to the Minister for Justice, Equality and Law Reform on whether such status should be granted. These offices are the Office of the Refugee Applications Commissioner and the Refugee Appeals Tribunal. Every asylum applicant is guaranteed an investigation and determination of his or her claim at first instance by the Refugee Applications Commissioner. Every asylum applicant is guaranteed a right of appeal to a statutorily independent and separate body, the Refugee Appeals Tribunal. Every asylum applicant is also guaranteed access to legal assistance provided by the Refugee Legal Service.

Under the provisions of section 17(1) of the Refugee Act 1996, the final decision in respect of an asylum application is a matter for the Minister for Justice, Equality and Law Reform based on the recommendation of the Commissioner or the decision of the Tribunal. However, under the legislative scheme of things I am obliged, save in exceptional circumstances, to accept a recommendation that a person should be given refugee status. Such a decision is made by the Minister as soon as possible following receipt of the relevant papers from the Commissioner or the Tribunal, as appropriate.

There has been a notable pattern of unaccompanied minors, that is, people under the age of 18, arriving in Ireland claiming refugee status. In the case of Nigerians, of which there were in the region of 105 unaccompanied minor asylum seekers for the past two years, since there are no direct passenger services between Ireland and Nigeria, these unaccompanied minors must have put in place elaborate travel arrangements involving transit through other safe countries in the European Union. Comprehensive safeguards are provided in the Refugee Act and in relevant procedures in ORAC [Office of the Refugee Applications Commissioner] and RAT [Refugee Appeals Tribunal] for dealing with asylum claims for unaccompanied minors. These include the minor being placed in the care of a Health Board on arrival in the State pending a decision being made on the making of an asylum application; dealing with such applications as a matter of priority by the Refugee Applications Commissioner; that the processing of cases is in line with child specific procedures having regard in particular to UNHCR [United Nations High Commissioner for Refugees] guidelines on best practice for dealing with unaccompanied minors; that unaccompanied minors are only interviewed in the presence of a Health Board representative; and to ensure that the special needs of minors and particularly unaccompanied minors are properly taken into account. A group of experienced ORAC interviewers has received additional specialised training to assist them in working on cases involving unaccompanied minors. This training includes the input of child care experts with a focus on issues such as psychological needs, child specific aspects of the refugee process, the role of the social worker and other issues particular to refugee determination for unaccompanied minors.

In this case, Deputy Cuffe stated that the person in question came here at the age of fifteen, but that is factually incorrect. In February 2002 the person referred to by the Deputies arrived in Ireland seeking asylum. The date of birth given in the asylum application indicated that he was seventeen years of age. On the basis of that date he was by no stretch of the imagination what newspapers have described as a schoolboy but was twenty years of age when he was deported. Moreover, he verbally indicated to the escorting Garda team that he was twenty-one years of age.

I am constrained by law from making public the exact details of the asylum claim and will not deal here with the credibility or strength of the person's original claim. The important point to note is that his claim was assessed by the two independent bodies that came to the same conclusion, that he was not entitled to refugee protection.

In October 2003 the person concerned was informed that he was found not to be a refugee and was informed of the three options then open to him, first, to leave the State before his case was considered for deportation, to consent to the making of a deportation order in respect of him or to make written representations, within 15 working days, to me as Minister for Justice, Equality and Law Reform setting out reasons he should not be deported, that is, why he should be allowed to remain temporarily in the State.

Representations were made by this person, which included the fact that he was a student. The case was examined under section 3 of the Immigration Act 1999 and section 5 of the Refugee Act 1996, prohibition of refoulement, including consideration of all representations received on his behalf and a deportation order was signed for him on 21 January 2005.

Ms Burton: The Minister did not examine the file.

An Leas-Cheann Comhairle: Order.

Mr McDowell: The deportation order was sent to the person at his home address and the accompanying letter instructed him to report to the offices of the Garda national immigration bureau on 3 March 2005.

Ms Burton: The Minister did not examine the file at any stage.

An Leas-Cheann Comhairle: Order, please.[26]

The two cases just cited share common themes. Other-regarding acts prevailed over self-regarding acts. In the case of Olukunle Eluhanla, sixth-year students rallied behind a fellow student. Taking on one of the most powerful Departments of State, the students were motivated by justice and fairness. Putting Olukunle's predicament before their own welfare (focusing on study and exams), their pleas struck a chord with the public. Deputy Higgins also appealed to the other-regarding and empathic impulses of citizens. Citizens not 'romanticists of the free market' reappeared if only momentarily. The public sphere

---

26 www.oireachtas.ie

was agitated via Dáil Éireann. Dáil Éireann triggered discursive accountability in the public sphere.

In both cases, the powerless and most vulnerable were given a voice. Agitated public spheres translated discursive spaces into concrete political outcomes. The Executive responded to public pressure, which was played out in the public sphere. Both episodes were very emotional in their dynamic. The participants appealed as much to the hearts (passions) as to the minds (rationality). Young's concept of communicative language which rejects a purely rational approach by incorporating the emotions and passions therefore possesses considerable theoretical and practical potential.

These cases demonstrate that it is feasible for Dáil Éireann to act as a normative vehicle in the public sphere.

SOCIAL PARTNERSHIP AND EXPERTS

I now focus on future possibilities. Concerns have already been raised in the previous chapter about the undemocratic nature of Ireland's social partnership model. Given that the model shapes many public policy outcomes, this democratic deficit ought to be redressed. I contend that the model can be democratised by deploying the norm of discursive accountability. Combining this norm with institutional innovation would be of further help. It will be recalled from the previous chapter that there are four phases to each partnership agreement, namely pre-negotiation, negotiations, agreement and implementation. Secrecy and non-transparency are the enemies of democracy. The key challenge, therefore, is to inject transparency into the process.

Transparency could be injected via a specialist Committee of Dáil Éireann; the Select Dáil Committee on Social Partnership would be assigned responsibility for bringing the process into the public arena.

Similar to the Public Accounts Committee, an Opposition Deputy would chair it. Generously resourced, it would be provided with adequate secretarial and research facilities. Before the commencement of negotiations, all social partners would be obliged to come before the Committee and make a formal submission and presentation. Subsequently, the Committee could examine each partner. These presentations could be broadcast live on the web, television and radio. Thus, discursive accountability in the public sphere could come into play at an early stage of the process.

Many legitimate objections might be raised about the democratic value of this exercise. Pre-negotiation submissions would be tactical and strategic in orientation. Strategically, the partners would not be revealing their true hand. Rather, the presentations would be designed to enhance their negotiating positions and presentations would be artificial in nature. Strategic power relations would merely have been transferred from one arena (the Executive) to another (the Parliament).

However, it is important to emphasise the following points about this process. The veil of secrecy which currently surrounds social partnership is removed, if only partially. Strategic relations are transferred from a closed arena to a public parliamentary arena. Partners are compelled to explain and justify their positions to democratically elected members of Dáil Éireann. The justifications are mediated to an observing and evaluating public through the media. It might be objected that subsequent to this public process the partners would return behind their veil of secrecy with the Executive making the previous parliamentary exercise a mere window-dressing exercise. Could it not become a parliamentary charade designed to confer democratic legitimacy to what is in democratic terms illegitimate? The question therefore arises whether anything can be done to inject the actual negotiations process with greater democracy.

There are several proposals which might be considered. The most radical proposal is that all negotiations should be conducted in public. Transfer the television cameras to Government Buildings and let the public witness the wheeling and dealing that pervades the process. This suggestion is rejected out of hand for one reason only: it is not feasible. An element of secrecy is probably required to reach an agreement. There is a danger that there might be perpetual 'playing to the cameras' resulting in a negotiating stalemate. Partners would frequently be required to speak on an 'off the record basis'. For actors accustomed to conventional negotiating techniques, it would be too much of a culture shock. However, a verbatim report of all contributions should be prepared and this report would become public after an agreement is reached. The process is therefore conferred with *retrospective* transparency. In overall terms, this is a circumstance where desired outcomes (efficiency) trump transparency (democracy).

Assuming the social partners reach agreement, the final package could then be sent back to the Committee on Social Partnership for consideration. The Committee could then invite submissions from Sectoral Committees such as Education, Environment, Agriculture and Social Affairs. The social partners could then appear before the Committee for a second time. During these hearings, the partners could once again be compelled to justify (discursive accountability) their positions publicly. Having completed these hearings the Committee could then compile a report of all submissions made seeking to place the common good at its normative and deliberative centre.

The social partnership agreement and report is then placed before both Houses of the Oireachtas for full plenary discussion. Finally, Dáil Éireann takes a vote to either reject or accept the agreement. Given the centrality of social partnership to the policy-making process, this vote has the same status as the annual budget vote. Were the Executive to lose the vote, it would be deemed the equivalent of being defeated on a motion of confidence. This vote would probably be a foregone conclusion. Executives rarely lose votes, crucial or otherwise, in the Irish parliamentary system. Since the foundation of the State, Executives have to date lost only two votes of confidence. Only one budget vote has been lost. Thus, the partners could be assured that once agreement is reached they would not have to enter a fresh round of negotiations. The important point to note is that the process will have been democratised.

The Committee on Social Partnership would be assigned a significant role in monitoring and reviewing the agreement's implementation, but primary responsibility for actual implementation of the agreement would remain with the Executive. However, the Committee would offer an important space to those partners who feel aggrieved by apparent deviance from the agreed terms. The Committee would also invite Ministers and officials to account for their actions or inaction. Sectoral Committees would from time to time be invited to submit their observations on the agreement's implementation. The Committee would from time to time lay reports before both Houses of the Oireachtas. Such reports would automatically spark plenary debates within a tightly specified time limit.

The previous chapter also raised democratic and financial concerns regarding the use of consultants and working groups by Government Departments. The process of appointing and monitoring the activities of consultants should be injected with a large measure of transparency. Dáil Éireann in its Committee guise is the most appropriate forum in this regard. The question arises whether there could be a prospective prudential role for Sectoral Committees in this sphere. In other words, could Committees intervene at the pre-spending stage? I argue that Committees should enter the prudential fray before the fact. The biggest bar to such a development is a cultural or attitudinal one and would most likely meet considerable resistance from Ministers and civil servants. It would be deemed a form of trespass upon functions which are properly in the Executive's domain, particularly those of a budgetary nature. Nevertheless, as has been iterated elsewhere throughout this book, there is evidence to suggest that attitudes within Leinster House are changing. It may therefore be a propitious time for Sectoral Committees to advocate their prudential credentials in this area.

I do not envisage a situation whereby the Sectoral Committees examine every proposal to hire consultants. Rather, at the prospective stage the Committees examine a small selection of proposals thoroughly and members would decide which proposals are prudentially suspect. This approach has a number of advantages. Committees would not suffer from overload. There is also the question of effective Government versus democracy. Committee involvement in all proposals would cause stasis, thereby preventing the Executive from hiring necessary experts. It is a question of achieving the right balance between democratic accountability and allowing the Executive to govern effectively. Of course, Committees would retain the right to examine decisions retrospectively. After all, it is highly probable that some prudentially suspect proposals would escape the prospective sifting process.

The Committees' work (prospective and retrospective) would of course be informed by the norm of discursive accountability. Government departments would have to give clear and cogent reasons in public as to why it is necessary to hire consultants rather than use in-house expertise. Clear budgetary parameters would be provided to the

Committee. There would also be an obligation on consultants to appear before the Committee to justify their fees. Initially, at least, it is envisaged that the Committee would be afforded powers of recommendation only. Government Departments would be afforded the final say when it comes to hiring and firing consultants.

This position is adopted for three very good reasons. Firstly, the salience of discursive accountability derives from the public articulation of reasons rather than the exercise of classic power relations. If the Committee were to be assigned ultimate decision-making authority in this sphere, it would quickly become an arena of strategic power relations for consultancy firms. Committee members would be targeted and lobbied. Secondly, to confer the Committee with decision-making powers in this arena would be too much of a systemic culture shock. It might also run into practical difficulties as the 1937 Constitution does not envisage such a role for Parliament. An incremental approach to reform is perhaps the wisest. Thirdly, the power of recommendation ought not to be dismissed or under-estimated. Should a departmental decision ultimately backfire, Ministers and civil servants would have some explaining to do. Recommendations are still imbued with the authority of a Parliamentary Committee which conducted its business in public.

When the project is completed, Ministers, civil servants and consultants would appear before Committee members again. All parties would be obliged to justify any imprudent expenditure of public monies. The Committee would produce periodic reports on its findings and recommendations. In accordance with standard practice, these reports would be laid before both Houses of the Oireachtas.

Dáil Éireann ought to act as an advocate for the common good via the contemporary public sphere. The Dáil can potentially achieve this objective. Given that Irish politics has historically been dominated by a clientelist orientation, and that a consumerist discourse is becoming firmly rooted in contemporary Ireland, this objective will not be realised with ease. Nevertheless, there is evidence to suggest that Dáil Éireann can make a difference. It will be recalled that Dáil Éireann agitated the public sphere in two specific cases, namely Gama workers and Olukunle Eluhanla. In each case, other-regarding acts prevailed over self-centred strategic interest. Similarly, discursive accountability was an important feature of each episode. I am not suggesting that these cases are typical, rather the cases demonstrate that it is feasible for Dáil Éireann to act as a normative vehicle in the public sphere.

I sketched future spaces (social partnership and expert sovereignty) where Dáil Éireann might conceivably act as an advocate for the polity's common good via the public sphere. I argued that the social partnership model suffers from serious democratic deficiencies. These deficiencies can be at least partly overcome by removing the cloak of secrecy surrounding social partnership. One way to achieve this objective is to assign Dáil Éireann an enhanced role in all stages of the process; in this way, it would move beyond its current spectator status. I envisage that its enhanced future role would be played out in the contemporary public sphere. In particular, Dáil Éireann's enhanced role under social partnership would challenge all actors involved in the process by measuring their contributions against the benchmark of the common good. The process would therefore be injected with a new dynamic.

The public sphere should not be perceived in purely abstract terms. In the contemporary communication society, it is a reality of everyday life. Like all facets of the empirical world, it may stubbornly resist efforts to impose rigorous conceptual order. Nevertheless, that is not to say it does not exist in the worlds of everyday political reality. As the section on Tony Blair elucidated, modern politicians live in a political world radically different to that of their predecessors. Contemporary politicians are compelled to be actors in a hyper-pluralistic public sphere. Their predecessors did not have to cope with the challenges of the contemporary public sphere.

In contemporary Ireland, consumerism is a major obstacle preventing the emergence of a framework centred on the common good. In the short to medium term, this obstacle may prove insurmountable. However, scholars and political activists must continue to search for those spaces in which other-regarding acts prevail. These spaces may provide a small springboard for greater things.

12

CONTEMPORARY DÁIL ÉIREANN

This is a peculiarity of ours: we do not say that a man who takes no interest in politics is a man who minds his own business; we say that he has no business here at all.[1]

But on every subject on which difference of opinion is possible, the truth depends on a balance being struck between two sets of conflicting reasons.[2]

We say that if the Dáil is to be a powerhouse of accountability, a true representative of the interests of the people, a place where maladministration leading to injustice can be investigated and rooted out, it has to be modern, efficient, dynamic and powerful.[3]

I believe that Dáil Éireann can most accurately be described as an institution of parliamentary governance. The position of Dáil Éireann as a participant in the processes of contemporary Irish governance has improved enormously in historical terms. Admittedly, coming from a weak base, it has acquired a stronger institutional identity within the political system. Improved resourcing combined with parliamentary

---

1 Pericles [430 BC], quoted in Crick, 2005.
2 Mill [1859], 1985: 98.
3 Rabbitte, 2003: 2.

professionalisation gives it a stronger voice. Dáil Éireann is not an example of a post-parliamentary institution. Dáil Éireann is not a spectator Parliament which is staid and static. On the contrary, my research suggests considerable institutional change.

The pace and depth of contemporary transformations are not leaving Dáil Éireann behind. In this regard, it is important that contemporary transformations not be cast in a negative light, as in Dáil Éireann's case they have acted as a catalyst for parliamentary reform. Once a primitive and impotent institution, Dáil Éireann has become an increasingly professional and potent actor. Dáil Éireann is no longer culturally and systemically subservient to the Executive.

There has been a vast increase in the number of actors involved in contemporary Irish politics. As such, the political system has expanded and this expansion has released Dáil Éireann from the shackles of a bilateral relationship with the Executive. Having escaped from this bilateral relationship, it has been able to build relationships on a multilateral basis; so a significantly expanded political system need not necessarily be a threat to parliaments. On the contrary, in Ireland's case this situation proved to be an opportunity rather than a constraint. Clearly, the presence of radical transformations *per se* in any political system cannot be held to be synonymous with post-parliamentary governance. Such transformations are a necessary but not a sufficient condition of post-parliamentary governance.

One could hardly challenge the post-parliamentary governance model's depiction that under conditions of contemporary governance collectively binding and authoritative decisions are made in a diverse range of non-parliamentary arenas. Even if this depiction is accepted, it is not to say, however, that such decisions are or ought to be beyond the reach of parliamentary scrutiny. And where meaningful scrutiny processes exist, it would be inaccurate to describe a parliament as marginal.

In chapters seven and eight I explored the position of the Dáil under three headings, namely resources, separation of powers and Standing Orders. Under all three headings significant progress was discovered. In respect of resources, this is particularly true if one adopts a longer-term view. Up until the late 1970s the House suffered serious resource deficiencies, making it nigh impossible to carve out a meaningful role for itself. The 2002 Deloitte and Touche Report was a significant milestone, signalling as it did a reform mood within Dáil Éireann.[4]

Under the separation of powers category, there is evidence of a shift from the Executive towards the Legislature. Subtle changes have occurred which suggest that the Executive is not displacing Dáil Éireann and there is a clear sense that the House is asserting itself. The single most important development in this regard is the establishment of an independent Commission for both Houses.

The Standing Orders of Dáil Éireann have changed radically since 1974. Bearing little resemblance to their predecessors, the 2002 Standing Orders have in overall terms improved Dáil Éireann's position. These include Leaders' Questions, a more inclusive Order of Business and a stronger Committee system. The 2002 Standing Orders demonstrate that the House is more outward looking. It is clearly envisaged in the Standing Orders that Committees should interact with civil society and this reflects what is currently taking place. The Committees have become an important space for civil society. Likewise, the televising of proceedings and the establishment of a public relations office demonstrate that Dáil Éireann is looking beyond Kildare Street.

In chapters nine and ten I explored the role of Dáil Éireann under four headings, namely European Union, civil society, social partnership

---

4   Deloitte and Touche, 2002.

and expert sovereignty. Both in law and practice Dáil Éireann currently enjoys a greatly enhanced scrutiny role of European Union legislation. With the advent of the European Union Scrutiny Act (2002) there has been a remarkable improvement at both legal and operational levels. Crucially, the 2002 Act affords the Dáil a form of prospective scrutiny. For the period 2002–2007, the Dáil chose to discharge these responsibilities via the Sub-Committee on European Scrutiny. This Committee scrutinised a huge volume of complex measures in a well-organised, structured and thoroughly professional approach. With the aid of more resources, it could undoubtedly do an even better job.

I clearly demonstrated that civil society, far from bypassing Dáil Éireann, is working through it. The emergence of a strong Committee system has facilitated this situation and Dáil Éireann in its Committee guise has become an important site for civic engagement. A symbiotic relationship exists between civil society and Parliamentary Committees, allowing Committees to carve out a distinct space in the political system.

Under the social partnership model, it is indeed accurate to state that Dáil Éireann has been crowded out: it is a passive spectator rather than a proactive participant. Dáil Éireann's exclusion from this vital policy sphere generates a democratic deficit. What is surprising is that, in an atmosphere which is conducive to Dáil reform, Deputies are blasé about remedying this deficiency. I have made specific suggestions on how this might be addressed.

I examined the widespread use of consultants and working groups by Government Departments. Democratic and financial concerns were expressed regarding the non-transparency of the appointments and monitoring process. I have suggested how Dáil Éireann's Sectoral Committees might inject the processes involved with transparency and democracy.

To the question of whether it is feasible for Dáil Éireann to become a proactive participant in the contemporary public sphere, I answer in the affirmative. I have clearly demonstrated, both theoretically and in practice, that such a role is feasible for Dáil Éireann. Furthermore, I have created a model which simultaneously moves beyond the liberal democratic framework and places the common good at its normative centre.

The key norm to be derived from this book is termed discursive accountability. The norm obliges actors, whether state or non-state, to provide reasons publicly for decisions made or not made. Crucially, reasons can be of both a passionate and dispassionate persuasion. As such, discursive accountability inspired by Young's theory of communicative democracy has made a sharp distinction between rational and reasoned discourse.

I have demonstrated that the norm of discursive accountability is capable of operating under conditions of contemporary governance. This is because the norm of discursive accountability provides a feasible real world role for Dáil Éireann by placing it at the political system's accountability centre rather than at its decisional centre. In a clear break with the normative underpinnings of the liberal democratic framework which expects the parliament to make all political decisions, Dáil Éireann's primary function becomes one of holding actors to account in the contemporary public sphere. Dáil Éireann thus provides a democratic and public forum where a range of actors would justify their decisions. These actors either receive the approval or condemnation of the public, depending on the quality of the reasons offered.

Significantly, the norm of discursive accountability also ensures that the reach of Dáil accountability extends to hitherto 'Parliament-free' zones of political activity such as social partnership and the appointment of consultants. The norm also assists Dáil Éireann's advocacy of the common good by obliging relevant actors to justify their decisions against benchmarks of public rather than selfish interest. In the case of consultants, for example, the benchmark might be a prudential one: Was the political system's money spent wisely? I draw on civic republican values in coming to an understanding of what constitutes the common good.

Whilst I conclude that Dáil Éireann possesses the capacity to act as a vehicle for the common good in the world of political reality, there remains one very significant barrier, a consumerist culture. Such a culture took root in Celtic Tiger Ireland. With its emphasis on self-maximising behaviour and uncritical consumption, it can prevent individuals from coming together to form a public sphere. Individuals behave as private actors rather than as public citizens. However, the current economic crisis may undermine this culture to some extent.

It should be emphasised that both the public sphere and the civic republican framework place the common good at their normative centre. As such, both positions seek to transcend an exclusively self-maximising and egotistical view of human behaviour. Both perspectives invite political actors to rise above their private preferences by engaging in other-regarding acts. There is, therefore, an unambiguous normative overlap between the public sphere and the civic republican framework.

Crucially, the norm of discursive accountability has proven capable of making the transition from the theoretical world to the world of political reality. In this context, I probed three real world settings, namely Tony Blair's premiership, the Gama workers controversy and the deportation and subsequent return of a young Nigerian refugee. Discursive accountability in the public sphere was an important feature in each case.

Young's theory of communicative democracy, in contradistinction to deliberative democracy, possesses considerable theoretical and practical potential. By lowering the ideal typical threshold, communicative democracy makes it a much more achievable ideal than deliberative democracy. Interestingly, in all three cases cited in chapter eleven communicative democracy possessed superior explanatory power and normative potential than its close relation, deliberative democracy. Deliberative democracy's emphasis on dispassionate and literal language disenfranchises all but the educationally privileged. That is not to say that deliberative democrats are misguided in their aversion to passionate discourse. Distorted speech in its multiple guises, be it rhetoric, sophistry, propaganda or contemporary public relations, should be treated with great circumspection and scepticism. But should such circumspection and scepticism lead us to displace our emotional essence as human beings? This book answers in the negative. Young offers a more humanistic interpretation of what constitutes communication. Crucially, her theory is also more effective at an operational level. Emotional ignition of the public sphere may be of particular discursive benefit for the voiceless and marginalised because it may resonate more with the observing and judging public. Equally, the dispossessed are better 'equipped' to communicate emotionally rather than deliberate dispassionately.

To date, the literature and public commentary has failed to capture the extent to which the position of Dáil Éireann has been enhanced within the polity. This book has endeavoured to inject a fresh approach, theoretically, empirically and normatively, by releasing the literature from a purely liberal democratic orientation. Noting the limitations of liberal democratic political understandings, I demonstrate that parliaments, including Dáil Éireann, do not enjoy a highly privileged space under the fluid conditions of contemporary parliamentary governance. Nevertheless, it does not follow from this assertion that Dáil Éireann, in line with the post-parliamentary governance model, is a peripheral and marginal institution. On the contrary, my analysis of Dáil Éireann concurs largely with Norton and Wood's appraisal of the British Parliament as 'a more active, more specialised, and less marginal House of Commons'.[5]

Presently, Dáil Éireann finds itself in a particularly strong position to engage as a proactive participant in the contemporary public sphere. As the polity's primary democratic forum, it is conferred with a high degree of democratic legitimacy. If talking is what a parliament does, it does so in a particular way. This is where Young's theory of an ideal communication community proves particularly insightful. Significantly, her model makes room for passionate and non-literal speech. In this regard, a parliament communicates more than it deliberates.

5 Norton and Wood, 1993: 3.

Appendix i

Pre-2009

Parliamentary salaries are payable monthly in arrears, on the last day of each month. There are three annual rates of salary: Basic €100,191; 1st Long Service Increment €103,389 (after 7 years combined service has been completed); and 2nd Long Service Increment €106,582 (after 10 years combined service has been completed). The salary rates quoted are rates effective from 1/9/2008. Salary is payable from and including polling day, on condition that the member signs the Roll of Members within 30 days of the election. Members who are promoted to ministerial positions are automatically reverted to the basic salary rate. Ministerial salaries are paid from their assigned departments.

2009

Section 2 of the Oireachtas (Allowances to Members) and Ministerial and Parliamentary Offices Act (2009) provides that Long Service Increments (LSI) will not be paid to those members of the Houses of the Oireachtas who would normally have qualified for an LSI on or after 13 May 2009.

Long Service Increments will not be paid to any member of the Houses of the Oireachtas after the next general election. Similar provisions will apply to members of the European Parliament who, being eligible to do so, opt to continue to be paid the same salary as TDs.

Specified Positions in Dáil Éireann (Annual Amounts)

The following allowances are also paid with Members' salaries: scheduled positions in the Dáil, Chairpersons, Vice-Chairpersons, Whips/Convenors, Rapporteurs and members of the Houses of the Oireachtas Commission.

Allowance Rates TDs

Ceann Comhairle	€125,005
Leas-Cheann Comhairle	€54,549
Taoiseach	€185,392
Tánaiste	€145,134
Minister	€125,005
Minister of State	€54,549

Specified positions in Dáil Éireann (Annual Amounts)

Assistant Government Whip	€16,027
Opposition Whip	€20,023
Whip to Labour Party	€16,027
Whip to Progressive Democrats	€6,380
Whip to Green Party	€6,380
Whip to Sinn Féin	€6,380
Assistant Whip to Fine Gael	€10,241
Assistant Whip to Labour Party	€6,380

Specified Positions on Oireachtas Committees (Annual Amounts)

Chairperson to Oireachtas Committee	€20,023
Vice-Chairperson	€10,241
Chairperson to Sub-Committee	€6,380
Whips to Committees	€6,380
Houses Commission Member	€20,023

New Rates from 22 July 2009

Chairperson to Oireachtas Committee	€10,016
Vice-Chairperson	€0
Chairperson to Sub-Committee	€0
Whips to Committees	€0
Houses Commission Member	€16,018

Other Allowances (Annual Amounts)

Miscellaneous Expense Allowance		€5,000.00
Constituency Travel Allowance	(A)	€2,500.00
	(B)	€5,000.00
	(C)	€8,000.00
Constituency Office Grant (Once-Off Payment)		€8,000.00
Constituency Office Maintenance Allowance		€8,000.00
Constituency Office Telephone Allowance		€5,700.00
Mobile Phone Allowance (every 18 months)		€750.00
Postal Facilities (Monthly Allocation)		1,750 prepaid envelopes

Travel and Subsistence

Daily Rate		€ 55.00
Overnight Rate		€126.00
Mileage	Up to 6,437	€0.5907
	6, 437+km in year	€0.2846

(Information Provided by Houses of the Oireachtas, September, 2009.)

Appendix 2

Dáil Questions on Experts and Consultants' Reports (6 October 2009)

Question:

To ask the Minister for the Environment, Heritage and Local Government the number of experts' and consultants' reports his department commissioned during 2008; the cost of each report; and if he will make a statement on the matter.

Joan Burton

Reply

Minister for the Environment, Heritage and Local Government (Mr Gormley):

Name of the Report	Cost
Independent assessment of proposed acquisition by the Irish Heritage Trust Limited of Anne's Grove House, Garden and Home Farm, Castletownroche, Mallow, Co. Cork	€14,520
Independent assessment of proposed acquisition by the Irish Heritage Trust Limited of 14 Henrietta Street, Dublin 1	€14,000[1]

Consultancy to develop a plan for the development of ENFO's Library and Information Service	€13,500
To provide a Communications Strategy for ENFO	€32,812
To review some of Ireland potential World Heritage Sites and provide a report on the viability of nominating such sites	€9,573
Limiting Thermal Bridging & Air Infiltration	€19,011
DEHLG review and spot checks of Capital Projects & Associated Training	€130,548
Quarterly construction Industry Indicators	€26,620
Construction Industry Review and Outlook report	€117,954
Gateway Innovation Fund Proposal Evaluation	€73,689
National Litter Pollution Monitoring System	€101,203
Assessment of Need for 'Living over the Shop' Tax Incentives to Support Urban Regeneration in NSS Gateways	€32,186
Knocknarea, Carrowmore and Carns Hill Conservation Study	€69,816
Study on Meeting the Requirements of European Regulation 842 on Certain Fluorinated Greenhouse Gases (F-gases)	€84,658
Irish Battlefields Project	€290,542
Monasterboice Conservation Study	€39,160
Geotechnical Consultancy – Rath Lugh	€4,734
Preliminary Study on the Establishment of an Electoral Commission in Ireland	€8,400

Regulatory Impact Assessment Report (Waste Facilities & Plastic Bags)	€72,341
Strategic Review of the Capital Funding Scheme for Voluntary & Cooperative Housing	€160,000[2]
Development of implementation plan for Homeless Strategy	€4,981
Waterford Youth Service – Research Project	€15,000
Screening Regulatory Analysis Report on the draft European Communities Environmental Objectives (Freshwater Pearl Mussel) Regulations 2009	€32,613
Preparation report on the nomination of Clonmacnoise as World Heritage Site	€50,232
National Archaeological Archive and Archaeological Object Resource Facility – scoping report	€54,407.00[3]
Former Irish Steel Plant Environmental Report (2008)	€394,949
Peer Review of White Young Green Irish Steel Plant Environmental Report 2008	€27,779
International Review of Waste Management Policy	€195,110
Regulatory Impact Analysis of a proposed Section 60 on a Ministerial Direction in relation to Volumetric Contractual Commitments	€22,216
Strategic Review of the Capital Funding Schemes for Voluntary and Co-operative Housing.	€160,000

1 No payment made to date.
2 €80,000 paid in 2008.
3 50% of costs to be met by the National Museum. €9000 paid to date.

Question:

To ask the Minister for Foreign Affairs the number of experts' and consultants' reports his department commissioned during 2008; the cost of each report; and if he will make a statement on the matter.

Joan Burton

Reply:

The Department of Foreign Affairs is responsible for two votes – Vote 28 (Foreign Affairs) and Vote 29 (International Cooperation). The following table sets out, for both votes, the details of experts and consultants commissioned to produce reports by the department in 2008 and the costs in each case.

My department, through Irish Aid (Ireland's official development assistance programme), occasionally commissions outside expertise where the specialised knowledge and/or skills are not available within the department and where the effective management and evaluation of the programme necessitates the presence of such skills. During the course of their engagements these consultants/experts may prepare reports and other documentation. However, as they would not have been commissioned specifically to furnish a report, these details have not been included in the table.

Vote 28: Experts/ Consultants commissioned to produce reports in 2008	Matter Reported On	Cost
Millward Brown	Research Project to establish reasons underlying the result of the Referendum on the Lisbon Treaty	€138,061

Communications Clinic	The preparation of a detailed Communication Action Plan to be used to direct spending under the Department's Communicating Europe Initiative (CEI) in 2009	€48,000
Richard Sinnott, Johan A. Elkink, Kevin O'Rourke and James McBride	Report on Attitudes and Behaviour in the Referendum on the Treaty of Lisbon	€11,800
Mr Jim O'Leary	Assessment of Value for Money Review of the Passport Service	€7,260

Vote 29: Experts/ Consultants commissioned by Irish Aid to produce reports in 2008	Matter Reported On	Cost
Copenhagen Development Consulting A/S	Evaluation of Irish Aid Support to Primary Education in the Rwenzori Region, Uganda	€96,665
Desam International Consultants – Uganda	Evaluation of Irish Aid Civil Society Programme – Uganda	€19,500
Debebe – Ethiopia	Civil Society Fund Audit	€3,000
PricewaterhouseCoopers Ltd	Develop Irish Aid Tanzania Private Sector Support Strategy	€ 36,414

National Forestry Authority Uganda	Environmental impact assessment of the construction improvement component of the post-primary education and training programme (PPET) in Karamoja	€21,666
J. Fitzpatrick Associates	External Review of Irish Aid Support to Kimmage Development Studies Centre	€66,550
Paud Murphy	Evaluation of Global e-Schools & Communities Initiative (GeSCI)	€33,200
FSG Social Impact Advisors	Evaluation of International Partnership for Microbicides	€139,000[4]
Helen O'Neill	Assessment of United Nations Industrial Development Organisation (UNIDO) as potential partner for Irish Aid	€4,000
Dr Larry Adupa – Uganda	Documenting the process of establishing the civil society fund for HIV/AIDS response in Uganda	€11,257
Prof. Amon Z. Mattee – Tanzania	Assessment of the performance of extension services delivery under ASDP in Tanzania	€19,235
ITAD Ltd	Evaluation of Ireland's Timor Leste Country Strategy 2004–2008	€130,000

The IDL Group – Mozambique	Analysis of Opportunities to Support Rural Livelihood Security and Pro-poor Growth through the Public Sector	£30,851
Alicia da Silva Calane – Mozambique	Analytic Study on process and indicators to address gender related obstacles to achieving PROAGRI goals	€10,000
Dr Barry Ryan	Review of the role of the Organisation for Security and Co-operation in Europe (OSCE) in the Partnership Programme for Eastern Europe and Central Asia (PPECA)	€15,000
Economics for the Environment Consultancy Ltd (EFTEC)	Review of Irish Aid's Strategic Partnership's Environment Programme 2006-2008	€30,000
Development Research Training (DRT) – Uganda	The Status of Chronic Poverty and Vulnerability in Karamoja	€ 2,857
J. Fitzpatrick Associates	Evaluation of Traidlinks	€30,250
FRR/ IDL Group	Review of Irish Aid Programme in Zimbabwe	€18,351
Dr Joseph Oonyu – Uganda	Mid Term Review of Irish Aid Support to Human Resources Development for Increased Access to Primary Health Care	$9640
Ishmael K.B. Kabanukye and others	Mapping exercise of Gender Based Violence (GBV) Programme in Uganda	€20,000

Mary Jennings	Copper Belt Government Programme Evaluation	€15,770
Albert Malama	Copper Belt Government Programme Evaluation	$10,800
Dr Henk J.W. Mustsaers	Review Operational Research for Food Security and Capacity Building and Evaluate Joint Mekelle and Cork Universities MSc Degree in Rural Development	€30,600
John O'Regan	Financial Assessment Component of an organisational assessment on partner NGOs for Multi-Annual Programme Scheme (MAPS), Civil Society Fund, Block Grants & other Civil Society Funding Schemes	€22,400
Declan O'Neill	Foreign Currency Transaction Review for Embassy in Tanzania	€ 15,000
Elim Serviços Lda	Evaluation of Irish support to Technoserve	€19,369
Health Tech Consulting – Mozambique	Evaluation of the Provincial Investment Plan 2004–2008 (PIPS) in Niassa Province (Mozambique)	€25,000
John O'Regan	Audit of Multi-Annual Programme Scheme (MAPS) Partnership grants awarded to Self Help Development International	€22,500

ITAD Ltd	Evaluation of the Uganda Country Strategy Paper 2007 –2009	€88,760
Catherine Butcher	Review of HIV AIDS programme in Northern Province (Zambia)	€18,600
AGEMA – Mozambique	Vulnerability & Agriculture Extension Study	€ 42,000
Jane Salvage	Feedback on evaluation of Irish Aids support to Health Rehabilitation Project for Marsh Arabs of Southern Iraq	€1,650
Integra Economic Development Consultants Ltd	Report to Inter-Departmental Committee on Development (IDCD) on development of skill sets	€18,300
Petrus Consulting Ltd	Quality review of draft HIV and AIDS Value for Money Report	€3.400
Prof. Ronan Conroy	Independent assessment of issues arising from review of a local HIV and AIDS Programme in Tanzania	€5,000

In addition, the Advisory Board for Irish Aid commissioned two research programmes in 2008. These were *Policy Coherence for Development and Agriculture* which cost €199,608 and *Policy Indicators Project* which cost €69,840. Both contracts were awarded to the Institute for International Integration Studies at Trinity College Dublin.

4 The Department of Foreign Affairs paid €139,000 towards the cost of this report. The remainder of the total cost of €342,000 was borne by other donors.

Question:
To ask the Minister for Social and Family Affairs the number of experts' and consultants' reports her department commissioned during 2008; the cost of each report; and if she will make a statement on the matter.

Joan Burton

Reply:
Minister for Social and Family Affairs (Mary Hanafin TD):
Details of experts' and consultants' reports commissioned by the department during 2008 are set out in the attached table.

Name of Reports	Date Finalised (or state ongoing if not yet complete)	Cost/ Estimated Cost €
Internal Penetration and Social Engineering Project	May 2008	23,500
Strategic Review of the Client Eligibility Services (CES) of the Department of Social and Family Affairs	September 2008	368,573
Strategic Review of Customer Facing Services	December 2008	183,781
Review of the Activation and Family Support Programme	March 2009	96,751
Review of IT Infrastructure Library (ITIL) processes in IS Services	December 2008	19,965
Report of the Expert Medical Group on Domiciliary Care Allowance	December 2008	8,517
Report on Green Paper Consultation Process	September 2008	13,552

Impact of Pension Reform Options	October 2008	3,448
Quality Assessment on VFM Review of Information Services	May 2009	8,334
Report on Indoor Air Quality in Government Building in Dundalk	July 2008	5,445
Air Quality in Goldsmith House	July 2008	6,159
Family Income Supplement Uptake Research	November 2008	65,606
National Employment Action Plan (NEAP) Evaluation	On-going	104,000*
Measurement of Consistent Poverty	On-going	240,933*

* Expected Costs – reports to be finalised

Appendix 3

Joint Committees of the Houses of the Oireachtas for the 30th Dáil

Joint Committee on Agriculture, Fisheries and Food
Joint Committee on Arts, Sport, Tourism, Community, Rural and
    Gaeltacht Affairs
Joint Committee on Climate Change and Energy Security
Joint Committee on Communications, Energy and Natural
    Resources
Joint Committee on the Constitution
Joint Committee on the Constitutional Amendment on Children
Joint Committee on Economic Regulatory Affairs
Joint Committee on Education and Science
Joint Committee on Enterprise, Trade and Employment
Joint Committee on the Environment, Heritage and Local
    Government
Joint Committee on European Affairs
Joint Committee on European Scrutiny
Joint Committee on Finance and the Public Service
Joint Committee on Foreign Affairs
Joint Committee on Health and Children
Joint Committee on the Implementation of the Good Friday
    Agreement
Joint Committee on Justice, Equality, Defence and Women's Rights
Joint Committee on Social and Family Affairs
Joint Committee on Transport

(Source: Houses of the Oireachtas Commission, 2008)

BIBLIOGRAPHY

Ahern, B. (1984) *Dáil Debates*, Vol. 349, Cols 1590–1591, 10 April.

Allen, K. (2000) *The Celtic Tiger: The Myth of Social Partnership in Ireland*, Manchester: Manchester University Press.

All-Party Oireachtas Committee on the Constitution (2002) *Seventh Progress Report: Dáil Éireann*, Dublin: Stationery Office.

Andersen, S.S. and Burns, T.R. (1996) 'The European Union and the Erosion of Parliamentary Democracy: A Study of Post-Parliamentary Governance', in S.S. Andersen and K.A. Eliassen (eds), *The European Union: How Democratic is it?* London: Sage.

Anderson, N. (2007) 'Do They Know It's (no longer) Christmas Time in the Dáil', *Irish Independent*, 25 January.

Ardagh, S. (2004) 'Launch of the Report of the Oireachtas Joint Committee on Justice, Equality, Defence and Women's Rights' Review of the Criminal Justice System', Dublin: Leinster House Public Relations Office, Press Release, 21 July.

Arkins, A. (1990) 'Legislative and Executive Relations in the Republic of Ireland', *West European Politics*, 13 (1).

Ayearst, M. (1970) *The Republic of Ireland: Its Government and Politics*, New York: New York University Press, London: University of London Press.

Bache, I. and Flinders, M. (2004) 'Themes and Issues in Multi-Level Governance', in I. Bache and M. Flinders (eds), *Multi-Level Governance*, Oxford: Oxford University Press.

Bagehot, W. ([1867] 1966) *The English Constitution*, Itacha, New York: Cornell University Press.

Bax, M. (1976) *Harpstrings and Confessions: Machine-Style Politics in the Irish Republic*, Assen: Van Gorcum.

Beck, U. (1992) *Risk Society*, London: Sage.

—— (1994) 'The Reinvention of Politics: Towards a Theory of Reflexive

Modernisation', in U. Beck., A. Giddens and S. Lash, *Reflexive Modernisation: Politics, Tradition and Aesthetics in the Modern Social Order*, Cambridge: Polity Press.

—— (2001) *World Risk Society*, Cambridge: Cambridge University Press.

Benhabib, S. (1996) 'Towards a Deliberative Model of Democratic Legitimacy', in S. Benhabib (ed.), *Democracy and Difference: Contesting the Boundaries of the Political*, Princeton: Princeton University Press.

Blichner, L.C. (2000) 'The Anonymous Hand of Public Reason: Interparliamentary Discourse and the Quest for Legitimacy', in E.O. Eriksen and J.E. Fossum (eds), *Democracy in the European Union: Integration through Deliberation*, London: Routledge.

Bohman, J. (1996) *Public Deliberation: Pluralism, Complexity and Democracy*, Cambridge, MA: MIT Press.

Bohman, J. and Rehg, W. (1997) *Essays on Reason and Politics: Deliberative Democracy*, Cambridge, Massachusetts and London: MIT Press.

Boothroyd, B. (2000) *Hansard*, Vol. 354, Cols 1113–1115.

Brennan, M. and McDonagh, P. (2008) 'McDowell Bagged €50,000 "golden parachute" Package', *Irish Independent*, 1 October.

Brennock, M. (2000) 'Fine Gael Proposals Radical and Thoughtful', *The Irish Times*, 13 September.

Broughan, T. (1996) *Dáil Debates*, Vol. 469, Cols 1752–1753, 9 October.

Browne, N. (1986) *Against the Tide*, Dublin: Gill and Macmillan.

Browne, V. (2009) 'Obama's Day in the Sun Shows Up Dull Dáil Tribute', *The Irish Times*, 21 January.

Bruton, J. (1991) *Dáil Debates*, Vol. 404, Cols 831–832, 30 January.

Bruton, J. and Mitchell, J. (2000) *A Democratic Revolution: A Thorough Overhaul of the Institutions of the State*, Dublin: Fine Gael.

Bryan, F.M. (2004) *Real Democracy: The New England Town Meeting and How It Works*, Chicago and London: University of Chicago Press.

Bryce, J. (1921) *Modern Democracies*, London: Macmillan.

Bunreacht na hÉireann (Constitution of Ireland), Dublin: Stationery Office.

Burke, E. ([1784] 1999) 'Speech at Mr Burke's Arrival in Bristol', in I. Kramnick (ed.), *The Portable Edmund Burke*, London and New York: Penguin Books.

Callinicos, A. (2000) *Equality,* Cambridge: Polity Press.

Carty, R.K. (1980) 'Politicians and Electoral Laws: Anthropology of Party Competition in Ireland', *Political Studies,* 28 (4).

—— (1981) *Party and Parish Pump: Electoral Politics in Ireland,* Ontario: Wilfrid Laurier University Press.

Chambers, S. (1996) *Reasonable Democracy: Jurgen Habermas and the Politics of Discourse,* Ithaca and London: Cornell University Press.

Chomsky, N. (2003) 'The Carter Administration: Myth and Reality', in C.P. Otero (ed.), *Noam Chomsky: Radical Priorities,* Oakland and Edinburgh: AK Press.

Chryssochoou, D.N. (2000) *Democracy in the European Union,* London and New York: I.B. Tauris.

Chryssochoou, D.N., Stavridis, S. and Tsinisizelis, M.J. (1998) 'European Democracy, Parliamentary Decline and the "Democratic Deficit" of the European Union', *Journal of Legislative Studies,* 4 (3).

Chubb, B. (1963) 'Going About Persecuting Civil Servants', *Political Studies,* 11 (3).

—— (1992) *The Government and Politics of Ireland,* London and New York: Longman.

Cigler, A.J. and Lommis, B.A. (1998) 'Introduction: The Changing Nature of Interest Group Politics', in A.J. Cigler and B.A. Lommis (eds), *Interest Group Politics,* Washington: Congressional Quarterly Press.

Coakley, J. (2003) 'The Election and the Party System', in M. Gallagher, M. Marsh and P. Mitchell (eds), *How Ireland Voted 2002,* Basingstoke, Hampshire: Palgrave Macmillan.

Cohen, J. (1991) 'Deliberation and Democratic Legitimacy', in A. Hamlin and P. Petit (eds), *The Good Polity: Normative Analysis of the State,* Oxford: Basil Blackwell.

—— (1997) 'Deliberation and Democratic Legitimacy', in J. Bohman and W. Rehg (eds), *Essays on Reason and Politics: Deliberative Democracy,* Cambridge, Massachusetts and London: MIT Press.

—— (1999) 'Democracy and Liberty', in J. Elster (ed.), *Deliberative Democracy,* Cambridge: Cambridge University Press.

Collins, C.A. (1985) 'Clientelism and Careerism in Irish Local Government:

The Persecution of Civil Servants Revisited', *Economic and Social Review,* 16 (4).

Collins, G. (2009) 'The New Hillary', *New York Times,* 24 January.

Collins, N. (2004) 'Parliamentary Democracy in Ireland', *Parliamentary Affairs,* 57 (3).

Collins, N. and Butler, P. (2004) 'Political Mediation in Ireland: Campaigning between Traditional and Tabloid Markets', *Parliamentary Affairs,* 57 (1).

Collins, N. and O'Shea, M. (2003) 'Clientelism: Facilitating Rights and Favours', in M. Adshead and M. Millar (eds), *Public Administration and Public Policy in Ireland,* London: Routledge.

Collins, S. (2003) 'Campaign Strategy', in M. Gallagher, M. Marsh and P. Mitchell (eds), *How Ireland Voted 2002,* London: Palgrave.

—— (ed.) (2007) *Nealon's Guide to the 30th Dáil and 23rd Seánad,* Dublin: Gill and Macmillan.

—— (2008) 'Politicians, Not Social Partners, Elected to Govern', *Irish Times,* 27 December.

Committee of Inquiry into Ministerial and Other Salaries (1937) *Reports Presented to the Minister for Finance,* Dublin: Stationery Office.

Connolly, G. (1996) *Dáil Debates,* Vol. 469, Cols 1754–1756, 9 October.

Cook, M. (2002) 'Five Arguments for Deliberative Democracy', in M.P. D'Entreves (ed.), *Democracy as Public Deliberation,* Manchester: Manchester University Press.

Cook, R. (2003) *The Point of Departure,* London and New York: Simon and Schuster.

Corbett, E.P.J. and Connors, R.J. (1999) *Classical Rhetoric for the Modern Student,* Oxford and New York: Oxford University Press.

Corrigan, P. (1997) *The Sociology of Consumption: An Introduction,* London: Sage.

Costa *v* Enel (Case 6/64) [1964] *Common Market Law Review,* 425.

Cotta, M. (1994) 'The Rise and Fall of the "Centrality" of the Italian Parliament: Transformation of the Executive-Legislative Subsystem after the Second World War', in G.W Copeland and S.C. Patterson (eds), *Parliaments in the Modern World: Changing Institutions,* Ann Arbor: University of Michigan Press.

Crick, B. (1965) *The Reform of Parliament*, New York: Anchor Books.

—— (2005) *In Defence of Politics*, London: Continuum.

Crossley, N. (2005) *Key Concepts in Critical Social Theory*, London, Thousand Oaks and New Delhi: Sage.

Crossman, R. (1966) ' Introcution', in W. Bagehot, *The English Constitution*, Ithaca, New York: Cornell University Press.

—— (1979) *The Crossman Diaries* (condensed version), London: Magnum Books.

Cullen, P. (2005) 'How Pupil Power Brings McDowell to Book', *The Irish Times*, 26 March.

Dahl, R.A. (1961) *Who Governs? Democracy and Power in an American City*, New Haven and London: Yale University Press.

—— (2000) *On Democracy*, New Haven and London: Yale University Press.

Dáil Éireann (2002) 'Electronic Voting in Dáil Chamber is Part of Major Oireachtas Reform Programme', Dublin: Oireachtas Public Relations Office, Press Release, 26 February.

Dáil Éireann: Minutes of Proceeding (1919–1921) Dublin: Stationery Office.

Dáil Éireann Standing Orders Relative to Public Business (1974) Dublin: Stationery Office.

Dáil Éireann Standing Orders Relative to Public Business (2002) Dublin: Stationery Office.

Dáil Éireann Standing Orders Relative to Public Business: Modifications and Amendments Thereto (2002) Dublin: Leinster House.

Dail Question addressed to the Minister for Social and Family Affairs by Deputy Joan Burton for Written Answer (2009) Ref: 33905/09, 6 October.

Dail Question addressed to the Minister for the Environment, Heritage and Local Government by Deputy Joan Burton for Written Answer (2009) Ref: 33900/09, No 6 October.

Dail Question addressed to the Minister for Foreign Affairs by Deputy Joan Burton for Written Answer (2009) Ref: 33902/09, 6 October.

Damgaard, E. (1994) 'The Strong Parliaments of Scandinavia: Continuity and Change of Scandinavian Parliaments', in G.W. Copeland and S.C. Patterson (eds), *Parliaments in the Modern World: Changing Institutions*, Ann Arbor: University of Michigan Press.

—— (2000) 'Conclusion: The Impact of European Integration on Nordic Democracies', in T. Bergman. and E. Damgaard (eds), *Delegation and Accountability in European Integration*, London: Frank Cass.

Davidson, R.H and Oleszek, W.J. (2000) *Congress and its Members*, Washington, DC: Congressional Quarterly.

Decker, F. (2002) 'Governance beyond the Nation State: Reflections on the Democratic Deficit of the European Union', *Journal of European Public Policy*, 9 (2).

Delanty, G. (1995) *Inventing Europe: Idea, Identity, Reality*, Basingstoke: Macmillan.

Deloitte and Touche (2002) *Houses of the Oireachtas: Final Report (Strand 2) Members' Services–International Benchmarking Review* (IBR), Dublin: Deloitte and Touche.

Denton, R.E. (1991) 'Political Communication Ethics: An Oxymoron', in R.E. Denton (ed.), *Ethical Dimensions of Political Communication*, New York and Westport, Connecticut: Praeger.

D'Entreves, M.P. (2002) 'Introduction: Democracy as Public Deliberation', in M.P. D'Entreves (ed.), *Democracy as Public Deliberation: New Perspectives*, Manchester and New York: Manchester University Press.

Department of Foreign Affairs (1972), *Into Europe: Ireland and the EEC*, Dublin: Department of Foreign Affairs.

Desmond, B. (1971) *Dáil Debates*, Vol. 257, Cols 1135–1136, 2 December.

—— (2000) *Finally and in Conclusion*, Dublin: New Island Press.

Dewey, J. (1927) *The Public and Its Problems*, Denver: Alan Swallow.

Dogan, R. (1997) 'Comitology: Little Procedures with Big Implications', *West European Politics*, 20 (3).

Dooley, C. (2005) 'More Inspectors to Protect Migrants', *The Irish Times*, 13 April.

Dror, Y. (2001) *The Capacity to Govern: A Report of the Club of Rome*, London: Frank Cass.

Dryzek, J.S. (1990) *Discursive Democracy: Politics, Policy, and Political Science*, Cambridge: Cambridge University Press.

—— (2001) 'Legitimacy and Economy in Deliberative Democracy', *Political Theory*, 29 (5), 651–659.

Economist Magazine (1997) 17 to 23 May.

Editorial (2007) 'Welcome Back Deputies', *Irish Independent*, 25 January.

Editorial (2007) 'Pernicious Curse of Clientelism', *The Irish Times*, 27 January.

Editorial (2008a) 'Challenge for Government and for the Dáil', *The Irish Times*, 21 June.

Editorial (2008b) 'The Return of Street Politics', *The Irish Times*, 23 October.

Editorial (2009a) 'Beverly Flynn Crosses the Line', *The Irish Times*, 7 January.

Editorial (2009b) 'Dáil Failings on Ceann Comhairle', *The Irish Times*, 17 October.

Elgie, R. and Stapleton, J. (2006) 'Testing the Decline of Parliament Thesis, Ireland, 1923–2002', *Political Studies*, 54 (1).

Elster, J. (1999) *Deliberative Democracy*, Cambridge: Cambridge University Press.

Eriksen, E.O. and Fossum, J.E. (2000) *Democracy in the European Union: Integration through Deliberation*, London: Routledge.

—— (2002) 'Democracy through Strong Publics in the European Union?' *Journal of Common Market Studies*, 40 (3).

European Community Act (1972) No. 27 of 1972.

European Communities (Confirmation of Regulations) Act (1973) No. 5 of 1973.

European Communities (Amendment) Act (1973) No. 20 of 1973.

European Union (Scrutiny) Act (2002) No. 25 of 2002.

Falkner, G. and Laffan, B. (2005) 'The Europeanisation of Austria and Ireland: Small Can Be Difficult?', in S. Bulmer and C. Lequesne (eds), *The Member States of the European Union*, Oxford: Oxford University Press.

Farrell, B. (1985) 'Ireland from Friends and Neighbours to Clients and Partisans: Some Dimensions of Parliamentary Representation under PRSTV', in V. Bogdanor (ed.), *Representatives of the People? Parliaments and Constituents in Western Democracies*, Aldershot: Gower.

—— (1994) 'The Political Role of Cabinet Ministers in Ireland', in M. Laver and K.A. Slepsle (eds), *Cabinet Ministers and Parliamentary Government*, Cambridge: Cambridge University Press.

Fearon, J.D. (1999) 'Deliberation as Discussion', in J. Elster (ed.), *Deliberative Democracy*, Cambridge: Cambridge University Press.

Featherstone, K. (1994) 'Jean Monnet and the "democratic deficit" in the European Union', *Journal of Common Market Studies*, 32 (2).

Festenstein, M. (2004) 'Deliberative Democracy and Two Models of Pragmatism', *European Journal of Social Theory*, 7 (3).

FitzGerald, B. (1996) *Dáil Debates*, Vol. 469, Cols 1717–1718, 9 October.

FitzGerald, G. (2000) 'Partnership Agreements Leading Us from Traditional Forms of Democracy', *The Irish Times*, 12 February.

—— (2003) *Reflection on the Irish State*, Dublin and Portland: Irish Academic Press.

—— (2006) 'Clientelism Still Blights Political Life of the Nation', *The Irish Times*, 15 July.

Flinders, M. (2002) 'Shifting the Balance? Parliament, the Executive and the British Constitution', *Political Studies*, 50 (1).

—— (2007) 'Analysing Reform: The House of Commons, 2001–2005', *Political Studies*, 55 (1).

Foot, M. (1959) *Parliament in Danger*, London: Pall Mall Press.

Frank, E. (1966) 'Introduction', in E. Frank, (ed.), *Lawmakers in a Changing World*, New Jersey: Prentice Hall.

Fraser, N. (1992) 'Rethinking the Public Sphere: A Contribution to the Critique of Actually Existing Democracy', in C. Calhoun (ed.), *Habermas and the Public Sphere*, London: MIT Press.

—— (2004) 'Institutionalising Democratic Justice: Redistribution, Recognition and Participation', in S. Benhabib and N. Fraser (eds), *Pragmatism, Critique, Judgment: Essays for Richard J. Bernstein*, Massachusetts and London: MIT Press.

—— (2007) 'Transnationalizing the Public Sphere: On the Legitimacy and Efficacy of Public Opinion in a Post-Westphalian World', *Theory, Culture and Society*, 24 (4).

Fraser, N. and Honneth, A. (2003) *Redistribution or Recognition: A Political-Philosophical Exchange*, London and New York: Verso.

Freeman, S. (2000) 'Deliberative Democracy: A Sympathetic Comment', *Philosophy and Public Affairs*, 29 (4).

Gallagher, M. (1996) 'Electoral Systems', in *Review of the Constitution Group*, Dublin: Stationery Office.

—— (1999) 'Parliament', in J. Coakley and M. Gallagher (eds), *Politics in the Republic of Ireland*, London: Routledge.

—— (2003) 'Stability and Turmoil: Analysis of the Results', in M. Gallagher, M. Marsh and P. Mitchell (eds), *How Ireland Voted 2002*, Basingstoke, Hampshire: Palgrave Macmillan.

—— (2005) 'Parliament', in J. Coakley and M. Gallagher (eds), *Politics in the Republic of Ireland*. London and New York: Routledge.

Gallagher, M. and Komito, L. (1999) 'The Constituency Role of TDs', in J. Coakley, and M. Gallagher, (eds), *Politics in the Republic of Ireland*, London: Routledge.

Gallagher, M., Laver, M. and Mair, P. (2001) *Representative Government in Western Europe*, London: McGraw-Hill.

Galston, W.A. (2004) 'Civic Education and Political Participation', *Political Science and Politics*, 37 (2).

Geoghegan-Quinn, M. (1998) 'Loss in Salary and Privacy Price of Becoming a TD', *The Irish Times*, 28 March.

Gibbon, P. and Higgins, M.D. (1974) 'Patronage, Tradition and Modernisation: The Case of the Irish "Gombeenman"', *Economic and Social Review*, 6.

Gibbons, J. (2008) 'Consumer Contagion Renders Us Vulnerable', *The Irish Times*, 3 July.

Giddens, A. and Hutton, W. (2001) *On the Edge: Living with Global Capitalism*, London: Vintage.

Gilmore, E. (2009) *Dáil Debates*, Vol. 690 6 October.

Glover, J. (2003) 'The Year in Politics', *The Guardian*, 30 December.

Goodin, R.E. (2003) *Reflective Democracy*, Oxford: Oxford University Press.

Goodin, R.E and Niemeyer, S.J. (2003) 'When Does Deliberation Begin? Internal Reflection Versus Public Discussion in Deliberative Democracy', *Political Studies*, 51 (4).

Gotoff, H. (1993) 'Oratory: The Art of Illusion', *Harvard Studies in Classical Philology*, 95.

Greenwald, C. (1977) *Group Power*, New York: Praeger.

Guidry, J.A and Sawyer, M.Q. (2003) 'Contentious Pluralism: The Public

Sphere and Democracy', *Perspectives on Politics*, 1 (2).

Gundersen, A.G. (2000) *The Socratic Citizen: A Theory of Deliberative Democracy*, Lanham, Boulder, New York and Oxford: Lexington Books.

Habermas, J. (1984, 1987) *The Theory of Communicative Action*, Vols 1 and 2, London and Cambridge: Heinmann and Polity Press.

—— (1989) *Structural Transformation of the Public Sphere*, Cambridge: Polity Press.

—— (1996) *Between Facts and Norms: Contributions to a Discourse Theory of Law and Democracy*, Cambridge: Polity Press.

Hague, W. (2000) *Hansard*, Vol. 353, Cols 1084–1179.

Hardiman, N. (2002) 'From Conflict to Co-ordination: Economic Governance and Political Innovation in Ireland', *West European Politics*, 25 (4).

Haughey, C. (1991) *Dáil Debates*, Vol. 404, Cols 1751–1752, 6 February.

Healey, D. (1989) *The Time of My Life*, London: Penguin.

Held, D. (1993) 'Democracy from City State to a Cosmopolitan Order?', in D. Held (ed), *Prospects for Democracy*, Palo Alto: Stanford University Press.

Hendricks, C.M. (2006) 'Integrated Deliberation: Reconciling Civil Society's Dual Role in Deliberative Democracy', *Political Studies*, 54 (3).

Hennis, W. (1971) 'Reform of the Bundestag: The Case for General Debate', in G. Loewenberg (ed.), *Modern Parliaments: Change or Decline*, Chicago and New York: Alding Atherton.

Heywood, A. (1992) *Political Ideologies: An Introduction*, Basingstoke and London: Macmillan.

Higgins, M.D. (1982) 'The Limits of Clientelism: Towards an Assessment of Irish Politics', in C. Clapham (ed.), *Private Patronage and Public Power, Political Clentelism in the Modern State:* London: Frances Pinter.

Hill, A. and Whichelow, A. (1964) *What's Wrong with Parliament?* Middlesex: Penguin Books.

Hollis, C. (1971) *Can Parliament Survive?* Washington, New York and London: Kennikat Press.

Houses of the Oireachtas Commission (2007) *Annual Report 2006,* Dublin: Stationery Office.

—— (2008) *Annual Report 2007*, Dublin: Stationery Office.

Houses of the Oireachtas Commission Act (2003) No. 28 of 2003.

Houses of the Oireachtas Commission Bill (2002) Explanatory Memorandum. Hudson, B. (2003) *Justice in the Risk Society: Challenging and Re-affirming Justice in Late Modernity,* London, Thousand Oaks and New Delhi: Sage.

Huitt, R.K. (1966) 'Congress, The Durable Partner', in E. Frank (ed.), *Lawmakers in a Changing World,* New Jersey: Prentice Hall.

Hunt, B. (2009) 'Time for Tough Decisions from Elected Leaders', *The Irish Times,* 8 January.

Issac, J. (2005) 'Republicanism: A European Inheritance', *European Journal of Social Theory,* 8 (1).

Joint Committee on European Affairs Sub-Committee on European Scrutiny (2007) *Fifth Report on the Operation of the European Union (Scrutiny) Act 2002, 1 January 2007 to 4 April 2007,* Dublin: Stationery Office.

Joint Oireachtas Committee on Justice, Equality, Defence and Women's Rights (2005) *Dáil Committee Debates,* Vols. 87 and 88, 22–23 March.

Jonas, H. (1984) *The Imperative of Responsibility,* Chicago and London: University of Chicago Press.

Judge, D. (1999) 'Representation in Westminister in the 1990s: The Ghost of Edmund Burke', *Journal of Legislative Studies,* 5 (1).

Katz, R.S. (1999) 'Representation, the Locus of Democratic Legitimation and the Role of National Parliaments in the European Union', in R. Katz, and B. Wessells (eds), *The European Parliament, National Parliaments and European Integration,* Oxford: Oxford University Press.

Keogh, D. (2005) *Twentieth Century Ireland: Revolution and State Building,* Dublin: Gill and Macmillan.

Kelly, V. (1987) 'Focus on Clients: A Reappraisal of the Effectiveness of TDs' Interventions', *Administration* 35 (2).

Kennedy, G. (2002) *Nealon's Guide to the 29th Dáil and Seanad,* Dublin: Gill and Macmillan.

Kitt, T. (2002) *Dáil Debates,* Vol. 554, Cols 575–576, 9 October.

Kogler, H.H (2005) 'Constructing a Cosmopolitan Public Sphere: Hermeneutic Capabilities and Universal Values', *European Journal of Social Theory,* 8 (3).

Komito, L. (1984) 'Irish Clientelism: A Reappraisal', *Economic and Social Review*, 15 (3).

—— (1989) 'Voters, Politicians and Clentelism: A Dublin Survey', *Administration* 37 (2).

—— (1992) 'Brokerage or Friendship? Politics and Networks in Ireland', *Economic and Social Review*, 23 (2).

—— (1997) 'Politics and Administrative Practice in the Irish Information Society', *Economic and Social Review*, 28 (3).

Laffan, B. (1996) 'Introduction', in B. Laffan (ed.), *Constitution Building in the EU*, Dublin: Institute of European Affairs.

—— (1999) 'Democracy in the European Union', in L. Cram, D. Dinan and N. Nugent (eds), *Developments in the European Union*, Basingstoke: Macmillan.

—— (2001) *Organising for a Changing Europe: Irish Central Government and the European Union*, Dublin: The Policy Institute.

Landy, D. (2001) In conversation with me during Tipperary South By-election.

Larsen-Jensen, K. (2002) Address in National Forum on Europe, *Report 17*, Dublin: Stationery Office.

Laski, H.J. (1927) *Communism*, London: Norgate Press.

Laursen, F. (2005) 'The Role of National Parliamentary Committees in European Scrutiny: Reflections Based on the Danish Case', *Legislative Studies*, 2 (3/4).

Laver, M. (1998) *A New Electoral System for Ireland?*, Dublin: The Policy Institute in association with the All-Party Oireachtas Committee on the Constitution.

Lee, J.J. (1993) *Ireland 1912–1985: Politics and Society*, Cambridge: Cambridge University Press.

Leib, E.J. (2004) *Deliberative Democracy in America: A Proposal for a Popular Branch of Government*, Pennsylvania: Pennsylvania State University.

Lemass, S. (1962) 'Statement to Ministers of the Governments of Member States of the European Economic Community, Brussels', in *The White Paper European Economic Community: Developments Subsequent to the White Paper of 30th June 1961*, laid by the Government before the Houses of the Oireachtas, Dublin: Stationery Office.

Lenin, V.I. ([1917] 1970) *State and Revolution,* Moscow: Progress.

Lewandowski, J.D. (2003) 'Disembedded Democracy? Globalisation and the "Third Way"', *Journal of European Social Theory,* 6 (1).

Loewenberg, G. (1971) *Modern Parliaments: Change or Decline,* Chicago and New York: Atherton.

—— (1972) 'Comparative Legislative Research', in S.C. Patterson and J.C. Wahlke (eds), *Comparative Legislative Behaviour: Frontiers of Research,* New York, London, Sydney and Toronto: Wiley-Interscience.

Loewenberg, G. and Patterson, S.C. (1979) *Comparing Legislatures,* Boston and Toronto: Little Brown Press.

Longley, L.D. and Davidson, R.H. (1998) 'Parliamentary Committees: Changing Perspectives and Changing Institutions', in L.D. Longley and R.H Davidson (eds), *The New Roles of Parliamentary Committees,* London: Frank Cass.

Lord, C. (1998) *Democracy in the European Union,* Sheffield: Sheffield Academic Press.

Lord, C. and Beetham, D. (2001) 'Legitimising the EU: Is there a "Post-Parliamentary" Basis for its Legitimation?' *Journal of Common Market Studies,* 39 (3).

Lord, C. and Magnette, P. (2004) '*E Pluribus Unum:* Creative Disagreement about Legitimacy in the EU', *Journal of Common Market Studies,* 42 (1).

Lynch, J. (1971) *Dáil Debates,* Vol. 257, Cols 1723–1724, 9 December.

—— (1972) *Dáil Debates,* Vol. 263, Cols 98–99, 25 October.

Lynch, K. (2001) 'Social Justice and Equality in Ireland', in H. Bohan and G. Kennedy (eds), *Redefining Roles and Relationships,* Dublin: Veritas.

Lyons, N. (2008) 'Snouts in the Trough', *Irish Daily Mail,* 5 July.

MacCarthaigh, M. (2005) *Accountability in Irish Parliamentary Politics,* Dublin: Institute of Public Administration.

Macpherson, C.B. (1988) *The Life and Times of Liberal Democracy,* Oxford: Oxford University Press.

McCraken, J.L. (1958) *Representative Government in Ireland: A Study of Dáil Éireann, 1919–1948,* London, New York and Toronto: Oxford University Press.

McGowan, L. and Murphy, M. (2003) 'Europeanisation and the Irish

Experience' in M. Adshead and M. Millar (eds), *Public Administration and Public Policy in Ireland: Theory and Methods*, London and New York: Routledge.

McMahon, B. and Murphy, F. (1989) *European Community Law in Ireland*, Dublin: Butterworths.

McSharry, R. and White, P. (2000) *The Making of the Celtic Tiger: The Inside Story of Ireland's Boom Economy*, Dublin and Cork: Mercier Press.

Mahoney, J. and Rueschemeyer, D. (2005) 'Comparative Historical Analysis: Achievements and Agendas', in J. Mahoney and D. Rueschemeyer (eds), *Historical Analysis in the Social Sciences*, Cambridge: Cambridge University Press.

Mair, P. and Weeks, L. (2005) 'The Party System', in J. Coakley and M. Gallagher (eds), *Politics in the Republic of Ireland*, London: Routledge.

Major, J. (2000) *Hansard*, Vol. 353, Cols 1084–179.

Malone, S. (1947) *Notes on Procedure in the Houses of the Oireachtas*, Dublin: Stationery Office.

Mann, T. and Ornstein, N. (2006) 'Our Pathetic Congress', *Los Angeles Times*, 26 September.

Manning, M. (2000) *James Dillon: A Biography*, Dublin: Wolfhound Press.

Mansbridge, J. (1980) *Beyond Adversary Democracy*, New York: Basic Books.

Mansergh, M. (2004) 'Grassroots Politicians Are Preferable to Ideologues', *The Irish Times*, 6 November.

Mansergh, N. (1934) *The Irish Free State: Its Government and Politics*, London: George Allen and Unwin Ltd.

Menzey, M.L. (1995) 'Parliament in the New Europe', in J. Hayward and E.C. Page, *Governing the New Europe*, Durham: Duke University Press.

Mill, J.S. ([1859] 1985) *On Liberty*, London: Penguin.

Miller, D. (1993) 'Deliberative Democracy and Social Choice', in D. Held (ed.), *Prospects for Democracy: North, South, East, West*, Palo Alto: Stanford University Press.

Mitchell, J. (1991) *Dáil Debates*, Vol. 404, Cols 833–834, 30 January.

—— (1999) 'Scandals Show Reform of Dáil is Badly Needed', *The Irish Times*, 17 December.

Montesquieu, C.L. ([1748] 1994) *The Spirit of the Laws*, Cambridge: Cambridge University Press.

Moxon Browne, E. (1996) 'Citizens and Parliaments', in B. Laffan (ed.), *Constitution Building in the European Union*, Dublin: Institute of European Affairs.

Murphy, G. (1999) 'The Role of Interest Groups in the Policy-Making Process', in J. Coakley and M. Gallagher (eds), *Politics in the Republic of Ireland*, London: Routledge.

Murphy, M.C. (2006) 'Reform of Dáil Éireann: The Dynamics of Parliamentary Change', *Parliamentary Affairs*, 59 (3).

Newman, C. (2005) 'Earlier Role for Parliaments in Scrutinising EU Measures Urged', *The Irish Times*, 8 April.

Nichols, M.P. (1987) 'Aristotle's Defence of Rhetoric', *The Journal of Politics*, 49 (3).

Norris, P. (1997) 'The Puzzle of Constituency Service', *Journal of Legislative Studies*, 3 (2).

Norton, P. (1993) *Does Parliament Matter?* London: Harvester Wheatsheaf.

—— (1994) 'Representation of Interests: The Case of the British House of Commons in Parliaments', in G.W. Copeland and S.C. Patterson (eds), *Parliaments in the Modern World: Changing Institutions*, Ann Arbor: University of Michigan Press.

—— (1997) 'Roles and Behaviour of British MPs', *Journal of Legislative Studies*, 3 (1).

Norton, P. and Wood, D.M. (1993) *Back from Westminster: British Members of Parliament and their Constituents*, Kentucky: University Press of Kentucky.

Ó Cinneide, S. (1998) 'Democracy and the Constitution', *Administration*, 46 (4).

O'Connor, T. and O'Halloran, A. (2008) *Politics in a Changing Ireland: 1960–2007. A Tribute to Seamus Pattison*, Dublin: Institute of Public Administration.

O'Dea, W. (1996) *Dáil Debates*, Vol. 469, Cols 1734–1735, 9 October.

O'Halloran, A. (2003) 'The Democratic Deficit and the European Parliament', *Working Paper No. 3*, Cork: Department of Government, University College Cork.

O'Halloran, M. (2001) 'Minister Warns against Politicians Pandering to Localism and Clientelism', *The Irish Times*, 27 August.

O'Halloran, M. (2005) 'Higgins Says "bonded labour" Used to Build Roads', *The Irish Times*, 9 February.

O'Halpin, E. (1996) 'Irish Parliamentary Culture and the European Union: Formalities to be Observed', in P. Norton (ed.), *National Parliaments and the European Union*, London: Frank Cass.

—— (1998) 'A Changing Relationship? Parliament and Government in Ireland', in P. Norton (ed.), *Parliaments and Governments in Western Europe*, London: Frank Cass.

—— (2002) 'Still Persecuting Civil Servants? Irish Parliamentarians and Citizens', in P. Norton (ed.), *Parliaments and Citizens in Western Europe*, London: Frank Cass.

O'Halpin, E. and Connolly, E. (1999) 'Parliaments and Pressure Groups: The Irish Experience of Change', in P. Norton (ed.), *Parliaments and Pressure Groups in Western Europe*, London: Frank Cass.

O'Hanlon, R. (2002) 'Foreword', in Deloitte and Touche, *Houses of the Oireachtas: Final Report (Strand 2) Members' Services – International Benchmarking Review (IBR)*, Dublin: Deloitte and Touche.

Oireachtas (Allowances to Members) Act (1938), No. 34 of 1938.

Oireachtas (Allowances to Members) Act (1962), No. 32 of 1962.

Oireachtas (Allowances to Members) and Ministerial and Parliamentary Offices (Amendment) Act (1973), No. 22 of 1973.

Oireachtas Sub-Committee on European Scrutiny (2007) *Fifth Report on the Operation of the European Union (Scrutiny) Act 2002*, Dublin: Houses of the Oireachtas.

O'Keeffe, J. (2002) *Dáil Debates*, Vol. 554, Cols 577–578, 9 October.

O'Malley, D. (1996) *Dáil Debates*, Vol. 469, Cols 1722–1726, 9 October.

Ó Snodaigh, A. (2002) *Dáil Debates*, Vol. 554, Cols 583–584, 9 October.

Ost, D. (2004) 'Politics as the Mobilisation of Anger: Emotions in Movements and in Power', *European Journal of Social Theory*, 7 (2).

O'Toole, F. (2007) 'A Culture TD Fixers Thrive On', *The Irish Times*, 30 January.

Ó Tuama, S. (2005) 'Respect and Dignity: Essential Guides to Successful Public Sector Innovation', *Administration*, 53 (3).

Parliamentary Inquiry into DIRT (1999) *First Report: Examination of the Report of the Comptroller and Auditor General of Investigation into the Administration of Deposit Interest Retention Tax and Related Matters during the Period 1 January 1986 to 1 December 1998*, Dublin: Stationery Office.

—— (2001) *Final Report: Examination of the Report of the Comptroller and Auditor General of Investigation into the Administration of Deposit Interest Retention Tax and Related Matters during the Period 1 January 1986 to 1 December 1998*, Dublin: Stationery Office.

Pateman, C. (1970) *Participation and Democratic Theory*, Cambridge: Cambridge University Press.

Patterson, S.C. and Copeland, G.W. (1994) 'Parliaments in the Twenty-First Century', in G.W. Copeland and S.C. Patterson (eds), *Parliaments in the Modern World: Changing Institutions*, Ann Arbor: University of Michigan Press.

Pattison, S. (2002) 'An Overview of Dáil Éireann Past and Present', Address to Department of Government, University College Cork, 22 February.

—— (2004) 'The Changing Role of Dáil Éireann Since 1961', Address to Department of Government, University College Cork, 1 March.

Pennington, M. (2003) 'Hayekian Political Economy and the Limits of Deliberative Democracy', *Political Studies*, 51 (4).

Peters, B.G. (1996) *American Public Policy: Promise and Performance*, New Jersey: Chatham House Publishers.

Putnam, R.D. (2000), *Bowling Alone: The Collapse and Revival of American Community*, London: Simon and Schuster.

Quinn, F. (2005) 'Oireachtas Returns but Who Cares?' *The Irish Times*, 28 September.

Rabbitte, P. (2003) 'Speech on Labour Party Dáil Reform Proposals', Press Statement, Dublin: Labour Party Press Office, 30 October.

Raunio, T. (2005) 'Holding Governments Accountable in European Affairs: Explaining Cross-National Variation', *Journal of Legislative Studies*, 2 (3 and 4).

Raunio, T. and Hix, S. (2001) 'Backbenchers Learn to Fight Back, European Integration and Parliamentary Government' in K.H. Goetz and S. Hix (eds), *Europeanised Politics and National Political Systems*, London: Frank Cass.

Raworth, P. (1994) 'A Timid Step Forward: Maastricht and the Democratisation of the European Community', *European Law Review*, 19 (1).

Regh, W. (1996) 'Translator's Introduction', in J. Habermas, *Between Facts and Norms: Contributions to a Discourse Theory of Law and Democracy*, Cambridge: Polity Press.

Report of the Informal Committee on Dáil Procedures (1972) Dublin: Stationery Office.

Report of the Joint Committee on the Remit of Ministers and the Allowance of Members of the Oireachtas (1929) Dublin: Stationery Office.

Reports of Proceedings of the Oireachtas Sub-Committee on European Scrutiny (2003) commencing on 16 January and concluding on 18 December, Available at www. oireachtas.ie/viewdoc.asp?DocID=1&StartDate=1+January+2003&CatID=74.

Ring, M. (1996) *Dáil Debates*, Vol. 469, Cols 1751–1752, 9 October.

Robinson, M. (1979) 'Irish Parliamentary Scrutiny of European Community Legislation', *Common Market Law Review*, 16 (1).

Roche, W.K. and Cradden, T. (2003) 'Neo-Corporatism and Social Partnership', in M. Adshead and M. Millar (eds), *Public Administration and Public Policy in Ireland: Theory and Methods*, London and New York: Routledge.

Rogers, J. (2001) 'Voters Should Not Be Blackmailed into Voting Yes to Avoid Giving Offence', *The Irish Times*, 19 May.

Rosamond, B. (2000) *Theories of European Integration*, Basingstoke: Palgrave.

Rumford, C. (2003) 'European Civil Society or Transnational Social Space? Conceptions of Society in Discourses of EU Citizenship, Governance and the Democratic Deficit: An Emerging Agenda', *European Journal of Social Theory*, 6 (1).

Ryan, J. (1962) *Dáil Debates*, Vol. 198, Cols 865–866, 6 December.

Ryan, R. (1972) *Dáil Debates*, Vol. 263, Cols 104–105, 25 October.

Sacks, P.M. (1976) *The Donegal Mafia: An Irish Political Machine*, New Haven and London: Yale University Press.

Scharpf, F.W. (1996) 'Democratic Policy in Europe', *European Law Journal*, 2 (2).

Scholte, J.A. (2000) *Globalisation: A Critical Introduction*, New York: St Martin's Press.

Schriver, K.A. (1989) 'Theory Building in Rhetoric and Composition: The Role of Empirical Scholarship', *Rhetoric Review*, 7 (2).

Schwarzmantel, J. (2003) *Citizenship and Identity: Towards a New Republic*, London: Routledge.

Shapiro, I. (2003) *The State of Democratic Theory*, Princeton and Oxford: Princeton University Press.

Sherlock, S. (2008) 'Dáil Committees Should Have Greater Role in Overseeing Quangos', Press Statement, Dublin: Labour Party Press Office, 15 September.

Sherwin, F. (1962) *Dáil Debates*, Vol. 198, Cols 870–871, 6 December.

Sinnott, R. (1999) 'The Electoral System', in J. Coakley and M. Gallagher (eds), *Politics in the Republic of Ireland*, London: Routledge.

—— (2005) 'The Rules of the Electoral Game', in J. Coakley and M. Gallagher (eds), *Politics in the Republic of Ireland*, London and New York: Routledge.

Smith, G. (2003) *Deliberative Democracy and the Environment*, London and New York: Routledge.

Smith, N. (2002) 'The Irish Republic: A 'showpiece' of Globalisation'? *Politics*, 22 (3).

Somers, M. (2000) 'Romancing the Market, Reviling the State: Historicising Liberalism, Privatisation, and the Competing Claims to Civil Society', in C. Crouch, K. Eder and D. Tambini, *Citizenship, Markets and the State*, Oxford: Oxford University Press.

Spring, D. (2008) Speech in Kilkenny Castle (5 June) on the occasion of the launch of O'Connor, T. and O'Halloran, A. (2008) *Politics in a Changing Ireland: 1960–2007. A Tribute to Seamus Pattison*, Dublin: Institute of Public Administration.

Stein, E. (1981) 'Lawyers, Judges and the Making of a Transnational Constitution', *American Journal of International Law*, 75.

Steiner, J., Bachtiger, A., Sporndli, M. and Steenbergen, R. (2004)

Deliberative Politics in Action: Analysing Parliamentary Discourse, Cambridge: Cambridge University Press.

Stoker, G. (2006) *Why Politics Matters: Making Democracy Work*, Hampshire: Palgrave Macmillan.

Stromer-Galley, J. (2003) 'Voting and the Public Sphere: Conversations on Internet Voting', *Political Science and Politics*, 36 (4).

Strydom, P. (2002a) *Risk, Environment and Society: Ongoing Debates, Current Issues and Future Prospects*, Buckingham and Philadelphia: Open University Press.

—— (2002b) 'Is the Social Scientific Concept of Structure a Myth? A Critical Response to Harre', *European Journal of Social Theory*, 5 (1).

Sweetman, G. (1962) *Dáil Debates*, Vol. 198, Cols 865–867, 6 December.

Third Amendment of the Constitution Act (1972).

Tordoff, L. (2000) 'The Conference of European Affairs Committees: A Collective Voice for National Parliaments in the European Union', *Journal of Legislative Studies*, 6 (1).

Torgerson, D. (1999) *The Promise of Green Politics: Environmentalism and the Public Sphere*, Durham and London: Duke University Press.

Treaty Establishing a Constitution for Europe (2005) 'Protocol on the Role of National Parliaments in the European Union', Luxembourg: European Communities.

Treaty of Amsterdam (1997) 'Protocol on the Role of National Parliaments in the European Union', *Official Journal of the European Communities*, 10 November.

Trenz, H.J. and Eder, K. (2004) 'The Democratising Dynamics of a European Public Sphere', *European Journal of Social Theory*, 7 (1).

Tully, J. (1972) *Dáil Debates*, Vol. 263, Cols 129–130, 25 October.

Turner, B.S. (2000) 'Liberal Citizenship and Cosmopolitan Virtue', in A. Vandenberg (ed), *Citizenship and Democracy in a Global Era*, London: Macmillan Press.

Upton, P. (1996) *Dáil Debates*, Vol. 369, Cols 1720–1721, 9 October.

Venturelli, S. (1998) *Liberalising the European Media: Politics, Regulation and the Public Sphere*, Oxford: Clarendon Press.

Walker, H. (2000, 2001, 2002) In Conversation with me in Cahir County Tipperary.

Ward, A.J. (1996) 'The Constitution Review Group and the "Executive State" in Ireland', *Administration*, 44 (4).

Ward, I. (2004) *The English Constitution*, Oxford: Hart.

Warleigh, A. (2004) *European Union: The Basics*, London: Routledge.

Weiler, J. (1995) 'Does Europe Need a Constitution: Reflections on Demos, Telos and the German Maastricht Decision', *European Law Journal*, 1 (3).

Weiler, J., Haltern, U.R. and Mayer, F.C. (1995) 'European Democracy and Its Critique', *West European Politics*, 18 (3).

Welton, M. (2001) 'Civil Society and the Public Sphere: Habermas Recent Learning Theory', *Studies in the Education of Adults*, 33 (1).

Wheare, K.C. (1968) *Legislatures*, London, Oxford and New York: Oxford University Press.

Whelan, N. (2009) 'Cutting Ministers of State Would Be Important Symbolic Gesture', *The Irish Times*, 17 January.

White Paper European Economic Community (1961) Laid by the Government before the Houses of the Oireachtas, Dublin: Stationery Office.

White Paper European Economic Community: Developments Subsequent to the White Paper of 30 June 1961 (1962) Laid by the Government before the Houses of the Oireachtas, Dublin: Stationery Office.

Whyte, J. (1966) *Dáil Deputies: Their Work, its Difficulties, Possible Remedies*, Pamphlet 15, Dublin: Tuairim.

Young, I.M. (1997a) *Intersecting Voices: Dilemmas of Gender, Political Philosophy and Policy*, Princeton: Princeton University Press.

—— (1997b) 'Difference as a Resource for Democratic Communication', in J. Bohman and W. Rehg (eds), *Essays on Reason and Politics: Deliberative Democracy*, Cambridge, Massachusetts and London: MIT Press.

—— (2001) 'Activist Challenges to Deliberative Democracy', *Political Theory*, 29 (5).

—— (2002) *Inclusion and Democracy*, Oxford: Oxford University Press.

Index

A

Accession of Ireland to the European Communities 168, 171, 172, 173, 182

Accountability 18, 19, 30, 41, 68, 118, 119, 120, 131, 135, 146, 147, 155, 167, 173, 181, 184, 187, 205, 207, 209, 210, 211, 222, 223, 227, 231, 232, 233, 235, 236, 237, 239, 243, 244

Accountability, discursive 130, 131, 209, 210, 211, 222, 223, 227, 231, 232, 233, 235, 236, 237, 243, 244

Accountability, executive 118, 167, 210

Additional member system 56

Aggregative model 104, 105

All-Party Oireachtas Committee on the Constitution 32, 57, 134

Allowances and expenses 25, 137, 139, 141, 143, 144, 150, 151, 152, 153, 248, 249

Amsterdam, Treaty of 183

Asylum 188, 190, 227, 228, 229

Australia 70, 148

Authoritative decisions 29, 66, 120, 240

B

Backbenches 24, 52, 222

Banking 14, 24, 35, 36, 135

BATU (bricklayers' union) 224

Bureaucracy 31, 51, 113, 197

C

Cabinet, Irish 43, 46, 55, 71, 78, 133, 160, 170, 182, 223

Canada 70

Ceann Comhairle 8, 14, 45, 142, 154, 158, 159, 161, 162, 163, 165, 166, 167, 203, 225, 226, 248

Celtic Tiger 35, 36, 40, 41, 57, 244

Centralised wage bargains 40

Centre right parties 47

Citizenship 12, 34, 58, 60, 61, 212, 213, 214, 215, 217, 218

Civic virtue 217, 218, 219, 220

Civil rights 95, 212, 213, 220

Civil service 28, 51, 53, 55, 73, 197, 210, 235, 236

Civil society 30, 31, 32, 40, 60, 89, 110, 111, 113, 114, 120, 125, 126, 167, 168, 193, 195, 196, 197, 198, 199, 210, 218, 241, 242

Clientelism 26, 53, 54, 55, 56, 214, 217, 237

Coalition government 47, 48, 49

Committee of grievances 75, 76

Committee of Inquiry into Ministerial and Other Salaries, 1937 141

Committee on Social Partnership 231, 232, 233, 234

Committees 149

Committee systems 42, 87, 88, 139, 167, 182, 194, 196, 197, 199, 241, 242

Common Agricultural Policy 39, 171, 174

Common good 19, 20, 26, 32, 34, 106, 117, 118, 119, 120, 121, 129, 131, 200, 209, 210, 217, 219, 220, 233, 236, 237, 238, 243, 244

Communications revolution 33, 58, 60, 113, 221

Communicative democracy 129, 130, 243, 245

Conference of European Affairs Committees [COSAC] 183

Constitution (1937) 32, 37, 38, 43, 45, 46, 57, 77, 78, 93, 134, 154, 166, 169, 170, 171, 172, 182, 200, 236
Constitution, 1922 77
Constitution, English 71, 72, 73
Constitutional referendum 16, 168
Consultants 43, 148, 165, 200, 205, 206, 207, 234, 235, 236, 242, 244
Consumerism 19, 34, 211, 212, 215, 216, 217, 218, 220, 238
Core-periphery model 113, 114
Criminal justice system 193, 195

D

Dáil Reform Committee 132
Decision-making 64, 116
Decisional centres 94, 95, 99, 116, 130, 209, 243
Decline of parliament thesis 30, 32, 68, 69, 70, 75, 76, 77, 78, 79, 81, 82, 83, 86, 90, 91, 92, 93
Deliberative democratic theory 19, 20, 21, 103, 105, 106, 107, 108, 109, 110, 114, 115, 117, 121, 122, 128, 129, 130, 210, 220, 245
Deloitte and Touche Report 139, 147, 149, 241
Democracy 17, 18, 19, 20, 21, 28, 30, 32, 33, 34, 35, 37, 39, 41, 54, 58, 69, 72, 76, 82, 84, 90, 91, 92, 93, 94, 95, 96, 97, 98, 99, 100, 101, 102, 103, 104, 105, 106, 107, 108, 110, 113, 114, 120, 129, 130, 131, 133, 134, 180, 181, 183, 184, 188, 199, 201, 204, 205, 207, 208, 209, 210, 211, 212, 213, 214, 215, 216, 219, 220, 231, 232, 233, 234, 235, 237, 242, 243, 245, 246
Democracy, parliamentary 18, 82, 92, 180
Denmark/Danish 42, 88, 118, 148, 176
Department of Enterprise, Trade and Employment 224, 225, 226
Department of Foreign Affairs 176, 190, 206, 253
Dialogical process 107, 108, 198

Discursive process 108, 109, 110, 116, 117, 122, 124
Dualistic analysis 125

E

Economic and Monetary Union 37, 39
Economic development/growth 35, 146, 172, 173, 176
Electoral democracy 104, 105
Electoral systems 27, 43, 44, 56, 57
Elites 97, 98, 103, 106, 112, 123, 169, 171, 184, 211, 212
Elitism 103, 189
Emotions 71, 106, 107, 109, 115, 121, 122, 123, 124, 125, 126, 127, 130, 131, 227, 231, 245
European Affairs Committees 88, 183, 184
European Central Bank 37, 39
European Communities (Amendment) Act (1973) 178, 179
European Communities (Confirmation of Regulations) Act (1973) 178, 187
European Communities Act (1972) 169, 170, 176, 177, 178, 179, 180
European Court of Justice 37, 38, 59, 176
European Economic Community (EEC) 36, 38, 39, 168, 169, 170, 171, 172, 173, 174, 175, 176, 177, 178, 179, 180, 181, 182, 191, 192
European Union (EU) 15, 36, 37, 38, 39, 40, 58, 59, 63, 88, 89, 133, 148, 168, 173, 183, 184, 185, 187, 188, 189, 190, 191, 192, 199, 229, 241, 242
European Union Committee 88
European Union Scrutiny Act (2002) 184, 185, 186, 187, 188, 189, 199, 242
Euro zone 37, 39
Excellence in Parliamentary Service 138
Executive (Irish) 51, 52, 56, 74, 76, 77, 78, 81, 83, 93, 117, 133, 134, 135, 136, 141, 153, 173, 182, 202, 203, 204, 210, 231, 232, 234, 235, 240
Executive–legislative relations 51, 52, 70, 71, 91, 241

Executive control 27, 33, 53, 63, 64, 68, 75, 76, 77, 78, 79, 80, 81, 83, 86, 92, 93, 94, 96, 97, 99, 116, 117, 118, 119, 120, 133, 134, 135, 136, 141, 166, 170, 177, 182, 186, 188, 197, 203, 231, 232, 234
Executive dominance model 81, 93
Experts 36, 41, 42, 43, 58, 63, 84, 85, 89, 102, 174, 205, 206, 207, 210, 229, 235

F

Fianna Fáil 26, 44, 47, 48, 49, 77, 151, 172, 175
Fine Gael 24, 44, 47, 48, 49, 143, 156, 184

G

Gama Construction 222, 223, 224, 237, 244
General elections 24, 43, 44, 45, 48, 49, 74, 96, 152, 156, 222
Germany 56, 148
Global governance 59
Globalisation 24, 29, 33, 35, 36, 39, 58, 59, 60, 61, 64, 65, 85, 89, 91, 101, 219
Golden age of parliament 73, 78, 86, 90, 91, 92
Governance, multi-level 58, 63, 64, 65, 85, 101
Greece 44, 78
Green Party 48, 49, 156
Guillotine procedure 117, 118

H

Health board 229
House of Commons 27, 43, 69, 71, 72, 73, 74, 79, 81, 88, 101, 145, 160, 221, 222, 246
Houses of the Oireachtas Commission 133, 137, 194
Houses of the Oireachtas Commission, Annual Report of the, 2007 152

I

Immigration Act (1999) 230
Inclusiveness 105
Incremental bounded reform 80, 91
Independent Commission 153
Information and Public Relations Service 165
Inter-Party Government 55
Interest groups 36, 40, 41, 42, 84, 85, 86, 87, 89, 97, 98, 102, 194, 200
International law 59
International Monetary Fund 59
Irish Independent 27
Irish law 37, 47, 168, 173, 174, 177, 200, 224, 225, 229, 242
Irish Times, The 25, 26, 55, 151

J

Joint Committee on Broadcasting and Parliamentary Information 164, 165
Joint Committee on European Affairs 187, 188
Joint Committee on European Affairs Sub-Committee on European Scrutiny 2007 189
Joint Committee on Justice, Equality, Defence and Women's Rights 193, 195
Joint Committee on the Remit of Ministers and the Allowances of Members of the Oireachtas 141
Joint Committee on the Secondary Legislation of the European Communities 179, 180, 181, 188

K

Knowledge economy 58

L

Labour Court 225
Labour Inspectorate 223, 226
Labour law 222, 226

Labour Party 47, 48, 49, 51, 146, 156,
172, 184, 248
Leaders' Questions 155, 156, 165, 167,
222, 223, 241
Leas-Cheann Comhairle 15, 139, 154,
165, 166, 230, 248
Legislation/Legislatures 19, 32, 37, 40,
45, 47, 52, 67, 68, 69, 70, 71, 74, 75,
76, 77, 82, 90, 91, 93, 111, 113, 116,
117, 118, 130, 133, 134, 137, 142, 153,
157, 164, 167, 169, 170, 173, 177, 178,
179, 181, 184, 187, 188, 189, 190, 195,
199, 200, 224, 228, 241, 242
Liberal democracy 35, 62, 63, 90, 91, 93,
94, 95, 96, 97, 98, 99, 100, 101, 102,
107, 213, 215, 216, 219, 243, 245

M

Maastricht Treaty 36
Macroeconomic policy 37, 39, 40
Marxist framework 97, 98
Monopolies 51, 64, 76, 85, 112, 167, 214
Motion of confidence 234
Multiple revolutions 33, 57, 66, 90

N

Nation state 58, 59, 61, 64, 65
National law 38, 177
Neo-classical framework 98
Neo-corporatism 63, 84
New Zealand 56, 148
Nice Referendum/Treaty 15, 173, 184,
188
Normative theory 15, 18, 19, 29, 33, 35,
51, 58, 68, 70, 88, 90, 91, 92, 93, 94,
95, 99, 100, 102, 105, 107, 110, 114,
120, 121, 122, 175, 215, 217, 219, 220,
231, 233, 237, 243, 244, 245
Northern Ireland 148, 157, 196

O

Oireachtas (Allowances to Members) Act
(1938) 144

Oireachtas (Allowances to Members) Act
(1962) 144
Oireachtas (Allowances to Members) Act
(2009) 247
Oireachtas (Allowances to Members) Bill
(1962) 139
Oireachtas Commission 133
Oireachtas Commission Act (2003) 137,
138
Oireachtas Commission Act (2006) 138
Oireachtas Public Relations Office 132,
193
Olukunle, Eluhanla 226, 227, 230, 237
Ombudsmen 75
Ontology 112, 126
Opposition, government 24, 46, 48, 49,
52, 116, 117, 118, 119, 134, 140, 141,
142, 143, 156, 157, 158, 159, 162, 167,
196, 197, 204, 222, 223, 232
Order of Business 46, 83, 134, 154, 155,
156, 157, 158, 167, 241
Order Paper 154, 155, 157, 159, 160

P

Parliamentary agitation 24
Parliamentary Committees 41, 42, 47,
87, 118, 135, 136, 137, 147, 149, 154,
164, 180, 184, 185, 187, 193, 194, 195,
236, 242
Parliamentary control 73, 74
Parliamentary democracy 18, 28, 82, 92
Parliamentary governance 101, 102, 209,
239, 245
Parliamentary government 35, 66, 73, 78,
86, 92, 95, 96, 97, 99, 100, 101, 102,
111, 112, 116, 120
Parliamentary Inquiry into DIRT 135
Parliamentary politics 17, 20, 40, 48, 57,
71, 117
Parliamentary privilege 163
Parliamentary questions 46, 202, 203
Parliamentary scrutiny 56, 66, 80, 147,
172, 173, 184, 188, 209, 240
Pluralism 97, 98, 112, 113, 220, 238
Political brokerage 69

Portugal 78

Post-parliamentary governance 12, 29,
    30, 35, 36, 42, 67, 84, 85, 86, 88, 89,
    90, 91, 92, 93, 99, 101, 102, 189, 199,
    205, 207, 240, 246

Power centres 80, 99, 100

Power relationships 98, 123, 217, 223

Private interests 56, 105, 106, 129, 218,
    219, 220

Private members' bills 47, 117, 184

Private Members' Business 46

Private notices 156

Programme for Prosperity and Fairness 40

Progressive Democrats 44, 48, 49

Propaganda 245

Proportional Representation by means
    of the Single Transferable Vote
    (PRSTV) 43, 44, 56, 57

Public Accounts Committee 135, 136,
    137, 146, 147, 164, 165, 194, 232

Public good 34, 105, 106, 216, 219

Public management 214

Public policy 35, 40, 42, 58, 94, 95, 96, 97,
    99, 100, 102, 105, 106, 120, 146, 201,
    202, 207, 231

Public sphere 19, 29, 30, 31, 32, 33, 34,
    35, 101, 103, 104, 110, 111, 112, 113,
    114, 120, 128, 209, 210, 211, 220, 221,
    222, 223, 227, 230, 231, 232, 236, 237,
    238, 243, 244, 245, 246

Q

Question time 46, 120, 133, 155, 156,
    159, 160, 181, 202, 203, 204, 223

R

Reform 14, 15, 27, 52, 53, 56, 79, 80, 91,
    92, 132, 133, 146, 147, 151, 155, 158,
    167, 236, 240, 241, 242

Reform Act (1867) 73

Refugee Act (1996) 228, 229, 230

Refugee Appeals Tribunal 228, 229

Refugee status 228

Republicanism 217, 219, 220

Resource deficiencies 142, 146, 147, 148,
    150, 153, 178, 241

Responsibility 37, 99, 116, 118, 165, 187,
    190, 200, 202, 209, 231, 234

Rhetoric 34, 109, 116, 126, 127, 128, 129,
    130, 131, 169, 171, 172, 173, 175, 216,
    245

Rhetoric, deliberative 129

Rhetoric, forensic 128, 129

Risk society 58, 61, 62, 65, 85, 91, 101

Rules of debate 160

S

Sanctions 107, 119

Scandinavia 67, 79, 81

Scotland 148

Seanad Éireann 14, 15, 41, 45, 137, 169,
    180, 193, 194

Secondary Legislation of the European
    Communities 179

Sectoral Committees 190, 191, 233, 234,
    235, 242

Select Committees 164, 194

Separation of powers 99, 133, 135, 137,
    153, 166, 241

Single European Act 36

Sinn Féin 43, 44, 48, 49, 156, 184

SIPTU 224

Socialist Party 156, 222

Social Partnership 36, 40, 41, 89, 116,
    168, 200, 201, 202, 203, 204, 207, 231,
    232, 233, 234, 237, 241, 242, 243

Socialist Party 223

Sovereignty 37, 38, 58, 65, 73, 168, 169,
    170, 171, 172, 174, 176, 182, 204, 205

Sovereignty, economic 172

Sovereignty, expert 42, 43, 168, 200, 205,
    207, 237, 242

Sovereignty, parliamentary 169

Spain 44, 78

Special Committees 47, 167, 194, 231

Standing Committees 194

Standing Orders 19, 118, 123, 154, 155,
    156, 157, 158, 159, 160, 161, 162, 164,
    165, 166, 167, 182, 194, 203, 241

State-centric citizenship 60, 61
State-centric government 58, 64, 65, 66,
     100, 169, 171, 175, 176
Sub-Committee on European Scrutiny
     189, 190, 199, 242
Sub-Committees 14, 135, 136, 137, 138,
     164, 187, 189, 190, 191, 199, 242
Sub-politics 62, 63
Suffrage 72, 73, 95, 212, 213
Supranational 29, 36, 38, 58, 59, 60, 61,
     64, 88, 116, 177, 181, 183
Supreme Court 45
Sustaining Progress 202

T

Technical Group 156
Third Amendment to the Constitution
     Bill 170
Trade unions 34, 50, 63, 70, 148, 225
Transnational movement 60
Transparency 119, 152, 205, 207, 210,
     231, 233, 234, 242
Transworld norms 60
Tribunals 49, 136, 228, 229

U

United Kingdom 27, 44, 54, 69, 70, 73,
     79, 81, 92, 102, 129, 148, 174, 176,
     212, 217, 220
United Nations 59
United States 35, 69, 79, 81, 82, 117, 128,
     166, 211, 212, 221
United States Congress 27, 79, 81, 82,
     117, 132

V

Vested interests 119

W

Wales 148
Welfare state 73, 212, 213
Westminster 42, 43, 47, 117, 145, 161,
     166
Westphalian principles 38, 58, 65, 170,
     171, 172
Whip, Chief 134, 157, 158
Whipped party system 52, 82, 116, 117,
     161
White Paper on the European Economic
     Community 173, 174
Working Group of Committee Chairmen
     164
World Bank 59
World Trade Organization 59